Yuktang Ch'oe Nam-sŏn
and
Korean Modernity

Yuktang Ch'oe Nam-sŏn and Korean Modernity

Hak Joo Choi
translated by Yer-ae K. Choi

YBM

Published by YBM, Inc.
55-1 Jongno 2-ga, Jongno-gu, Seoul 110-772, Korea
Tel: 82-2-2000-0515
Fax: 82-2-2265-7573
Website: www.ybmbooks.com

ISBN: 978-89-17-21433-8

Printed in Korea

To the memory of my grandfather

My grandfather, Yuktang Ch'oe Nam-sŏn (1890–1957).
He posed for me at his Myo-dong residence during his illness in 1956.

Extended Ch'oe family on New Year's Day in 1912. My great-grandfather, Ch'oe Hŏn-gyu, sits in the front row (third from right). In the back row, from right to left, stand his three sons: Tu-sŏn (age 18), Nam-sŏn (age 23), and Ch'ang-sŏn (age 25). My great-grandmother, in a headdress, sits in the front row holding Han-ok, Nam-sŏn's daughter. In the same row, second from left, sits my grandmother (age 26). This photograph was taken during the period of mourning for my great-great-grandfather, Ch'oe Chŏng-sŏb (1833–1911), who, at his own peril, opposed Taewon'gun's isolationist policies and fought for the enlightenment of Korea.

The family celebrates Great-grandfather's sixtieth birthday, *hwan'gap,* in 1917. Great-grandfather continued his own father's enlightenment efforts by funding the various modernization projects undertaken by his young son Nam-sŏn. In this photograph, Nam-sŏn stands in the back row(fourth from right) in a traditional long coat and black top hat.

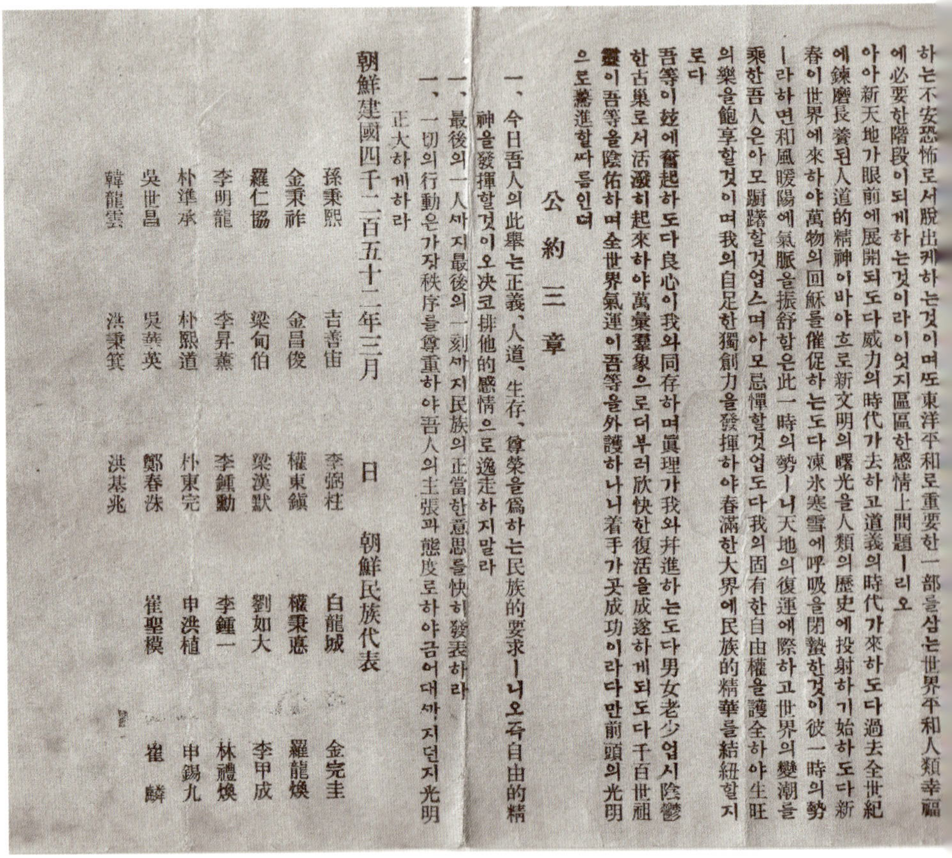

하는不安恐怖로서脫出케하는것이며또東洋平和로重要한一部를삼는世界平和人類幸福에必要한階段이되게하는것이라이엇지區區한感情上問題ㅣ리오

아아新天地가眼前에展開되도다威力의時代가去하고道義의時代가來하도다過去全世紀에鍊磨長養된人道的精神이바야흐로新文明의曙光을人類의歷史에投射하기始하도다新春이世界에來하야萬物의回穌를催促하는도다凍氷寒雪에呼吸을閉蟄한것이彼一時의勢ㅣ라하면和風暖陽에氣脈을振舒함은此一時의勢ㅣ니天地의復運에際하고世界의變潮를乘한吾人은아모躕躇할것업스며아모忌憚할것업도다我의固有한自由權을護全하야生旺의樂을飽享할것이며我의自足한獨創力을發揮하야春滿한大界에民族的精華를結紐할지로다

吾等이玆에奮起하도다良心이我와同存하며眞理가我와幷進하는도다男女老少업시陰鬱한古巢로서活潑히起來하야萬彙羣象으로더부러欣快한復活을成遂하게되도다千百世祖靈이吾等을陰佑하며全世界氣運이吾等을外護하나니着手가곳成功이라다만前頭의光明으로驀進할따름인뎌

公約三章

一、今日吾人의此擧는正義、人道、生存、尊榮을爲하는民族的要求ㅣ니오즉自由的精神을發揮할것이오決코排他的感情으로逸走하지말라

一、最後의一人까지最後의一刻까지民族의正當한意思를快히發表하라

一、一切의行動은가장秩序를尊重하야吾人의主張과態度로하야금어대까지던지光明正大하게하라

朝鮮建國四千二百五十二年三月 日

朝鮮民族代表

孫秉熙 吉善宙 李弼柱 白龍城 金完圭
金秉祚 金昌俊 權東鎭 權秉悳 羅龍煥
羅仁協 梁甸伯 梁漢默 劉如大 李甲成
李明龍 李昇薰 李鍾勳 李鍾一 林禮煥
朴準承 朴熙道 朴東完 申洪植 申錫九
吳世昌 吳華英 鄭春洙 崔聖模 崔麟
韓龍雲 洪秉箕 洪基兆

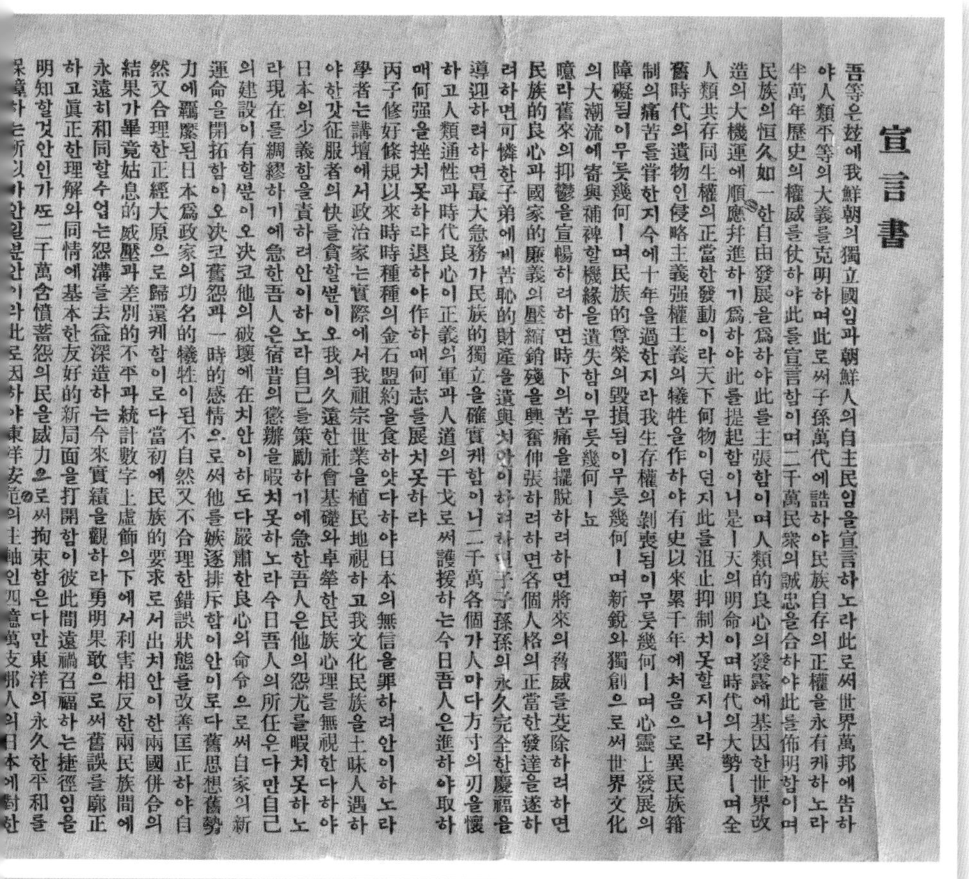

宣言書

吾等은玆에我鮮朝의獨立國임과朝鮮人의自主民임을宣言하노라此로써世界萬邦에告하야人類平等의大義를克明하며此로써子孫萬代에誥하야民族自存의正權을永有케하노라
半萬年歷史의權威를仗하야此를宣言함이며二千萬民衆의誠忠을合하야此를佈明함이며民族의恒久如一한自由發展을爲하야此를主張함이며人類的良心의發露에基因한世界改造의大機運에順應幷進하기爲하야此를提起함이니是ㅣ天의明命이며時代의大勢ㅣ며全人類共存同生權의正當한發動이라天下何物이던지此를沮止抑制치못할지니라
舊時代의遺物인侵略主義强權主義의犧牲을作하야有史以來累千年에처음으로異民族箝制의痛苦를嘗한지今에十年을過한지라我生存權의剝喪됨이무릇幾何ㅣ며心靈上發展의障礙됨이무릇幾何ㅣ며民族的尊榮의毁損됨이무릇幾何ㅣ며新銳와獨創으로써世界文化의大潮流에寄與補裨할機緣을遺失함이무릇幾何ㅣ뇨
噫라舊來의抑鬱을宣暢하려하면時下의苦痛을擺脫하려하면將來의脅威를芟除하려하면民族的良心과國家的廉義의壓縮銷殘을興奮伸張하려하면各個人格의正當한發達을遂하려하면可憐한子弟에게苦恥的財產을遺與치안이하려하면子子孫孫의永久完全한慶福을導迎하려하면最大急務가民族的獨立을確實케함이니二千萬各個가人마다方寸의刃을懷하고人類通性과時代良心이正義의軍과人道의干戈로써護援하는今日吾人은進하야取하매何强을挫치못하랴退하야作하매何志를展치못하랴
丙子修好條規以來時時種種의金石盟約을食하얏다하야日本의無信을罪하려안이하노라學者는講壇에서政治家는實際에서我祖宗世業을植民地視하고我文化民族을土昧人遇하야한갓征服者의快를貪할뿐이오我의久遠한社會基礎와卓犖한民族心理를無視한다하야日本의少義함을責하려안이하노라自己를策勵하기에急한吾人은他의怨尤를暇치못하노라現在를綢繆하기에急한吾人은宿昔의懲辨을暇치못하노라今日吾人의所任은다만自己의建設이有할뿐이오決코他의破壞에在치안이하도다嚴肅한良心의命令으로써自家의新運命을開拓함이오決코舊怨과一時的感情으로써他를嫉逐排斥함이안이로다舊思想舊勢力에羈縻된日本爲政家의功名的犧牲이된不自然又不合理한錯誤狀態를改善匡正하야自然又合理한正經大原으로歸還케함이로다當初에民族的要求로서出치안이한兩國倂合의結果가畢竟姑息的威壓과差別的不平과統計數字上虛飾의下에서利害相反한兩民族間에永遠히和同할수업는怨溝를去益深造하는今來實績을觀하라勇明果敢으로써舊誤를廓正하고眞正한理解와同情에基本한友好的新局面을打開함이彼此間遠禍召福하는捷徑임을明知할것안인가또二千萬含憤蓄怨의民을威力으로써拘束함은다만東洋의永久한平和를保障하는所以가안일뿐안이라此로因하야東洋安危의主軸인四億萬支那人의日本에對한

Facsimile of original document "The Declaration of Independence" that Grandfather composed, typeset, and printed in 1919. In his great haste to have the document ready, he missed the transposition of the two characters in the word *Chosŏn* in the first sentence.

Grandfather(age 31) was incarcerated at Sŏdaemun prison in 1919 as one of the leaders of the March First Independence Movement. The prisoner number "757" appears on his prison garb. During his two-year imprisonment, he sought to establish Korean identity, as well as to explore the origin of Northeast Asian civilization.

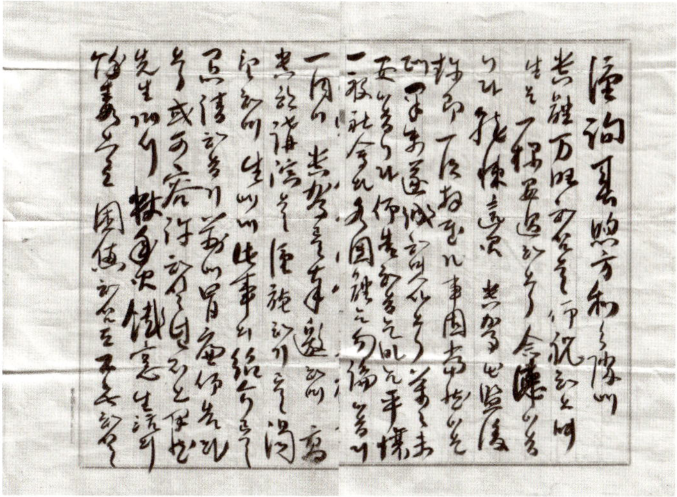

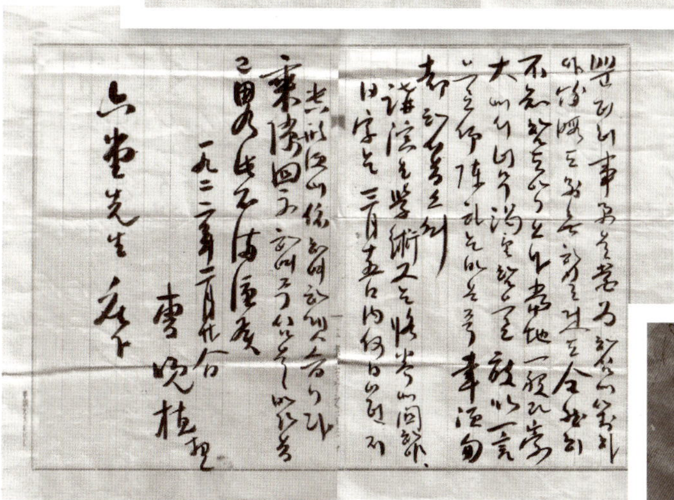

Letter that Cho Man-sik's sent Grandfather in 1922.
In the letter Cho offered him a teaching position at Sungshil College in Pyongyang (present capital of North Korea).

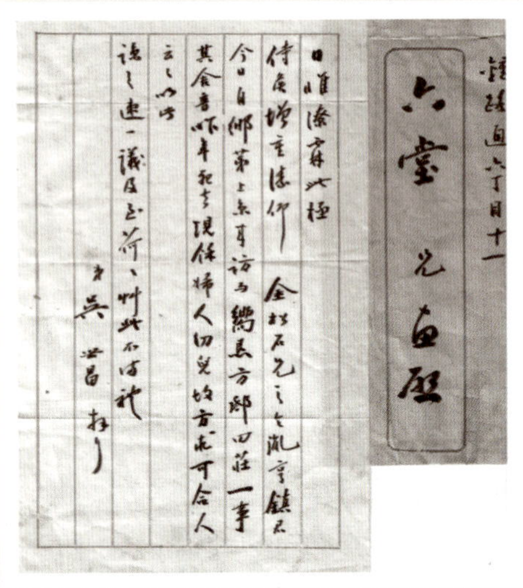

Letter that O Se-ch'ang, a famed calligrapher, sent Grandfather in 1925.
The O family, like the Ch'oe family, promoted the modernization of Korea for several generations.

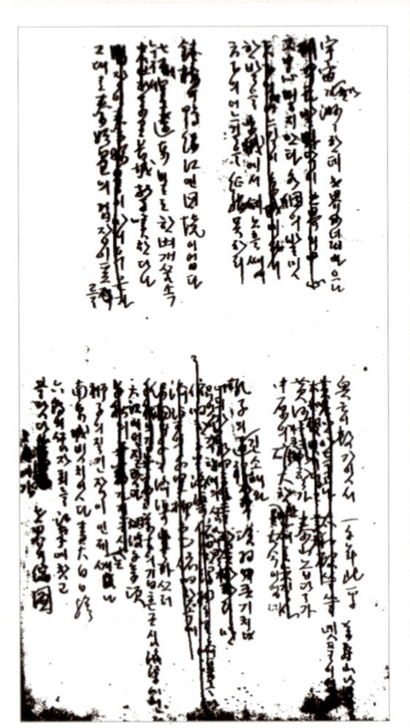

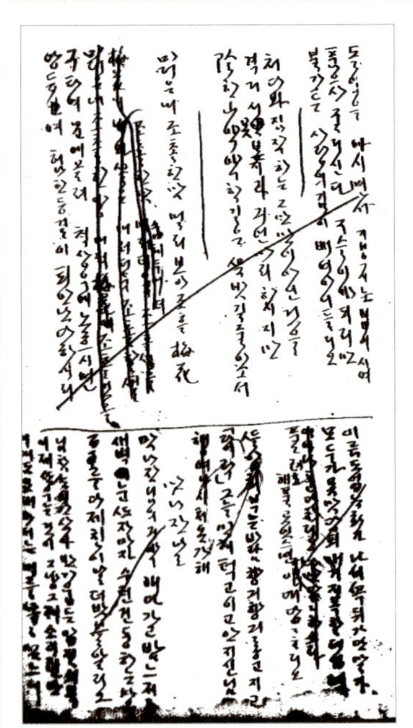

Drafts of Grandfather's sijo written in 1926.
These sijo were discovered in his notebook in 2007, and are published here for the first time.

Grandfather(left) at the top of Paektu Mountain, with Venerable Pak Han-yŏng(middle) in 1926. In the background is Ch'ŏnji Lake. Grandfather viewed the mountain as the cradle of Korean culture.

My great-grandfather, Ch'oe Hŏn-gyu (1857–1933). He spent his entire fortune to promote the modernization of Korea at the beginning of the twentieth century. He also established the *Chŏng'an'gongpa* branch of the Dongju Ch'oe-ssi family line. He was 71 years old when this photograph was taken in 1927.

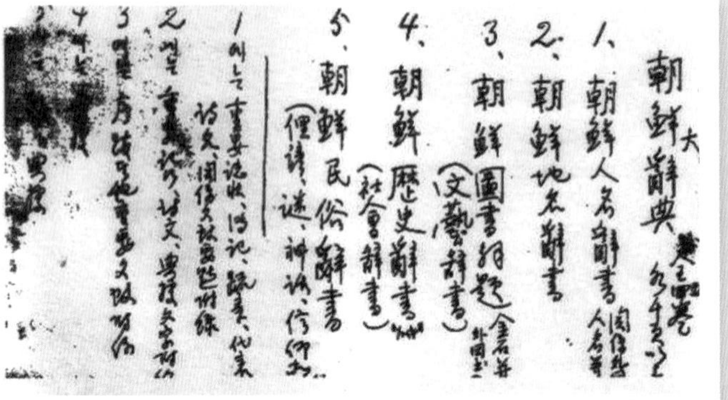

朝鮮大辭典

1. 朝鮮人名辭書
2. 朝鮮地名辭書
3. 朝鮮圖書解題 (文藝辭書)
4. 朝鮮歷史辭書 (社會辭書)
5. 朝鮮民俗辭書

Page from a notebook Grandfather kept during the 1920s and 1930s. In this notebook he mapped out his grand plan for an encyclopedia of Korea.

In 1932, Grandfather let his hair grow in preparation for his trip to France, later cancelled by his father's sudden illness. This family portrait had been taken as a keepsake for the trip. His daughter(Han-ok, 24) and his three sons(Han-gŏm,11; Han-ung,16; Han-in,18) stand in the back. Grandmother, Grandfather, and their son-in-law(Kang Kŏn-ha, 27) sit in the front.

Ch'oe Tu-sŏn and his wife, Kim Sun-yŏng.
Ch'oe Tu-sŏn, Nam-sŏn's younger brother, engaged in various "nation-saving" projects during the Japanese colonial rule. After the Liberation, he served as diplomat, journalist, and statesman. In 1933, he married Kim Sun-yŏng, who, behind the scenes, made a significant contribution to the women's rights movement in Korea.

The wedding of Ch'oe Nam-sŏn's eldest son, Han-in (my father), in 1936. Directly behind the newly married couple stand Grandfather and Grandmother.

My father, Han-in, and his younger brother, Han-ung. The brothers were avid basketball players during their college years. My father was also a figure-skating champion.

Photograph taken on my first birthday in 1942. My father was 28 and my mother, 26. The photograph was sent to Grandfather, who was then teaching in Manchuria.

Grandfather and his three sons in Ui-dong, 1947. It is a rare photograph that shows Grandfather with a happy smile.

Grandfather at his Ui-dong residence in 1945.
Immediately after the Liberation, he wrote *A History of Chosŏn for the Korean People*, the first book about Korean history he was able to write free of colonial censorship.

This photograph was taken on the day of Han-gŏm's marriage in 1950. It was also the day of Grandfather's *hwan'gap*. Grandfather sits in the front row(third from left), and I, then nine years old, stand to his right. Two months later, the Korean War broke out.

My cousin Kang Ho (age 21), the eldest son of my aunt Han-ok, at Yŏido Airport in 1955. His younger siblings joined him for a family portrait before he left for the United States to study medicine. His medical research during his career won him the Hoam Award in 2001.

Grandfather and his brother, Tu-sŏn. In April of 1957, Tu-sŏn, then president of *Dong-a Ilbo*, visits his older brother, who was bedridden due to a paralyzing stroke.

Grandfather's funeral mass at Myong-dong Catholic Church in October of 1957. I stand behind the casket carrying a framed photograph of Grandfather. Grandmother is to my left and Second Uncle (Han-ung), in funeral headgear, stands behind me. Han-sŏk (son of Tu-sŏn, who later became the dean of the College of Engineering at Korea University) stands to the left of Grandmother.

Second Uncle (Han-ung) and his wife (Yi Mu-hi). In 1970, they visited me in Boston during his sabbatical leave from his professorship at Seoul National University's School of Medicine. After the Liberation, he managed the family business, Tongmyŏng Publishing Company. He also published a memoir in which he recorded many memories of his father.

Third Uncle, Han-gŏm, in North Korea(199?). In his sixties, he shows a stronger resemblance to his mother than to his father. He majored in philosophy at Tokyo Imperial University and later taught at Kim Il Sung University in Pyongyang, North Korea.

My family in the United States. In the back are, from left to right, my son-in-law (Jae-hoon), my daughter (Hahng-sun), my daughter-in-law (Ji-sun), and my son (Hahng-sok). In the front, my wife and I sit with our grandchildren. This photograph was taken on New Year's Day in 2010 after we performed our yearly ancestral memorial rites.

Translator's Note

- Korean words and names have been romanized according to the McCune-Reischauer system.
- The romanization of some well-known personal names and place names, such as "Syngman Rhee" and "Seoul," is in accordance with the standard usage.
- Most Korean, Chinese, and Japanese personal names adhere to the East Asian order, with the surname first, followed by the given name.
- The numbers indicating people's ages follow the Korean custom in which a person is one year old at birth.

CONTENTS

PART THREE
The Future of Yuktang Study

Preface

Who is Yuktang Ch'oe Nam-sŏn (六堂 崔南善)? Where does he stand in modern Korean history? To this day, there are no clear answers. From both the scholarly and historical viewpoints, the task of "getting to know" Ch'oe Nam-sŏn remains unfinished. This is true for me as well. Even as I approach the age of 70, I still find I have much to learn about my grandfather. Along with many people of my generation, I have many lingering questions about Ch'oe Nam-sŏn, the man and the time he lived in.

When I was born as his first grandson in 1941, my grandfather was 51, so there is a half-century span between his time and mine. That half century was a time of unprecedented turbulence for the Korean people. Without having lived it myself, it is next to impossible for me to even imagine the hardships my grandfather endured while living and working under such conditions. In this book, I have merely attempted to recapture my early memories of him and to revisit my thoughts as I came across his writings later in life. The content of this book is indifferent to public opinion and scholarly debate, both past and present.

My purpose in writing this book is, in fact, very simple—to paint a picture of my grandfather, whose steadfast gentleness guided my childhood, and to record my personal response to his writings as I grew into adulthood. In the process, I have tried to express my own understanding of the vast and passionate body of work he dedicated to the modernization of his country.

Prior to becoming my grandfather, Ch'oe Nam-sŏn was already a leading public figure in the forefront of his time. In a broader sense, his time is still in the present progressive tense, and I firmly believe that we are standing right on the extension of his time. For this reason, I feel very proud of my grandfather and also deeply grateful for the painstaking work he has undertaken and bequeathed to us.

I have received a great deal of help in writing this book. Fully aware that mere words cannot repay my indebtedness, I would especially like to express my heartfelt gratitude to my good friend, the columnist Cho Kyu-suk, and to the esteemed historian Dr. Lee Young-hwa, both of whom provided me with meticulous reviews of my manuscript, along with their invaluable comments, opinions, and suggestions. Also, I would like to extend my special thanks to President Cho Sang-ho of Nanam Publishing Company and its superb editorial team for bringing this book to publication. In addition, I would like to thank my wife of 40 years, Yer-ae K. Choi, who has undertaken an English translation of this book so that it may reach a wider audience.* It is my sincere hope that the collaborative effort that went into this book will bear fruit by sparking a larger and more nuanced discourse on Yuktang Ch'oe Nam-sŏn, the man and his work.

Hak Joo Choi
New York
January 23, 2011

*I am most grateful to Dr. Sunshik Min, president of YBM, Inc., for bringing the English translation of this book to publication.

June 20, 2012

INTRODUCTION

Seventeen Years with My Grandfather

Until I was of elementary school age, I grew up in Ui-dong, located on the outskirts of Seoul, where Grandfather owned a piece of land. On it stood his house and study, surrounded by a large rice field and some vegetable patches. He named the place Sowŏn, "a humble grove."

In the spring, the cherry trees in their full bloom lined the stream that flowed in from Paek-un Mountain. The berries in the backyard tasted extra sweet when picked by my tall grandfather. In the summer, the days flew by as I looked for crayfish in the stream. In the fall, my pockets would burst from all the chestnuts I picked up from the ground as I walked. In the winter, a section of the harvested rice field became an icy playground. My father, who was then teaching at a university in Seoul, would visit and practice figure skating to the music blaring on the RCA Victor gramophone.

There was a little distance between Grandfather's study and the main house. At mealtimes, as he went back and forth between the two buildings, he would pull out the chestnut burrs stuck to my bare feet, and put ointment on my knees, scraped from catching crayfish. One winter day, he put a band-aid on a cut I got on my finger while whittling a piece of wood into a top to spin on the ice. His gentle hands always felt good, and I would look for him first at the most minor hurt. He had *yak-son*, "medicine hands."

To all appearances, Ui-dong epitomized the peace and tranquility of rural life. However, even as far back as several years before the Korean War (more commonly referred to in Korea as *Yuggio*, which means "6/25"), I became, as young as I was, aware of a nagging undercurrent of tension around me. Nobody told me explicitly, but my growing sense of unease had a definite source. At the time, Grandfather and Third Uncle took turns being incarcerated at Sŏdaemun prison, Grandfather as a "pro-Japanese collaborator" and Third Uncle, as a "Red." Perhaps I was unhappy with the recurring absence of my mother, who had to make frequent trips to Seoul to supply them with food and clothing. Although I came to realize it only much later, there were already strong portents of the tragedy that Yuggio, several years before it actually broke out, would unleash on our family. I don't think even Grandfather could foresee how everything would play out in the end.

The war resulted in near total evisceration of our family. Grandfather's eldest daughter was murdered by North Korean soldiers; his son-in-law was abducted to the North, his whereabouts unknown thereafter; his eldest son, my father, died suddenly as a refugee in Pusan; and his youngest son crossed over to the North voluntarily. In the face of all this tragedy, Grandfather did not waver in his determination to bring the *Encyclopedia of Korean History* to completion. In addition, neither diabetes nor hypertension deterred him from pursuing this goal.

Around the time of the Armistice, I was in fifth grade, and our family moved to a house in Myo-dong in Seoul, where Grandmother had stayed with Third Aunt during the war. Grandfather returned to Seoul earlier than most of the other refugees. His lifelong collection of 170,000 books had been napalmed by United Nations Forces during the Red Chinese Offensive in the spring, and he wanted to restart his

Grandfather(Ch'oe Nam-sŏn) and Grandmother(Hyŏn Yŏng-ch'ae), 1956.

library by buying up books that were being sold in the streets as scraps in the aftermath of the war. In order to raise funds for his work on the *Encyclopedia of Korean History*, as well as for daily living expenses, a mill was set up at the house. In my mother's management of household expenses, buying books for Grandfather often took precedence over food.

Grandfather was on the heavy side. His hands were always warm, and he perspired heavily in the summertime. Constitutionally, he took after his mother, who was more sensitive to heat than cold. He avoided tobacco as something that caused "a hundred harms without a single benefit." As for alcohol, he derived the same effect from one glass as from ten glasses, and could effortlessly join in the merriment with heavier drinkers. He was a prodigious drinker of tea, though. In the front yard, a black iron kettle sat on two flat stones between which the fire never went out. He treasured the tea leaves from Chiri Mountain, and brewed Chaksŏl tea from Mudŭng Mountain himself, to which he often treated himself and his guests. On several occasions, he would point out to me the differences among the shapes, colors, and fragrances of the various tea leaves, but the niceties escaped me then, and they still do now.

From early morning to late afternoon, a good portion of Grandfather's day was taken up with receiving and entertaining guests, but whenever possible, he took time out to play with his grandchildren. Around the time of the Armistice, he often played jumprope with my sister, who was three years younger than I was and in third grade. He would take me to the nearby Pagoda Park, hauling the old bicycle and teaching me how to ride it. I often marveled at how agile he was, considering his heft. As I watched him zipping around on the bicycle, I envied him his dexterity.

Grandfather always wore white rubber shoes over traditional white cotton socks, which he tied with strings around his ankles. When he rode the bicycle, I would worry that the strings would untie or the rubber shoes fly off the pedals. I would also worry that the bicycle might collapse under his considerable weight. Grandfather seemed to know, however, that my main concern was not his rubber shoes or his weight, but my most prized possession, the bicycle. It was something of which Grandfather and I had joint ownership.

Except on the days when events intruded, Grandfather took his daily walk to Pagoda Park, and often took my sister and me with him. On his way back, he would sometimes stop by old bookstores in Nagwŏn-dong or Iksŏn-dong to look for certain books. Returning home, he stayed at his desk working until quite late at night. Sometimes, at my pestering, he would play a quick game of *chang'gi* (Korean chess), giving me a couple of handicap points. He derived greater pleasure from my wins than his own. He would try to explain my winning moves to Grandmother, but when she didn't show much interest in the grandfather-grandson match, he would look very disappointed. He never played more than one game of chang'gi with me, though. When his older grandchildren played *paduk* (go), he wasn't very pleased because the game required a long stretch of time, which he thought could be spent more fruitfully.

In 1954, I was chosen at my school to give a farewell speech at the graduation ceremony. Worried, I pleaded with Grandfather to write the speech for me. At first he said that if I came up with a draft, he would look it over, but finally giving in to my repeated entreaties, he wrote the speech, five or six Korean manuscript pages long. I then copied it onto a white piece of paper in my best handwriting.

The graduation ceremony took place in the auditorium of Ch'ŏndogyo Church. As I was reading the speech, I spied Grandfather sitting right next to the principal! He had come to the ceremony, I found out later, as a "distinguished guest" of the principal. I already had butterflies in my stomach, and Grandfather's unexpected presence heightened my nervousness. I hadn't noticed while transcribing the speech the previous evening, but as I was delivering it on the podium, one of Grandfather's lines struck me as being too difficult. I haltingly replaced it with my own words and continued on with my speech.

On the way back home after the ceremony, Grandfather exclaimed, "*Goyan nyŏsŏk* (Naughty boy), you changed my words! Even the Japanese wouldn't dare do that!" My speech, titled "Farewell Speech by the Representative of the Graduating Class of 1954, Kyo-dong Elementary School," if it still exists somewhere, is written by my grandfather, Yuktang Ch'oe Nam-sŏn.

After I entered middle school, my mother started a business selling school uniforms in Iksŏn-dong, a neighboring district. The business became quite successful, unlike the mill business right after the Armistice. Second Uncle was working as a doctor at an air force base in Taegu, and Third Aunt (the wife of Third Uncle who went over to the North) opened a pharmacy near Myo-dong. Although the country as a whole was still in the grip of the war's devastation, my family had overcome the immediate financial hardship. Day and night, Grandfather poured all his energy into the *Encyclopedia of Korean History*. Probably as a result of overwork, he had a paralyzing stroke in the spring of 1954. I was a first-year middle school student when Grandfather became bedridden.

I moved my desk and bedding to his room. There I read newspapers to him, and took dictations of his writings to be published in various magazines. There was, of course, a caregiver who tended to his everyday needs, but the job of finding the various reference materials necessary for his writing fell to me. It was perhaps the desire to free myself from the demands of the sick room that led me to join a rock-climbing club, which enabled me to spend every weekend outdoors with my friends. Grandfather never said a chiding word about my spending more than 60 days out of the year in the mountains. Nor did I mention my rock-climbing exploits to him.

During his illness, whenever his symptoms abated, Grandfather expressed a wish to pay a visit to Kim Sŏng-su, his longtime friend, who lived in nearby Kye-dong. Because Kim passed away before Grandfather did, I could not help him fulfill his wish. My grandfather, who had by then converted to Catholicism, died on October 10, 1957, with Grandmother, Second Uncle, and myself at his bedside. He had his usual gentle expression on his face.

PART ONE

Modern Korea in Yuktang's Family History

Chapter 1

My Great-Grandfather and the Enlightenment Movement

1. Every Year on New Year's Day

My family celebrates the New Year's according to the solar calendar. All the family members gather to perform memorial rites for our ancestors and bow to one another afterwards. This ritual was conducted at Ui-dong when I was a little boy, and now it is held in New York, since I am the *chongson*, the eldest male descendant, of the Ch'oe family line.

The first "table" (symbolic meal) of the rite is for General Ch'oe Yŏng (崔瑩: 1316-1388). First, on a piece of paper to be placed at the head of the table, I write, *Koryŏ paldo dotongsa/Chosŏn mumin'gong* (高麗八道都統使 朝鮮武愍公: Commander of the Eight Provinces of Koryŏ/ Honorary General of Chosŏn). Next, I lay out three sets of spoons and chopsticks for him and his two wives. Together we bow, light incense, offer food and wine, and bow again. Every year I tell my children that he held the two government positions and had two wives. I go on to explain why this Ch'oe ancestor attempted, six centuries ago, to reclaim Manchuria, a land that had once belonged to Korea. Then I tell them the reason I repeat this information every year, namely, to carry out the dying directive of my great-great-grandfather, Ch'oe Chŏng-sŏb (崔廷燮: 1833-1911). Just as my own grandfather, Ch'oe Nam-sŏn (崔南善: 1890-1957), passed this information on to my generation, I pass it along to my own children. In addition, I remind them once a year that my grandfather is a 20th-generation descendant of General Ch'oe Yŏng

Yuktang Ch'oe Nam-sŏn's (六堂 崔南善) Family Tree

Progenitor Ch'oe Chun-ong (崔俊邕: ca.900)
10th **Generation** Ch'oe Yŏng (崔瑩:1318–1388)

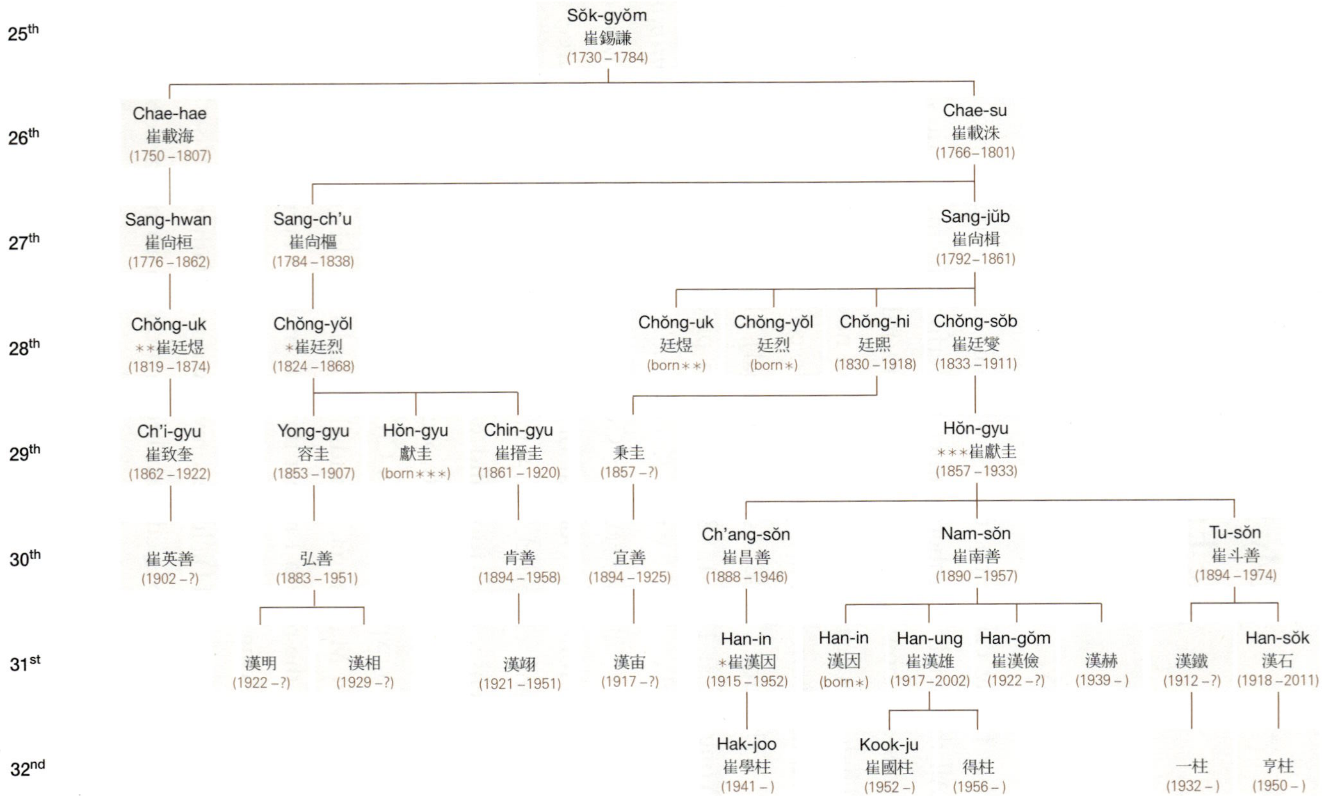

* denotes adoption within families to maintain blood-lines.

of the Koryŏ dynasty.

Since our family honors up to four generations of our ancestors, the second table is for my great-great-grandfather, Ch'oe Chŏng-sŏb, and his wife. On another piece of paper, I write *chong'ipum kaŭidaebu chungch'uwŏn ch'anŭi* (從二品嘉義大夫 中樞院贊議: Second Rank: Palace Assistant Secretary) and next to it I write "Yang-ssi (woman with the surname Yang) from Namwŏn." Chŏng-sŏb inherited his father's (Ch'oe Sang-jŭb, 崔尙楫: 1792–1861) herbal medicine business, and his brothers, Chŏng-uk (廷煜: 1819–1874) and Chŏng-yŏl (廷烈: 1824–1868), passed the civil service examinations and became government officials. I explain to my children how this Ch'oe generation lived through turbulent times in Korean history, starting from the seclusionist era of Taewŏn'gun (1820–1898), to the Kanghwa Treaty of 1876, to the failure of the Kapsin Coup of 1884, and to the Kabo Reform of 1894. I go on to explain what part these historical events played in our family's celebrating the New Year's by the solar calendar. Every year I repeat all this information to carry out the dying directive of my great-grandfather, Ch'oe Hŏn-gyu (崔獻圭: 1857–1933). I also tell my children that since 1896, the Ch'oe family has not celebrated the New Year's by the lunar calendar, the Chinese New Year's traditionally celebrated by most Koreans. My grandfather repeated this information in Korean to me, but I repeat it in English to my children so that they can understand it fully and remember it.

The next "table" is for my great-grandfather, Ch'oe Hŏn-gyu, and his wife. On still another piece of paper, I write *chong'ipum kasŏntaebu sijongwŏn pukyŏng* (正二品嘉善大夫 侍從院副卿: Second Rank: Undersecretary of the King's Court) and next to it, I write "Kang-ssi from Chinju." Together we bow, light incense, offer food and wine, and bow again. Then I continue, in both English and Korean:

> To follow Ch'oe Yŏng's dying words, we must reclaim our ancient land of Manchuria. Our ancestor Ch'oe Sang-jŭb and his descendants were the pioneers of the Korean modernization movement at the end of the nineteenth century, when the Western powers tried to take over the East. In order to save their country and enlighten its people, his grandson, Hŏn-gyu, and his wife dedicated their entire hard-won fortune to the movement.

Then, remembering my grandfather Yuktang Ch'oe Nam-sŏn who stood at the forefront of that movement at the beginning of the twentieth century, I add these final words:

> All of us live in the historical present that is given to us, and most of us live our lives without much focus or sense of purpose, but a few among us must take it upon ourselves to build a foundation for the lives of generations to come.

2. My Great-Grandfather, Ch'oe Hŏn-gyu, a Self-Made Man

My great-grandfather, Ch'oe Hŏn-gyu (1857–1933), was born the second son of Ch'oe Chŏng-yŏl, but was adopted into my family line because it lacked a male heir. At the time, our family, with its meager business in herbal medicine, was quite poor in comparison to his birth family. Perhaps for this reason, Hŏn-gyu did not marry Kang (1859–1925) until he was 23 years old, much later than was customary at the time. Kang's father, Kang Wi-yŏng, a former mayor who had retired to the vicinity of Ch'ŏlwŏn in Kangwŏn Province, had initially turned down Hŏn-gyu's marriage proposal due to the poverty of the young man's family. He finally relented when his daughter demurred, "Father, is it the fault of the groom that his family is poor?"

After a brief wedding ceremony at the bride's home, the couple left for Seoul. When the bride's mother opened the marital chest the groom had left behind and saw that it was all but empty, she broke into loud sobs. The couple, turning a corner on the village road, heard the mother's sobs, and the bride followed suit. At this moment, according to family lore, the groom resolved to make a fortune for himself.

The year he got married, Hŏn-gyu passed the civil service examination in the meteorology division. He quickly rose to the position of Assistant Secretary of Palace Administration. Soon afterwards, by printing and selling farming calendars, as well as trading in herbal medicine, he began to accumulate a sizable fortune. By the time he agreed to support his two young sons in their "nation-saving" publishing ventures, he had 50,000-bushel rice fields in Kyŏnggi Province and in the Honam region. In Seoul proper, he owned about 80 houses and building lots.

Hŏn-gyu and his wife had three sons and three daughters: the eldest daughter, Hwa-gyŏng; the second daughter, Wŏl-gyŏng; the eldest son,

Great-grandfather(Ch'oe Hŏn-gyu), 1927. Great-grandmother(Kang-ssi from Chinju), 1919.

Ch'ang-sŏn; the second son, Nam-sŏn; the third son, Tu-sŏn; and the youngest daughter, Sŏl-gyŏng. Hŏn-gyu was 32 when his eldest son, Ch'ang-sŏn (1888–1946) was born, and his second son, Nam-sŏn (1890–1957), followed two years later.

Hŏn-gyu and his wife had an unconventional approach to raising their children. The couple constantly reminded them, just as all the Ch'oe forebears had done during the 500 years of Chosŏn dynasty, that during the Koryŏ dynasty the Ch'oe line had produced as many as nine prime ministers and one vice-prime minister, and that General Ch'oe Yŏng, at the end of the dynasty, was the most eminent ancestor of the Ch'oe line.

In addition to this drill, there was yet another unusual routine in Hŏn-gyu's upbringing of his sons. Every night, before they went to bed, he gave them each a swat with a rod on their bare calves to spur them to contemplate the right and wrong of their actions during the day. My grandfather used to tell me that, his father's bedtime swat, which continued until he got married at age 12, had a strangely calming effect on the excitement of the day.

Hŏn-gyu's wife was also unconventional in the way she went about her domestic affairs. She insisted that her daughters-in-law pay more than the asking price when buying produce from the peasants. She also cautioned them not to waste even a single grain of rice by washing it down the drain. My grandmother, one of the daughters-in-law, used to tell me how hard it had been to adhere to these two injunctions.

The amount of money that Nam-sŏn, as a 17-year-old youth, received from Hŏn-gyu, his father, for his publishing ventures in 1906 was 70,000 won. With this money, Nam-sŏn purchased a printing press and other necessary equipment from Shueisha, a major publishing company in Tokyo. After hiring and bringing back a couple of Japanese technicians with him, Nam-sŏn set up a printing factory and an office at his parents' house in Seoul. From 1906 to 1924, Nam-sŏn spent another 90,000 won of his father's money, as well as 170,000 won in bank loans, which he later had to repay by selling off family property. All told, the expenses incurred for "nation-saving" endeavors, such as the preservation of ancient Korean texts and various other cultural and enlightenment projects, had wiped out almost all of the Ch'oe family assets, which amounted to approximately 400,000 won (40 billion won in today's Korean currency, approximately 40 million US dollars).

Grandfather embarked on his cultural endeavors at the age of 17, the age at which most of today's youths graduate from high school. *What kind of man was Ch'oe Hŏn-gyu who, without hesitation, gave his young son such an enormous sum, a sum that even the government of a country might find prohibitive? How did he accumulate such wealth?*

The government position Ch'oe Hŏn-gyu held as a meteorologist had allowed him access to the yearly calendar sent by the Chinese emperor, which Hŏn-gyu used to create a calendar that farmers could use. By block-printing it and selling it countrywide, he made a considerable profit. With the profit as seed money, he started an herbal medicine business with Chinese merchants. As it happened, his purchase of medicines often coincided with epidemic breakouts, driving up prices. In addition to business sense, Hŏn-gyu seems to have been blessed with luck. With an easygoing, pleasant personality and a solid reputation, even the hard-to-please Chinese merchants often chose him as their trading partner. His relationships with these merchants led to frequent contact with China, which opened his eyes to the world beyond Korea's shores.

At this time, Northeast Asia was grappling with Western encroachment. In China, which had just emerged from the Opium War (1840), the Yangwu (洋務: self-strengthening) movement, had been in full swing since the early 1860s. O Kyŏng-sŏk (吳慶錫: 1831-1879), as translator, was exposed to this movement during his trips to China and began to feel the dire need for Korea to open up its ports for trade. Yu Tae-ch'i (劉大致: 1831-1884?), of *chung'in* (class between the aristocrats and commoners) origin, fully appreciated the reasons for Japan's Meiji Restoration. Together, these two men initiated modernization efforts in Korea. With his theory of *tongdo sŏgi* (東道西器: Eastern ways, Western technology), O Kyŏng-sŏk won over the moderate progressive Pak Kyu-su (1807-1877) in the Yi government, who then played an important role in opening up Korean ports as part of the 1876 Treaty with Japan. Yu mentored Kim Ok-gyun and Sŏ Jae-pil, who, during the Kapsin Coup of 1884, spearheaded a radical reform movement.

Through his trading relationships with Chinese merchants, Ch'oe Hŏn-gyu gained knowledge about the international political scene and thus enthusiastically supported the efforts of O Kyŏng-sŏk and Yu Tae-ch'i. Moreover, he wanted his two sons to be a part of the movement as well. Having embraced the enlightenment endeavor as his own, he willingly supported his sons, despite their young age, in their foundation of Sinmun'gwan (新文館: The Institute for New Learning) and the publication of the first popular modern magazine in Korea, *Sonyŏn* (少年: Boys).

In 1884, the year of the Kapsin Coup, Ch'oe Hŏn-gyu (then 28) was a contemporary of Kim Ok-gyun (then 33) and Sŏ Jae-pil (then 21), the leaders of the radical enlightenment movement. When success eluded these two men, he was devastated. The movement was a failure, not because its leaders had failed to gain political power, but because Korea's sovereignty itself was lost soon afterwards. It is more than likely that Hŏn-gyu himself was a student of Yu Tae-ch'i, who had mentored the leaders of the Kapsin movement. The fact that Hŏn-gyu frequently talked about the movement to his young son Nam-sŏn leaves little doubt that he himself was an enthusiastic supporter of the movement, if not an active participant.

3. The Tragic Trailblazer, Ch'oe Chŏng-uk

It was the summer of 1953, soon after the first anniversary of my father's death. Grandfather had some business to take care of at the ancestral burial ground at Ssang'gyeri and asked me to accompany him. I had been assigned an insect collection for summer vacation homework, so I decided to go along. This trip with Grandfather is still vivid in my memory.

> We go by streetcar to Ch'ŏng'nyang'ni and from there take the Ŭijŏngbu-bound train. We get off at Ch'angdong Station, since the ancestral burial ground in Ssang'gyeri is about a 10-*ri* (2.5 mi.) walk from the station. Not far from the station, we reach a shallow stream, which we cross barefoot. After crossing the stream, I simply put my sneakers back on, since my bare feet will dry in no time. For Grandfather, though, it is a little more complicated since he has to wait until his feet dry before he can put back on his white cotton socks and then his rubber shoes. While Grandfather sits on a bank of the rice paddy drying his feet, I catch grasshoppers. We resume our walk under the hot summer sun. Grandfather, who perspires easily, sweats through his shirt.
>
> We arrive at Ssang'gyeri, but the keeper, Yi, is nowhere to be seen. He and his family must have gone to work in the fields. Grandfather tells a child who was left behind to fetch Yi. Then we head for the burial sites and, on entering, bow two times. On the southwest slope are the graves of the "Chŏgsŏng" ancestors and on the southeast side, the graves of the direct ancestors of my family line. I notice that every Chŏgsŏng grave has a tombstone, whereas most of the graves of our direct family ancestors have no tombstones.

I ask, "Grandpa, why don't we have tombstones in front of our ancestors' graves?"

Grandfather answers in a way that a 12-year-old can understand, "That elder family line had many generals who held government positions, but our family had many doctors who didn't hold any government positions."

Then Grandfather continues, "Look. See how the graves are positioned according to the generations. Here, on the very bottom row, is the generation of ancestors with names that have the character "sŏn"; above that row are the names with "gyu"; above that are the names with "chŏng"; above that are the names with "sang"; and at the very top are the names with "chae." Then, pointing to each grave, Grandfather cites the name of each buried ancestor.

"The first row is Ch'ang-sŏn and Hong-sŏn; the next row is Hŏn-gyu, Chin-gyu, and Yong-gyu; the next row is Ch'ŏng-sŏp, Chŏng-hi, and Chŏng-yŏl; and the next row is Sang-ch'u, Sang-jŭp, and Chŏng-uk."

A-ha! I think to myself, Grandpa made a mistake! I ask him, "Why is 'chŏng' in the 'sang' row then?"

"You're quite right," replies Grandfather, and begins to tell me the story behind the apparent misplacement.

On our way back home, Grandfather told me that the Ch'oe family line produced nine prime ministers and one vice prime minister during the Koryŏ dynasty, but after the overthrow of General Ch'oe Yŏng by General Yi Sŏng-gye (who founded the Yi dynasty in 1392), the family stopped seeking government posts during the Yi dynasty. However, one of the ancestors was credited with ousting Yŏnsan'gun (reign: 1494–

1506), and in recognition of this service was called to Seoul by the new king, Chungjong (reign: 1507–1544). At that time, the family burial site was set up at what is now the area around Sŏkgwan-dong and Changwi-dong. Then, during King Yŏngjo's reign (1725–1776), our family line, having more or less established itself as *chung'in*, purchased the burial site at Ssang'gyeri. During the reign of Taewŏn'gun, Chŏng-uk fell into disfavor because of his advocacy of modernization, and the Ssang'gyeri burial site was confiscated. Thanks to Hŏn-gyu's wealth, however, the family was able to buy it back and hold onto it. For this reason, Hŏn-gyu is regarded to this day as an eminent ancestor of the Ch'oe line.

The reason that Chŏng-uk's grave sits not *under*, but *next* to, his father's is related to the reason that Hŏn-gyu was able to fund his young son's cultural endeavors. Based on what Grandfather told me that summer day at Ssang'gyeri and on what I have learned since then, the history of our family during the Chosŏn era is as follows:

In the fifteenth century, Ch'oe O-bok, a descendant of Ch'oe Yŏng, refused to serve in the Chosŏn court out of loyalty to the Koryŏ dynasty. Then, in the sixteenth century, Ch'oe Yŏng-ho, having performed a meritorious service in ousting Yŏnsan'gun, was called to Seoul by the new king. During the seventeenth century, after the Imjin War (1592, against Japan) and the Pyŏngja War (1636, against Manchuria), the Ch'oe family members from Dongju (present-day Chŏlwŏn) entered government service as military officers. In the eighteenth century, during the reigns of Yŏngjo (reign: 1725–1776) and Chŏngjo (reign: 1777–1800), Chae-hae (1750–1807), the first son of the military officer Ch'oe Sŏk-gyŏm (1730–1784), passed the civil service examination in the military division and rose to the position of general. With the second son,

Chae-su (1766–1801), passing the medical division of the civil service examination, the male members of the Ch'oe line began their service to the central government as medical doctors and technocrats.

Ch'oe Chae-su, Supervisor of the Palace Medical Facility, had two sons: Sang-ch'u (1784–1838) and Sang-jŭb (1792–1861), who passed the civil service examination's medical and accounting divisions respectively. Sang-jŭb had four sons, Chŏng-uk, Chŏng-yŏl, Chŏng-hi, and Chŏng-sŏb. The eldest, Chŏng-uk (1819–1874), was adopted into his elder uncle's family, which lacked a male heir.

Chŏng-uk grew into a young man of great promise, on whom the entire Ch'oe clan laid high expectations. At age 25, he won the highest place in the legal division of the civil service examination and rose swiftly within the government service. He was about ten years older than translator O Kyŏng-sŏk (1831–1879), but both were equally committed to modernizing Korea. During the reign of Taewŏn'gun, Chŏng-uk was driven out of his position for his opposition to the king's seclusionist policies. Banished to a rural village called Chŏgsŏng in Kyŏnggi Province, he lived out his life in lonely isolation. On his death, he was buried on an unnamed nearby hill. This is why the burial site of the Chŏng-uk family line became known as the "Chŏgsŏng" site. Chŏng-uk died at age 56 without witnessing the fulfillment of his cherished desire for an open, enlightened Korea.

My great-grandfather Hŏn-gyu worked as an apprentice at the herbal medicine shop owned by his adoptive father Chŏng-sŏb, and began in time to venture into an herbal medicine business of his own. According to the custom of the day, Chŏng-sŏb and his three brothers all lived under one roof. His uncle Chŏng-uk helped open the way for Hŏn-gyu to start a herbal medicine trade with China. Through his daily contact with his uncle, Hŏn-gyu came to understand the necessity for Korea's modernization and became one of its most enthusiastic advocates.

With Chŏng-uk's death, his family fortune inevitably declined. He himself had been buried unceremoniously on an unnamed hill in Chŏgsŏng, and in time, the burial site for his family line was also shut down. Years later, Hŏn-gyu, my great-grandfather, troubled that his uncle had not been properly buried in his ancestral burial ground, had his remains moved to Ssang'gyeri, next to the grave of his birth father, Sang-jŭb.

This is the story I learned from Grandfather that summer day, the story that explains why Chŏng-uk's grave does not sit in the "chŏng" row, but in the row above, next to his father's grave.

4. The Stories My Grandmother Told Me

My grandmother, Hyŏn Yŏng-ch'ae (1887-1971), was born the sixth daughter of Hyŏn Chŏng-un, a translating officer of Chinese in the court. At age 15, she married my 12-year-old grandfather Nam-sŏn. When Grandfather passed away in 1957, my mother, my sister, and I moved to a house in Samsŏn'gyo, and Grandmother and Third Aunt (wife of Han-gŏm) stayed on at Myo-dong. The barbershop I frequented was located in Myo-dong, and after my haircuts, I visited my grandmother, often staying late into the evening.

I distinctly remember a conversation I had with her when I was 20, just after I entered college. At the time, Grandmother was well into her seventies. Wishing to have a written record of her recollections, I brought her a notebook and asked her to jot down whatever came to mind. She never did use the notebook, but on each of my many visits, she would dig deep into her memory and pull up strands of her amazing life story. To the extent that memory will allow, here I recount her recollections:

> Before my grandmother married my grandfather at age 15, she was told that her groom was born "in Nugakggol under Inwang Mountain in the Year of the Tiger," but contrary to what his birth information suggested, she found her 12-year-old husband to be gentle and mischievous, not at all fierce like a tiger. To her surprise and bafflement, she found her parents-in-law extremely frugal in spite of their wealth, and found it very difficult at her age to manage all the household servants. She was heartbroken when she had to give up her first-born (Han-in) to be adopted by her elder brother-in-law, whose wife could not bear him a son. Above all, she found it exhausting to take care of the unending

stream of writers and scholars who visited Sinmun'gwan, preparing one meal after another for them. On many a day, she would go through two bushels of rice, cooking for them.

When her husband was incarcerated at Sŏdaemun prison after the March First Movement, she had to rent a room nearby to take care of him, cooking meals and sewing clothes. Years later, when her husband's venture in *Sidae Ilbo* (Times Daily) failed, she was mortified that her husband had incurred such a huge debt. She and her husband moved out to Yangsakkol on the outskirts of Seoul, where she went through a time of severe financial hardship. When her husband, at the "advanced" age of 43, announced his "immature" plan to go to France, she was not happy. Then, he went to Manchuria to teach, leaving her to manage the Hyojedong household all by herself for four years. On his return, she learned that he had had a child with another woman.

When the family moved out to Ui-dong, she enjoyed a period of comparative contentment, but it was marred by her nagging worry over her youngest son's (Han-gŏm's) socialist leanings. Many scholars, writers, and politicians came to Ui-dong to confer with her husband, so many that she could hardly remember them all. Yuggio soon broke out, during which her eldest daughter (Han-ok), to her unspeakable horror and grief, was murdered. She was worried sick when her daughter-in-law (Yi Sŏn-yŏng, my mother) was taken to the police station for questioning about her (Grandmother's) husband's whereabouts. Then, the lowest point of her life came when she learned of the death of her beloved eldest son in Pusan. In her seventies, following in her husband's footsteps, she became a Catholic.

Standing beside her husband, Grandmother had endured the most turbulent half century in Korea's history. She passed away in May of 1971 in Ui-dong, leaving me an oral narrative of her eventful life. She was 85 years old. She had lived a life of vicissitudes, and as wife, daughter-in-law, mother, and grandmother, she had experienced more than her share of pain as well as pride. At the moment of her passing, I was unable to be at her bedside, but to this day I can clearly hear her voice as she shared with me her extraordinary life story.

When Grandmother arrived as a bride at the Ch'oe household, the family owned more than 80 houses and building lots in Seoul. The property all but disappeared while her husband immersed himself in his work at Sinmun'gwan, Kwangmunhoe, and *Sidae Ilbo*. The family wealth had been created not only through her father-in-law's business acumen, but also through her mother-in-law's frugality and management skills. One reason that her father-in-law had not passed the civil service examination until the late age of 23 was the family's poverty, but another reason was the family's involvement in the enlightenment movement. Her grandfather-in-law and his brothers had all passed the civil service examinations with flying colors, but had incurred the displeasure of Taewŏn'gun through their enlightenment activities. As a result, they banded together to start a medicine business of their own and then to open trade with China. Her father-in-law had run errands for these family ventures, and as times gradually changed, he had been able to take and pass the civil service examination, aiding his prospects for marrying his wife (my grandmother's mother-in-law). When they married, both were much older than was customary, but together they had worked assiduously to build a fortune. Now their son, Grandmother's husband, had spent it all for the sake of the country.

After more than 50 years of observation at close proximity, she had this assessment of her husband and of her father-in-law's role in her husband's work:

> Your grandfather never worried about making money. Instead, he concentrated on how to spend the money well. How could he have done what he did without your great-grandfather?

For her husband's many achievements, Grandmother gave all the credit to her parents-in-law.

5. Grandfather's Notebook

Grandfather claimed that he had never kept a diary. Quite sure he had one hidden away, I asked him several times to show it to me, but he insisted that he didn't have one. He said, "I'm committed to one thing and one thing only in my life, and if I were to be arrested by the Japanese police, they would take me to task because of it."

In retrospect, of the 67 years of his life, Grandfather lived the first 58 years under foreign tyranny, fighting for Korean independence. After the establishment of the South Korean government in 1948, he spent four to five years in a maelstrom of fratricidal madness. In his last three years, he was felled by a stroke. He had lived, in effect, all of two years as "a free person in an independent country," and during those two years he labored on the *Encyclopedia of Korean History*. He simply never had the time to write anything resembling a memoir.

I do, however, have a notebook with a black cover that belonged to him. This notebook contains the drafts of his *sijo* (traditional Korean vernacular poetry), and I have come to look upon it as his diary. On the cover, the title *Chasŏngrok* (自省錄: A Book of Contemplation) appears in his own handwriting. This title, Grandfather once told me, was taken from Toege Yi Hwang's *Chasŏngrok*, which my great-grandfather used to keep on his desk. On opening the cover, I find miscellaneous everyday items tucked away, such as letters that need to be answered, bills to pay, and newspaper clippings. As I turn the pages, I notice that he recorded, in sijo form, the day's events as well as his thoughts and feelings about them.

During the three years that Grandfather was bedridden, my cousin Kang Ho (1934–) and I took turns taking dictation from him. He rarely went to sleep without recording the day's happenings. Most of the for-

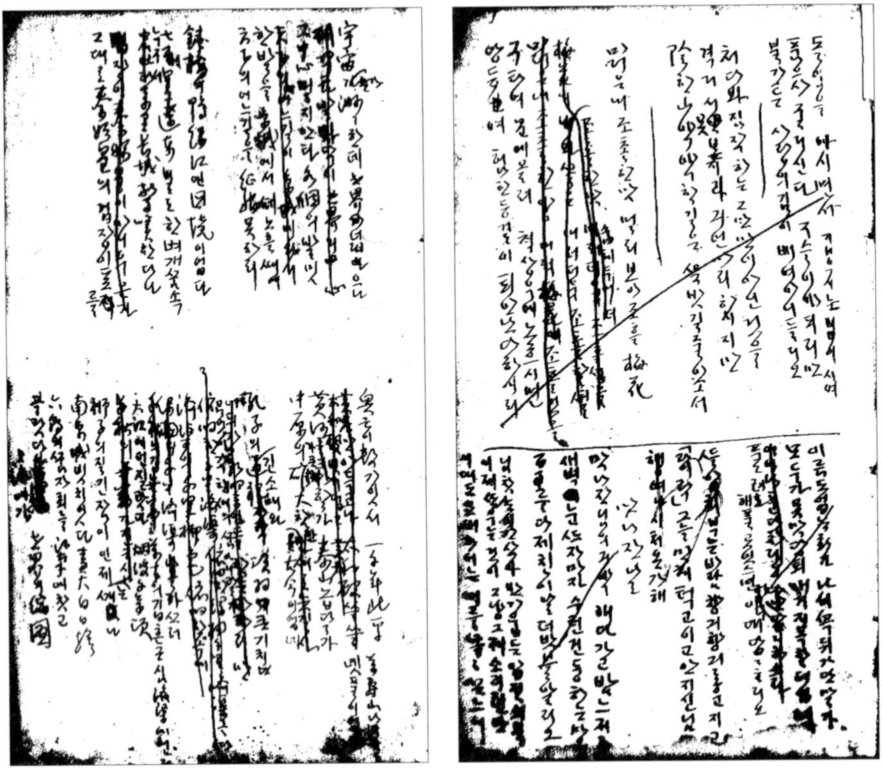

Drafts of Grandfather's sijo, published here for the first time.

(the third sijo in the upper right-hand corner)

From afar, the apricot tree is fragrant and graceful.
Planted in a pot and placed on a table in a room,
Would the roughness of its trunk turn invisible?

merly unpublished works of sijo that were included in the 15-volume *The Complete Works of Yuktang Ch'oe Nam-sŏn*, published in 1973 by Korea University, appear in this notebook. Using the sijo form, he had kept a record of his everyday life. I realize now that this little black notebook *is* his diary.

Here are a few pieces of sijo he wrote in 1919 during his incarceration in Sŏdaemun prison for his independence activities. They show the depth of his love and respect for his parents:

(On his mother's *hwan'gap*, 60th birthday)

With diligence and decorum, you built a tower.
Draped in virtue and decked with love,
You are like the sun, warm and radiant.

Your six branches each are full of buds.
Each bud will blossom into a splendid flower.
May you enjoy sixty years sixty times over.

You have borne me whole,
but now I can't move my body at will.
I want so much to make you smile,
but my hands don't obey my heart.
I'm ashamed of my weak hands
as they hold up the wine cup to you.

A letter Grandfather wrote to his mother who, braving the cold weather, had just visited him in prison. It begins, "I worry that you have returned home safely in the bitter cold. The image of you as you turned to leave stays with me. . . ." (published in *Dong-a Ilbo*, March 1, 1921)

(Commemorating his father's *hwan'gap*, two years before)

You carry with yourself everything noble and strong.
Standing before the mirror you shined for sixty years,
By comparison, how childish and feeble I appear.

Your hard-won possessions are all but gone now.
Though the wine you receive is thin and cold,
I'm moved to see you smile, happy and content.

So that the flowers would bloom, you planted and weeded.
Spring will return, but I see the grey in your beard.
So that you may enjoy Youth returned, I'll tie up Time.

In 1925, Grandfather wrote this sijo a few months after his mother had passed away:

By the day my longing for your warm bosom grows.
The desolate winds of fall already sway in the trees.
Oh, where shall I turn when my hands and feet freeze?

6. Grandfather's "Self-Reminders"

Grandfather did not leave any grand precepts for his children and grandchildren to follow. Instead, he modeled for me frugality and *musilyŏkhaeng* (務實力行: Do your utmost with the task at hand). In his twenties, he included in *Simun Tokpon* (時文讀本: A Reader of Modern Writing, published by Sinmun'gwan, January, 1916) a list titled "Yuktang's Self-Reminders." They were, as the title indicates, reminders to himself, but were surely also precepts he had hoped for his children to follow as well.

Here I include the list in its entirety. The list delineates a true picture of Grandfather as I knew him.

1. Be pure of heart and steady of purpose. Stand tall.
2. Be hot as the sun, untiring as the stream, and lighthearted as the skylark.
3. Do the thing. Do it yourself. Take the first step.
4. Be industrious. Set laziness as life's worst enemy.
5. Do things bit by bit. Nothing gets done in one fell swoop.
6. Do more, then some more, continuously.
7. Be miserly with time, greedy with health, and stubborn with truth.
8. Never regret what is in the past; have faith in the future.
9. Always jump into the center of the problem, and don't tarry in its periphery.
10. Never lay blame on others. Do not think of excuses. Do not get into situations that call for excuses in the first place.
11. Make plans with allowances, but execute them to the letter.
12. Actualize philosophical ideals in ways that produce real benefits.

13. Lay your eyes on the big picture, your feet at the center, and your hands in the details.
14. Find light in the darkness. Wrest greatness from small things. Create huge spaces out of tiny spots.
15. Embrace everything, and let everything embrace you.
16. Be satisfied with the present in order to be content. Do not be content with the future so that it may spur greater effort.
17. Congratulate yourself for work done with great care. Reward yourself for work done to the best of your ability.
18. Do not think small in the wide open space that is heaven and earth. Do not act small in a world so large.
19. Know that you are small. Do not be self-important because the world will go on as before without you. At the same time, know that you are big. Be proud that you, as small as you are, will play a big role indispensable to the world's destiny.
20. Open your eyes and feel what you see. Open your ears and feel what you hear. Throw open your heart and fill it with the mystery and grandeur of the universe. Let your breaths flow into the universe and feel your connection to it.

Chapter 2

The Intersection of Ideologies

1. Grandfather and My Father

My father, Ch'oe Han-in, was born in 1915 as the eldest son of Ch'oe Nam-sŏn. He grew up, however, as the adopted son of Grandfather's elder brother, Ch'ang-sŏn, because Ch'ang-sŏn's wife could not bear him a son. It was the custom of the time for the second son to present his firstborn male child to the first son if he lacked a male heir. Grandmother, who had to give up her first son to be adopted by the elder brother-in-law, once told me, "Your father was taken away from me before I even had a chance to put him to my breast." As a result, my father grew up in a household that included both his birth mother and his adoptive mother, an environment conducive to some uneasiness on his part. He also must have experienced another kind of uneasiness when some people pointed their finger at his famous father for "turning pro-Japanese."

My father was a man of high intelligence and many talents. Graduating in the class of 1929 from Cheil High School (present-day Kyunggi High School), he graduated at the top of his class from the School of Medicine at Kyŏngsŏng Imperial University (present-day Seoul National University). He received his doctorate at age 28, and at the time of Yuggio, was teaching at his alma mater as professor of internal medicine. His medical training notwithstanding, he seems to have been more interested in politics. My father, who died at the early of age 38, was not a man who lived a life of his own choosing. From the extreme repressive rule at the end of the Japanese occupation and to the tumult of Yuggio, my father probably found being the eldest son of my famous grandfather somewhat onerous, certainly more so than I found being the famous man's grandson.

In 1982 my mother gave me a small chest that contained some family memorabilia. Among them were a number of official-looking letters that my ancestors had received on their appointments to government posts, two old books of the Ch'oe genealogy, a few documents of unknown origin, several family seals, an ink stone and brushes that had belonged to my great-grandfather, a thick pocket-sized notebook that Grand-father had used after his incarceration, a dozen or so faded family photographs taken after 1920, the rain-stained calligraphy sign that had hung in front of Sinmun'gwan, and a copy of the original "Declaration of Independence" distributed on March 1, 1919. Also among the memorabilia were my father's diary and college notebooks, as well as a dog-eared notebook he had kept during his refugee days in Pusan. On perusing his diary entries, I discovered that he had often grappled with complicated feelings towards his father and what he stood for.

This family memorabilia survived the fiery destruction of Grandfather's library at Ui-dong in 1951 because my mother had, in the previous spring, taken them with her when she moved her family to Samsŏn'-gyo in order to enroll me in elementary school. Going through the memorabilia, I also found several letters that Grandfather had sent to my father from Manchuria in 1938, when my father was working in a physiology research laboratory in Seoul. Also, from 1943 to the Liberation in 1945, Grandfather sent many more letters to my father, who by then had evacuated to Puan in North Cholla Province. All together, there were about 30 letters, and from these I could glean the nature of the father-son relationship. Each worried about the other's health and safety, and they exchanged surprisingly detailed information about household finances and various family events, including the naming of grandchildren.

Among the memorabilia, my father's diary held the greatest interest for me. As if in a composition notebook, he wrote in a random fashion about his daily issues, switching often from Korean to English, and sometimes German. Not one line was in Japanese. Now and then, he wrote poems in Korean that showed his sensitivity to the nuances of old Korean expressions. He wrote at length about his two-year courtship of my mother, their eventual marriage, and the raising of their young children. The most affecting entry was the one in which he wrote about his eldest daughter, Yŏng-ju, who brought great joy to Grandfather with her sweet playfulness, and the sorrow and helplessness that he, as a medical doctor, felt when she died of dysentery at age 3.

My father would have never, in his wildest dreams, imagined that his son would be reading his diary 70 years later. Through his written words, I could sense that he thought of his father as someone he would have to share with the rest of the world and that he felt somewhat conflicted about being unable to monopolize his father's love.

You make me warm–how, I do not know.
You make me strong wherever I go.

If my father is the father to his country
The way he is the father to his son,
Who among my countrymen
Would deem himself unfortunate?

Today, whether or not a child gains admission to a good college determines the happiness of the entire family. This fact of life was no different in my father's time, and my family appears to have been no exception. My father's diary entry from March 25, 1935, shows a snapshot of a close-knit family that includes a fun-loving grandmother. It was the spring of the year when Grandfather turned 46 and Grandmother, 49. In the entry, my father gives a detailed description of the family as it reacts to the news of his younger brother, Han-ung, being admitted to the Preparatory College of Medicine at Seoul National University. Han-ung, born in 1917, is my second uncle, the second son of Ch'oe Nam-sŏn.

> It didn't quite sink in at first when someone cried, "Ung made it!" showing me the newspaper extra. Immediately afterwards, I heard everyone in the room shouting, "Hooray!" Gŏm, who had been crying at the top of his lungs for one reason or another, stopped crying, sensing the sudden change of atmosphere in the room. I took hold of Ung's hand, and we shook hands for the first time in our lives. I teased him that he owed his admission to me, the tutor, and therefore owed me a bow. He immediately got up and gave me a deep bow, kneeling on the floor. Soon we found ourselves overcome with the euphoria that had swept over us. It took a while for us to actually believe that the good fortune was indeed ours. Again and again, I pored over the newspaper announcement. Yes, there was his name, all three characters of it!
>
> We all waited anxiously for our father's return. Had his shoes suddenly gotten heavy? Had the cotton cloth of his outfit suddenly turned into heavy gold? Had anyone stopped him during his walk to prevent his speedy return to us? Then we made a pact

among ourselves to withhold the good news for a brief moment so that we could savor the moment when his expression would change from disappointment to joy. We would tell him upon his return that the list of admitted students had been reported, but that it did not include Ung's name.

At last, he came home. Mother said, "*Yobo* (Dear), the newspaper's here, but it looks like Ung has . . . not made it." Father, ever considerate of the feelings of those around him, just gazed at the newspaper with a deep sigh, not wanting to hurt his son's feelings. Then, pointing to a spot in the newspaper, he said, "Something's not right–I see Ung's name here. . . ." We sensed that his immediate response was not what we had expected it to be. He seemed rather preoccupied, possibly with something that might have happened during his walk. But soon, his preoccupation dispersing, he got happier and happier by the minute. Watching him, we couldn't help feeling a bit sorry for him. Oh, the pressures of fatherhood!

At the time of this entry, Grandfather and Grandmother had just moved to a smaller house in Hyoje-dong. Both were deeply troubled with their respective worries, Grandmother with household finances and Grandfather with the larger issues affecting the country.

2. My Father's Diary Entry of April 2, 1934

In his diary entry of April 2, 1934, my father writes a rough summary of what he heard from Grandfather about why he, a few years before, had joined the Commission for the Compilation of Chosŏn History. My father had obviously planned to revisit this entry at a later date, but unfortunately his own death preceded his father's. I read the entry, thinking, *What father would tell his son something that is not true?* Between the lines of the entry, I was able to read the innermost feelings and struggles of the intellectuals of the day.

> Back in my room, I have a reason to sit down promptly at my desk and lift my pen. It's to record the emotions that are welling up inside me upon hearing, face to face, Father's view on religion, which, in one blow, demolished my own childish views on the subject. The narrow-minded ideas that I long held, along with the sundry ideas that I came across in my readings, all came tumbling down. His certainty definitely trumped my own.
>
> As soon as Father taught himself the Korean alphabet at age five, he read old Korean novels. He soon read the New Testament, laboriously translated by Western hands. It was a feast like he had never laid eyes on before, and having feasted on it, he was mesmerized by it until he reached his mid-teens.
>
> When he went to Japan with the other Korean students, there was yet another feast laid out before him. All 700–800 Korean students aspired to go into law with an eye to public positions, with two exceptions–Father and Chang Ŭng-jin. Their interests lay in literature and philosophy. The new ideas they encountered broadened their thinking horizons. Their world view, once bound

by Chinese learning, opened up in Japan, a country that had incorporated Western ideas before China. The new trend of the time, socialism, did not leave them untouched, either. At age 17 and 18, Father followed the likes of Sakai Toshihiko, founder of the Japanese Communist Party.

During his studies in Japan, Korea never left his mind. He thought hard about Korean national identity and the development of Korean national character. At this time, he was stimulated by the ideas of Tolstoy, then 78. *A Confession* left a huge impression on him. Yi Kwang-su followed him in his admiration of Tolstoy, but Hong Myŏng-hi was more attracted to Turgenev. Steeped in these new ideas, the three resolved to become trailblazers in the study of Korean culture.

As a first step, Father began to introduce Western books to Korea. Soon afterwards, however, the Resident-General of Japan arrived in Seoul, turning Korea into a semi-Japan. Father struggled against this situation for over a decade. The money he spent during this time had been accumulated by his own father by the sweat of his brow. During these years, he began to study history. He was not interested in history for its own sake. He came to believe firmly that the only way to establish Korean identity is through history. However, on opening the first of page of history books, he was shocked to discover that Tan'gun was nowhere to be found. The very beginning of Korean history had been excised out of existence. Indignation soon followed shock. For over ten years, he tried to correct this omission, without much success.

After the March First Independence Movement, while in prison, he completed his theory of Tan'gun. On his release, he published his well-researched thesis on Tan'gun, but the public was not interested and called him a "Tan'gun-ist." At this juncture, he bid farewell to the first half of his life, which had been filled with a dizzying array of activities. There was nothing left for him to do, but he couldn't just sit idly by. He found the only thing left for him in the side branch of history, so he picked it up. By this time, his approach to history had undergone a sea change from his earlier days.

I have written all this without stopping to make any changes or corrections.... I'll have time to do that later....

When Grandfather joined the Commission for the Compilation of Chosŏn History, which was affiliated with the Japanese Government-General of Korea, some pointed a critical finger at him. Grandfather, who was a historian and not a politician, had a valid reason for his actions, however. When a falsehood appears in print, it has a way of morphing into truth. Because Grandfather was cognizant of the power of the printed word, he put all his energy and resources into his efforts to save the nation through publishing. He could not sit idly by when it had become obvious to him that the aim of the Commission was to publish a falsified version of Korean history. Moreover, Grandfather was in the process of preparing his manuscript for the *Encyclopedia of Korean History*, and he felt he needed to confront the aim of the Commission in person.

For two decades prior to 1928, Grandfather had been single-minded in his involvement with various nation-saving endeavors, such as the founding of Sinmun'gwan (The Institute for New Learning) and Chosŏn Kwangmunhoe (The Institute for the Illumination of Chosŏn Culture), the publication of the magazines *Sonyŏn* (Boys), *Ch'ŏngch'un* (Youth), *Tongmyŏng* (Dawn), and the newspaper *Sidae Ilbo* (Times Daily). Through all these years, his commitment to the study of Korean history was steadfast. There was no other reason that would have persuaded him to abandon these single-minded efforts to join the Commission. It is true that his financial situation was somewhat constrained at this time, but he and his family had enough to eat from the proceeds of the land owned by his elder brother. It is not entirely impossible that his straitened circumstances could have opened a crack for Japanese manipulation, but his financial situation simply was not that desperate. He had been able to send his four children to college, and he himself was not a stranger to a life of austerity.

Grandfather once told me that while he was incarcerated, he received, as a political prisoner, fairly decent treatment. His chores were to sweep the floors and arrange the books in the prison library, and after finishing with that, he was free to read. Away from the business of the outside world, he had the luxury of time to study the origins of Korean history. His concentrated study and research led him to a moment of clarity about Korea's origin. It was the concept of "park (밝)," *bright* or *light*, which was based on the names of the mountains in Northeast Asia, and this concept became central to his study of Korean history. I truly believe that Grandfather became involved with the Commission in order to confront and refute the historical falsification perpetrated by the Japanese Government-General. His aim was to replace their fabrications with his own concept of Korean origins. My father's diary entry from April 2, 1934, irrefutably confirms Grandfather's motivation for joining the Commission.

3. Grandfather's Advice: "Don't Major in the Humanities"

Grandfather was appointed professor at the National University of Manchuria in 1938 and resigned from the post in November of 1942 for health reasons. Considering the political situation at the time, his health probably was not the sole reason for his resignation, but it is true that his health had suffered significantly during his stay in Manchuria. My father sent him a letter detailing the diet he should follow for diabetes. Grandfather replied, letting his son know how his move was progressing and detailing his departure schedule. Enclosed in Grandfather's letter dated December 13, 1942, was a letter that his youngest son, Han-gŏm, had sent Grandfather from Tokyo.

> Dear In,
>
> I have studied the meal plan that you sent me the other day, but it appears that a diet of rice porridge will have to do until I return to Seoul. I regret that I'll have to present myself to the family in my weakened state. I heard the sad news about Mr. Noh, but I could not send a telegram. I've mailed a condolence note instead, but I'm not sure if it has been received.
>
> Mr. Yi Tae-jong will leave Manchuria on the 15th to recruit teachers in Seoul and will arrive in the city the next day. I have sent a couple of boxes to check in and a package of books to travel with him. (You'll need a receipt to claim the boxes at the station, and the books are rather heavy, so I suggest you take someone to help you.) I trust you will thank him properly for his troubles.
>
> The bigger items will be packed in the next four or five days and will be taken to the shipper. I'm so relieved that whatever

needs to be done on the home front is done. It looks like Gŏm is determined to change his major (see his letter enclosed). He plans to arrive in Seoul a day or two before my arrival. I'll leave here around the 20th.

December 13, from a hotel in Xinqing

In his letter, Grandfather expressed concern about the worry he would cause the family with his unhealthy appearance, the heavy packages his son would have to pick up, and his youngest son's resistance to his advice about not majoring in the humanities. What interested me most was the enclosed letter from Han-gŏm, who had apparently asked his elder brother, Han-in, to intercede for him with his father. Judging from the content of Han-gŏm's letter, Grandfather had sent him a letter listing the reasons he should not major in the humanities.

There were four reasons he had spelled out for his son: first, the future prospects for a humanities major were poor; second, teaching lifestyle conflicts with scholarly pursuits; third, he himself was not ready for a scholarly life, and nor was society; and lastly, the state of his health could not handle its rigors. I can infer from these four reasons that Grandfather was speaking from his own experience. He was warning his son about the challenges he himself was facing at the time. However, his son was adamant that somebody had to stand up to reality and do what needed to be done. Going against his father's advice, he enrolled at the department of philosophy at Tokyo Imperial University. It was a classic case of "like father, like son."

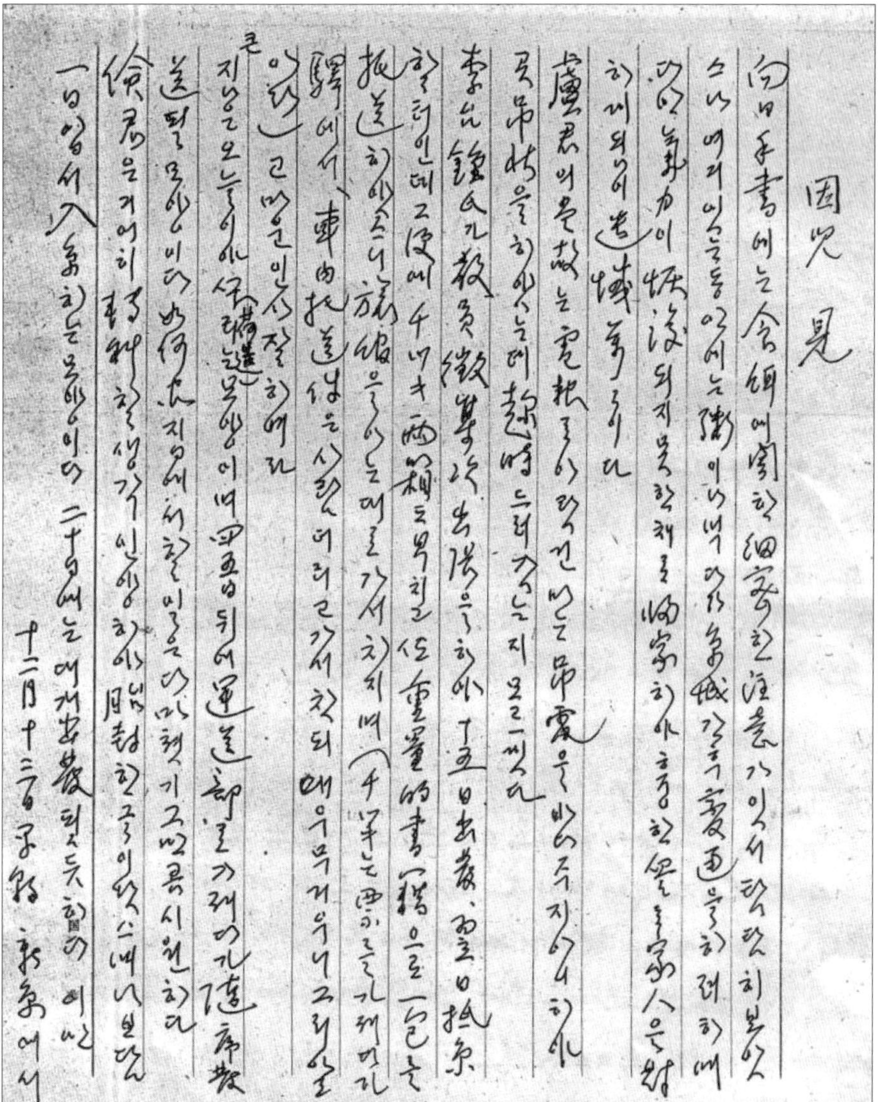

A letter Grandfather sent from Manchuria to my father on December 13, 1942, in which he tells his son about his imminent return to Seoul.

The following is the letter that Han-gŏm sent his father on December 7, 1942. It shows self-confidence typical of a spirited 21-year-old. I often wished, however, that my uncle had taken Grandfather's advice. Later in this book, I will write about his tumultuous life.

Dear Father:

I have just received your much awaited reply. It concerns me greatly that your health isn't improving. I'm so worried I don't know what to do. My winter recess is from December 24 to January 5. I had planned to stay in Tokyo, but have changed my mind and will return to Seoul. Due to train schedules, I will leave Tokyo on the 19th and will arrive in Seoul on the 20th.

Please forgive me for bothering you in your poor health with this matter, but since it has been occupying my thoughts day and night, I feel I must bring it up in my letter. Although the four reasons you have pointed out make me wince with their great acuity, here I want to present, with all due respect, my own thoughts on the matter.

1. Poor future prospects for humanities majors

In this regard, I feel there is little difference between law majors and humanities majors. Although it is true that there is a significant difference between the two majors in terms of being able to make a living, it is not impossible for humanities majors to make a decent living. Actually, in the worst cases, there is very little difference between them. For me, there is a good chance I would be one of the worst cases if I chose law.

2. Conflict between teaching and scholarship
I don't think there would be a problem if teaching does not interfere with my scholarly pursuits. It is one of the legacies of my esteemed high school that we should try to ascribe meaning to whatever we choose to pursue in life.

3. Personal ability and the readiness of society
I have the weakest argument to this point, but I do have a modicum of trust in my own ability. As for the readiness of society, I have no choice but to entrust myself to the society I was born into.

4. My health
I have little to say on this subject since it is somewhat beyond my control.

I understand that it is impossible for a man, who is tied to reality, to completely ignore it. However, if he were to simply prostrate himself before this reality, where would the energy come from to drive its progress? Do you think that going along with the tide will provide this energy? I doubt very much that it comes from those who, lacking passion for improvement, simply bow down before reality. While I am aware I have to face a reality over which I have little control, can I not at least expect it to make small compromises with my own dreams?

I'll be sure to give more thought to this matter when I get home.

Your son, Gŏm

4. My Maternal Grandfather, Yi Ik-sang

In 1936, my father, Ch'oe Han-in, married my mother (Yi Sŏn-yŏng, 1917-2006), the eldest daughter of Yi Ik-sang (1895-1935). According to my father's diary, Pak Yŏng-hi, the daughter of Pak Sŏk-yun (Ch'oe Nam-sŏn's brother-in-law) had introduced them to each other. After two years of courtship, when my father announced his wish to marry my mother, his family opposed the match because my mother's family had six daughters and no sons. My mother's family also had reservations because the prospective father-in-law was "too famous." The marriage took place, however, in spite of the two families' initial opposition. Apparently, the

The gathering of the entire Ch'oe family at the wedding of my parents in November of 1936. Directly behind the bride and bridegroom stand Ch'oe Nam-sŏn and his wife (my father's birth parents) and to their left, in formal attire, stand Ch'oe Ch'ang-sŏn and his wife (my father's adoptive parents). Ch'oe Tu-sŏn, my great uncle, stands in the front row, to the far left.

two families were flexible enough not to impede the marriage.

My maternal grandfather, Sŏng-hae Yi Ik-sang, journalist and novelist.

A year before her marriage, my mother's father passed away. He died of tuberculosis at age 41. He was from Chŏnju, and his pen name was Sŏng-hae, meaning "a sea of stars." I often wondered why he had given himself such a pen name. I never met him, of course, but he seems to have been someone who inhabited a world of ideals. He went to Tokyo for his college education, and after graduating from the department of sociology at Nihon University, he returned to Seoul and worked as a reporter at *Chosŏn Ilbo*, as the head of the culture section at *Dong-a Ilbo*, and then as the editor-in-chief at *Maeil Sinbo*.

Yi Ik-sang's literary output represents the "new wave" or the socialist trend of the time. Along with Kim Pal-bong and Pak Yŏng-hi, he was one of the eight founders of the PASKYULA literary movement. Two years later, in 1925, as one of the founders of the Korean Artists Proletarian Federation, he wrote about the class struggle in Korea. His works have all but disappeared in South Korea, but in North Korea, they appear in *The Anthology of Chosŏn Literature*. The short stories of his that I have read mainly explore the theme of rural inequities. Through these works, he wanted to raise the consciousness of the Korean peasants who, crushed by extreme poverty, were oblivious to their own victimhood.

My maternal grandfather, Yi Ik-sang, was of slender build. He married his wife (Sin Kye-jŏng, 1899-1954) at age 21, and they had a happy marriage, according to my mother. My grandmother, from Puan, was gentle and affectionate. She was the cousin of Sin Sŏk-jŏng, one of the first modern Korean poets, who became famous for his poem "The Candlelight."

My maternal grandfather and grandmother had six daughters. The story behind how my mother married my father remains unclear in my mind. Based on my father's diary, it appears that they married for love, but according to my mother, she decided to marry my father for a less romantic reason. She felt that, with her father's passing, she had little chance of going to college and therefore decided to marry. Now, as I ponder the life they led together, with both of them long gone, the differing accounts of how they came to marry seem little more than a footnote.

Yi Ik-sang's eldest daughter, Sŏn-yŏng, married my father, and the second daughter, Sŏn-ok, married Kim Kak-hun, a friend of my father's from the Cheil High School days. Unlike my father, Kim had studied law. At the time of the Liberation, he was the manager of the Chinnampo branch of the Chosŏn Central Bank, and after the establishment of the North Korean government in 1948, he managed the national currency at the Chosŏn Bank in Pyongyang. At the beginning of Yuggio, during the North Korean occupation of Seoul, he visited my mother to deliver news of his wife, my mother's younger sister, and left two photographs of their two sons, In-gi and Mun-gi. I still have my cousins' photographs tucked away in my desk drawer.

The third daughter, Sŏn-dong, who had an outgoing personality, married a man named Kang Pil-jin from Kongju, who was in the pharmaceutical business. A well-known businessman in Ch'ungch'ŏng Province, he was a dyed-in-the-wool anti-communist.

After the marriage of her three eldest daughters, my maternal grandmother moved back to her hometown of Puan. Among all the "grandmothers" (elderly female members of the extended family), I loved my maternal grandmother the most. In turn, she attended to my every wish. After the war when food was scarce, she killed the last chicken she had in her yard and cooked it for me to eat. I enjoyed visiting her home in Puan. At the back of the her house, there was a bamboo forest that swayed in the cool breeze, and during summer vacations, my aunts often took me to Pyŏnsan Beach and Naesosa Temple, which were nearby.

The fourth daughter was somewhat poor in health, and after graduating from Chŏnju Girls' High School, she married a man named Kim Chŏng-gu, who later became the son that my grandmother never had. Committed to the enlightenment movement for the peasant population of rural Korea, he worked as the principal of an elementary school in Chŏlla Province. In the mountainous regions of this province, the vestiges of the Tonghak Rebellion (the peasant uprising of 1894) still remained. Many bright young men who had returned from studying in Japan felt it their duty to lead the rural movement. Kim was one of them.

As Yuggio drew to a close, Kim went to Chiri Montain to join the North Korean Army led by Yi Hyŏn-sang and was later captured by the South Korean police. Unknown to him at the time, North Korea had abandoned Yi's partisan unit. The young men who had followed Yi into the recesses of the mountain never dreamed that they would be so easily abandoned. At my grandmother's earnest and repeated appeals during his captivity, Kim eventually renounced his communist ideas.

I would sometimes run into Kim during my visits to my grandmother's house, and whenever I did, I couldn't help feeling incredibly sad for him. After his wife, my aunt, died from complications of childbirth with her second son, Kim remarried. A few years later, his eldest son came to see my mother, his mother's eldest sister. On this occasion, I learned the history of my mother's family. Even after his remarriage, Kim took care of my maternal grandmother, his one-time mother-in-law, until the day she died.

As I learned the divergent life histories of my maternal aunts' husbands, I began to get a vague understanding of the consciences and aspirations of Korea's young educated youths as they lived through the Japanese occupation, the Liberation, and Yuggio, as well as the agonies they must have suffered during these historical events. Theirs was indeed a time fraught with unimaginable challenges, with no one correct choice to be made, even with the benefit of hindsight.

Later in my youth, I learned that my maternal grandfather also had a son. He had six daughters with his wife, and a son with a Japanese woman. While he was studying in Tokyo, the 1923 Kanto Earthquake almost destroyed the city, and the Japanese blamed the Koreans. In danger of losing his life, Yi was saved by a Japanese friend who hid him in his home. During his hiding, he fell in love with his friend's elder sister, Yamaguchi Nobuko, and together they had a son. I learned later that Yamaguchi had worked as a journalist in Xinqing until the early 1940s.

In the summer of 1959, a man approaching middle age came to see my mother. In Japanese, he introduced himself to my mother, "My name is Shō. My father is Yi Ik-sang of Chosŏn. And I am your half brother."

I was then a high school student with a passing knowledge of English, and we conversed in halting English. He said that he had come to Korea on official business. His business card indicated that he was a government official. His mother must not have married because she had given her son her maiden name. He also told us that she had inherited, after the war, a sizable fortune from her parents and that she was then living comfortably in her maiden home. Since the meeting, Shō and my mother exchanged letters a few times, but their correspondence gradually came to a stop. One day my mother said softly, "Don't hate the Japanese so much. One of them is your uncle, and his children are your cousins. The world needs to change."

My mother's life in her father's house had been difficult, but her married life in the Ch'oe household was even more so. While she took care of her elderly parents-in-law in Ui-dong, she also had to look after her brother-in-law, who was repeatedly incarcerated at Sŏdaemun prison for his communist activities. Upon learning that he wished to marry a girl from Ulsan, she made the trip to the girl's parents' home to gain their approval. During Yuggio, she was persecuted by the Korean Youth Corps who wanted to find out the whereabouts of her husband. With his death during the war, she became a widow in 1952. She returned to Myo-dong to live with her in-laws and managed their household. It was not until Grandfather's death in 1957 that she was able to move to her own home in Samsŏn'gyo.

My mother was an able woman. She ran a business to support her two children, my sister and me. She was a close friend of Sim Chae-wan, the daughter of Sim U-sŏp, who was a good friend of Grandfather's since childhood. The two friends became partners in a school uniform business. Kim Wŏn-gyu, who was an English teacher at Kyunggi Girls' High School, helped them grow their business with his contacts. Soon their business supplied uniforms to Kyunggi Middle School and High School, Seoul Middle School and High School, and other secondary schools in Seoul. She also opened a branch in Sinsin Department Store.

Thanks to my mother's business sense, I grew up in material comfort, lacking nothing.

When my great-uncle Tu-sŏn died, he left his house to me, the *chong-son* of the Ch'oe Hŏn-gyu family line, out of appreciation for my mother who, as the eldest daughter-in-law, had contributed in no small measure to the peace and well-being of the extended Ch'oe family through tumultuous times. My mother passed away at age 90 in the United States. Following in the footsteps of her parents-in-law, she had become a Catholic in her seventies.

5. My Great-Uncle, Ch'oe Tu-sŏn

It was one fine day in the spring of 1960. The previous fall, on the second anniversary of Grandfather's death, a ceremony had taken place at Sowŏn in Ui-dong to erect a monument in his memory. Complications from a recent surgery had prevented me from attending the ceremony. That spring day was the day of the *chesa* (ancestral rite) for my great-grandfather, Ch'oe Hŏn-gyu, so all the family members had gathered together at my house, the house of the *chongson*. Tu-sŏn and Sŏl-gyŏng came with their spouses to take part in the memorial rite for their father. The sons and daughters of relatives who had benefitted over the years from my great-grandfather's generosity also came, making the gathering the largest one since Yuggio.

After the rite was over, Tu-sŏn, the eldest living member of the Ch'oe family, told everyone to sit down and announced that I had just entered college, adding that the *chongson* of the Ch'oe family had now reached maturity. With my college entrance, I had suddenly become a full-fledged grown-up, who had the responsibility of tending to all Ch'oe family matters, big and small. Among the matters that were discussed that day was the problem of the ancestral burial ground at Ssang'gyeri, which had fallen into disrepair during the war. Adding to this problem was the increasing number of visitors who came to pay their respects to Grandfather since his death. The situation had actually become more than just a family problem.

What kind of a man was my great-uncle Tu-sŏn who, with one brief announcement, had just handed me this huge responsibility? My mother, the eldest daughter-in-law of the family, regarded him with the utmost respect and admiration. A close friend of her own father, Yi Ik-sang, she had known him since before her marriage. Tu-sŏn,

The two brothers, Nam-sŏn and Tu-sŏn, in April of 1957. Grandfather died later that year, on October 10.

she thought, was the most refined of the three brothers, with the comportment of a "typical European gentleman." According to my mother, Ch'ang-sŏn, the eldest brother, was a rather taciturn man with a stubborn mien, while Nam-sŏn, her father-in-law, was a rugged-looking man with a booming voice. In contrast, Tu-sŏn, the youngest, always had a gentle and open smile, giving the impression that he could converse with anyone on just about any subject.

In 1917, Tu-sŏn graduated from Waseda University at the top of his class, recipient of a gold watch given by the Japanese Emperor each year to students of exceptional academic merit. Around this time, a rumor spread among the Korean students in Tokyo that Tu-sŏn had abruptly returned to Korea for some unknown reason. He had, however, hastily returned to Korea with a clear mission: At his brother Nam-sŏn's urging, he had joined Kim Sŏng-su in his education efforts.

When Kim was incarcerated for his participation in the March First Movement, Tu-sŏn took over his work, serving as principal at Chung'-ang High School. After Kim's release, Tu-sŏn went to Germany to study philosophy. Upon receiving his doctorate, he returned to Korea in 1925. He discovered that Nam-sŏn had been struggling with a debt of 200,000 won (20 million US dollars) incurred during his involvement with the publication of *Tongmyŏng and Sidae Ilbo*. With his father's approval, Tu-sŏn paid a portion of the debt by selling some of his father's property. After his father's death, in spite of the worldwide depression, Tu-sŏn paid off the rest of the debt by selling the family's land. His elder brothers' protests notwithstanding, he did not inherit one single piece of land from his father's estate. Worldly possessions simply did not interest him.

During his study in Europe, Tu-sŏn was not impressed by the prevailing materialist ideas. On his return, he built on his experience as principal of Chung'ang High School and, in 1932, became one of the executive directors of Posŏng Institute, founded by Kim Sŏng-su. Posŏng Institute later grew into Korea University under Tu-sŏn's leadership.

Although he had little political ambition, Tu-sŏn served as ambassador-at-large of South Korea to the United Nations during the war years, as Kim's Hanmin Party supported Syngman Rhee during his presidency. Also, working in tandem with the Min'guk Party (an offshoot of Kim's Hanmin Party), he successfully brought *Dong-a Ilbo* to the forefront of the struggle for freedom of speech against Rhee's dictatorship. However, throughout the years of political storm that raged from the Liberation to the national division, Yuggio, the Pusan political crisis, and, finally, to the demise of the Chayu Party, Syngman Rhee and Ch'oe Tu-sŏn refrained from inflicting harm on each other.

Inch'on Kim Sŏng-su and Kakch'ŏn Ch'oe Tu-sŏn(October 1925). On his return from Germany, where he studied philosophy, Tu-sŏn collaborated with Kim Sŏng-su to further the cause of Korean education, journalism, and business.

It was the early spring of 1957, the year Grandfather passed away. I was taking dictation for Grandfather's eulogy of Kim Sŏng-su, which was going to be published in the newspaper on the second anniversary of his death. Ever since Grandfather had become bedridden after his stroke, I would read the daily newspapers aloud to him, and therefore had a vague idea of Kim Sŏng-su as a public figure who had preceded Sin Ik-hi and Cho Byŏng-ok, politicians who had died during the previous presidential election. I asked Grandfather to tell me more about Kim Sŏng-su. He said, simply, "On Kim's left side stood Song Chin-u and on his right, Ch'oe Tu-sŏn."

It is not clear whether Grandfather first met Kim through Song during the March First Movement, or whether he himself introduced Song to Kim. At any rate, the four men–Ch'oe Nam-sŏn, Song Chin-u, Kim

Sŏng-su, and Ch'oe Tu-sŏn–had all attended Waseda University within a few years of one another during the 1910s, and it is quite likely that they, as educated young men of spirit, resolved to shoulder the burden of the times together. When Kim needed his father's money in order to take over Posŏng Institute, he asked Grandfather to intercede for him. With Grandfather's visit to Ch'ŏng'ŭp, where Kim's father lived, the matter was settled. Kim's father, a landowner of great wealth who had an abiding interest in the study of Korean history, had immediately assented. It was also Grandfather who urged his youngest brother, who had recently graduated from Waseda University, to join Kim in his education projects.

Koha Song Chin-u, journalist and president of *Dong-a Ilbo*.

For more than 30 years, until the establishment of the Korean government in 1948, these three men–Kim Sŏng-su, Song Chin-u, and Ch'oe Tu-sŏn–worked tirelessly in various fields ranging from education, journalism, and industry to politics. Ch'oe Tu-sŏn, being the youngest, outlived the other two, and served as the first prime minister of the Third Republic after the May 16 Coup, playing an indispensable role in stabilizing the country.

In 1963, Park Chung Hee, hoping, as president-elect, to persuade Tu-sŏn to head his government as prime minister, paid a visit to Tu-sŏn at his home in Sŏngbuk-dong. During the visit, which lasted about 50 minutes, no beverage was served. As he was leaving, Park, curious,

My great-uncle, Ch'oe Tu-sŏn, and his wife, Kim Sun-yŏng.

asked why he had not been given anything to drink. Tu-sŏn respectfully replied, "I was concerned about the possibility of something untoward happening to the head of state."

Tu-sŏn was circumspect in all matters and showed astute judgment in all situations. Even though he served as prime minister, he put distance between himself and politics. The proudest moment of his career, he said, was when, as president of the Korean Red Cross, he successfully arranged a meeting whose objective was to search for separated family members in North Korea and South Korea. If he had any political ambition at all, it was the reunification of his country.

When Tu-sŏn left Korea in 1922 to study abroad, he left behind the marriage that his parents had arranged for him in his early teens. Many progressive young men of the day found themselves in similar situations. Three years after he returned from Germany, at age 32, he sought out

Kim Sun-yŏng (1899–1975), whom he had met while she was studying at Tokyo Teacher's College for Women (class of 1925). After graduating, she had returned to Seoul and started teaching Japanese language and history at Chŏngsin Girls' High School and Tongdŏk Girls' High School, and had moved on to Hosudon Girls' High School in Kaesŏng. Ch'oe and Kim married in 1933, and on her marriage, Kim retired from public life.

One day while I was in college, I asked Kim, who was then in her mid-sixties, "Have you ever felt that all your education was wasted?" She answered, "Of course I have, but it couldn't be helped." Fully aware of her husband's role as a leading public figure, she, even though personally supportive of feminist causes, was concerned that her public career might adversely affect her husband. Her withdrawal from public life was a reflection of the inviolable wall that a modern woman of intelligence faced at the time.

In the private sphere, Kim helped her husband in no small measure, especially with her fluency in Japanese and English. Born and raised in Pusan, she had retained a hint of a Kyŏngsang accent, which many people found appealing. With the inheritance she received from her well-to-do parents, she made generous contributions to Ewha Women's College, Dŏksŏng Women's College, Chinmyŏng Girls' High School, and many other educational institutions for women. During her tenure as financial officer and then vice-president of the Association of University Graduate Women, the scope of its activities widened. At the same time, she made a considerable contribution to the land purchase and to the construction of a building that the Association needed.

In 1975, one year after the death of Kim's husband, the building was completed, and the Association members dedicated it to her in her name. She was 77 years old then. Having relinquished her own public career, she promoted, both directly and indirectly, the advancement of Korean women in a variety of fields, including education, politics, culture, and art. Out of public view, Kim played a significant role in paving the way for the women's liberation movement in Korean society.

6. My Great-Aunt's Husband, Pak Sŏk-yun

My great-aunt Sŏl-gyŏng (1899–1989) is Ch'oe Nam-sŏn's youngest sister. On graduating from Kyunggi Girls' High School in Seoul, she traveled to Tokyo to pursue a college education. There she met Pak Sŏk-yun (1896–1950), who was attending Tokyo Imperial University after graduating from Hwimun High School in Seoul. Due to the existing custom of men marrying in their early teens, it was difficult for educated women to meet men "without a past." Sŏl-gyŏng, however, had the unusual good fortune to meet a bachelor. She once said, "I decided to marry Pak because he had not been previously married, a rare thing in Korean men." They were two years apart in age, and had four children. The couple lived in Myŏng'yun-dong, right next to my maternal grandfather, Yi Ik-sang. Pak and Yi became good friends, bonding over their shared commitment to Korean journalism.

Pak is known for having introduced baseball to Korea. In 1925, while he was in Kyoto, he formed a baseball team of Korean students, which won a game against a team representing the Japanese students. In addition, he created a sensation in Korea when a newspaper published a picture of the winning team holding a flag with the *t'ae'gŭk*, the central element of the Korean flag. For a time, he was a Korean hero, much like Son Ki-jŏng, who became a national hero by winning the gold medal in the marathon at the Berlin Olympics of 1936.

I remember Pak as a good-looking man with masculine features and an athletic build. I also remember him as a man who acted on his beliefs. Because he threw himself wholeheartedly into everything he did, my great-aunt often worried that her husband "did too many things too much."

My great-aunt, Ch'oe Sŏl-gyŏng, and her husband, Pak Sŏk-yun.

In February of 1930, *Maeil Sinbo*, having instituted a new policy of hiring a Korean as its vice-president, invited Pak to fill the position. This caused a furor in the Japanese conservative wing, and soon developed into what was called "the Rose of Sharon" incident. A design showing a rose of Sharon, the Korean national flower, had been inserted in the masthead of the newspaper since Pak's appointment. Previously, the masthead design had shown a map of Japan that included Korea and Taiwan. To make matters worse, the newspaper had allocated more space for a statement by the incoming vice-president than for the official celebratory statement for the anniversary of the inception of the Japanese Empire. An order came down from above that the original design be reinstated in three days. This time, Pak responded by simply deleting the design from the masthead altogether. He was a man of true grit.

Pak was an expert on international politics, with a genius for languages. After majoring in German Law at Tokyo Imperial University, he went to

France and Germany to study political science and European languages. On his return, he spent time studying international law and politics at a research institute at Tokyo Imperial University and then at Cambridge University in England. His stellar academic background later sent him all over the world, to places including Europe, the United States, Russia, and China. Pak, whose original aspiration had been to become a scholar of international law, believed that Korean independence was possible through the restructuring of international power, not by an armed insurrection by the Korean people.

In 1937, while doing research on China in Beijing, Pak was appointed Counselor of Foreign Affairs of Manchukuo, a position equivalent to today's vice-minister. Puyi, the last emperor of the Qing dynasty, was the nominal head of the newly founded Manchukuo. Although a puppet government of Japan, Manchukuo needed the trappings of an independent state. The ministers in the cabinet were Chinese or Manchu, but the vice-ministers, who were Japanese, were the ones who held the real power over all areas of the government. Within this organization, a Korean had been appointed vice-minister. Pak had been recommended by the Minister of Foreign Affairs in Japan, Matsuoka Yosuke, who was an alumnus of Tokyo Imperial University. Pak apparently had an excellent reputation in Tokyo political circles.

In 1933, Pak traveled to Geneva as part of the group that negotiated the Arms Reduction Treaty at the League of Nations, and on this trip he developed a close friendship with Lieutenant Colonel Ishihara Ganji, who participated in the negotiation as a military attaché. When Ishihara later took over the reins of the Kwantung Army as well as Manchukuo, many people surmised that Ch'oe Nam-sŏn went to Manchuria by way of Pak's connection to Ishihara. This is not true, however. His teaching post in Manchuria was arranged by Lieutenant Colonel Tsuji of the Kwantung Army, who had earlier visited him in Seoul to negotiate the terms of his appointment to professorship in the newly founded National University of Manchuria. The Governor-General of Korea at the time, Minami Jirō, had vehemently objected to Ch'oe Nam-sŏn's appointment because of his earlier involvement in the March First Movement. In the end, his appointment was cleared after a much contested debate between the generals in the Kwantung Army and the top officials in Japan.

According to my great-aunt, Pak was not on good terms with Governor-General Minami, whom he had alienated by bitterly criticizing his rice-rationing policy of "5 *hops* (1 hop=3 oz.) for the Japanese, 4 *hops* for the Koreans." Koreans would receive 5 *hops* only if they adopted Japanese names. At her husband's request, my great-aunt always wore a *hanbok* (Korean short jacket and long skirt) at official diplomatic functions. The Japanese government offered Pak a professorship at Kyŏngsŏng Imperial University to entice him to change his name to a Japanese one, but he resisted to the end, as Ch'oe Nam-sŏn did. At one time, while he was traveling in China, his Korean name caught the attention of the Japanese police and landed him in prison.

In 1939 Pak was appointed Manchukuo's Consul General to Poland. Soon after Germany occupied Poland, he went to Germany. He visited Korea briefly, and in 1941 he returned to China and, until 1945, he served as Manchukuo's Consul General in Nanking, Shanghai, Chindao, and Beijing. Throughout this period, he remained in constant contact with the Korean Provisional Government as it moved its headquarters from Shanghai to Chungqing.

There is scant record of Pak's activities between 1941 and 1945. However, his contact with the Korean Provisional Government has been verified in Kang Ch'ang-yŏng's deposition dated July 7, 1949, which was presented to the court of Anti-National Law. In the deposition, Kang, who was being tried for collaboration with the Japanese, stated that he had met with Pak in Shanghai, where they decided that Pak would contact the Provisional Government in Chungqing, while he himself would return to Korea. Before they parted, Pak gave him money for his activities in Korea. According to Pak's son, Hyo-wŏn (1929-), who was attending high school in Beijing at the time, Pak mainly stayed in Nanking during the period of 1941-1945. Hyo-wŏn recalls the time when he delivered, at his father's request, a document of some sort to an underground resistance group in Xinqing.

On his return to Korea in May of 1945, Pak worked with Yŏ Un-hyŏng in the Committee for the Preparation of Korean Independence. Highly knowledgeable about the geopolitical scene and with his wide international connections, he was probably able to predict the fall of Japan sooner than most people. With Japan's defeat all but certain, the top officials of the Japanese government ordered the Government-General of Korea to prepare for the immediate transfer of power and to make plans for the evacuation of Japanese citizens from Korea. The Government-General had three prominent Koreans in mind for the delicate job, and secretly started to approach them. The first was Song Chin-u, the second, An Chae-hong, and the last, Yŏ Un-hyŏng. The Government-General finally chose Yŏ Un-hyŏng and started the transfer negotiations with him.

I believe that the Government-General chose Yŏ Un-hyŏng partly because of his close relationship with Pak Sŏk-yun. It had requested Pak, then in Shanghai, to return immediately to Seoul, and Grandfather also recommended Pak to Yŏ Un-hyŏng when they met on the morning of the Liberation. The purpose of Yŏ's visit was to persuade Grandfather to work with him in the Committee for the Preparation of Korean Independence. Grandfather declined Yŏ's invitation, recommending instead his brother-in-law, Pak.

August 15, 1945, brought defeat to Japan and liberation to Korea. However, with the subsequent advances of both American and Russian troops toward the 38th Parallel, there were already signs of national division. General Hodge of the Tenth Army invited Pak to become an advisor to the American Military Administration in Seoul, but he declined. He felt the urgent need to do something for his newly liberated country, now buffeted with unprecedented confusion and turmoil.

In March of 1946, he crossed the 38th Parallel in a bold but risky attempt to prevent the bifurcation of his country. I believe that he, after consulting with Yŏ, went to the North to have a face-to-face meeting with Kim Il Sung. Pak dared to hope that he would be able to reach a compromise with Kim about the future of their country. He had probably planned to meet with Cho Man-sik, the leader of the Chosŏn Democratic Party, as well. Pak knew that Cho had felt an abiding respect for his brother-in-law, Ch'oe Nam-sŏn, ever since the days of the March First Movement.

It is not clear whether Pak did, in fact, have a meeting with Kim Il Sung. What is clear is that North Korea had a very different idea in mind. In North Korea, Pak was viewed as "a high official in the puppet government of Manchukuo, as well as an arch-reactionary and collaborator, whose creation of Minsaengdan (Organization for the People's Livelihood) in Manchuria thwarted the Korean independence movement." Now "the enemy" had just walked into their headquarters on his own accord. Within weeks of his arrival, Pak was arrested, and my great-aunt was forced to make numerous trips across the 38th Parallel with food and clothing for her incarcerated husband.

In South Korea, as the furor over the trusteeship intensified, Yŏ was assassinated on July 19, 1947. Pak's long-awaited dream of an independent unified country had died along with his good friend. Soon afterwards, his trial began in North Korea, and thanks to this, more records about him can be found in North Korea than in South Korea. Of special interest among the existing records is the detailed account of the "anti-Minsaengdan struggle" in Manchuria, which appears in Kim Il Sung's memoir, *With the Century*. Perhaps Kim gave special attention to the struggle because he had himself had experienced a demotion because of it.

I started reading Kim Il Sung's memoir because I wanted to understand the role communism, an idea largely rooted in Western history and philosophy, had played in the modernization of Northeast Asia at the beginning of the twentieth century. To me, it seemed absolutely necessary for present-day Koreans to understand the relationship between the Korean intellectuals under colonial rule and the "non-compromising" nationalists within the larger framework of Northeast-Asian intellectual history. To my disappointment, Kim's *With the Century* was too "movement"-oriented to provide me with a fundamental explanation for Korea's national division. Kim's memoir reinforced my feeling that in modern Korea, political decisions were often made without the benefit of a full historical consciousness, resulting in tragic consequences for its people.

Much is misunderstood about Pak Sŏk-yun, especially his involvement with Minsaengdan. In September of 1931, with the Japanese occupation of Manchuria, the life of Koreans living in Kando (the region north of Tumen River) changed drastically. Instead of Chinese overlords, now they had Japanese overlords. Pak, then vice-president of *Maeil Sinbo*, went to Manchuria to set up an organization that would provide assistance to the 400,000 Koreans in Kando. According to his testimony during his trial in North Korea, he stated that he came up with the name of "Minsaengdan" from "The Three Principles of the People" of Sun Yatsen, who had advocated *minjok* (statehood), *min'kwŏn* (rights), and *minsaeng* (livelihood) for the Chinese people. True to its name, the aim of the Minsaengdan that Pak established was to ensure the livelihood of the Korean people in Manchuria.

Two weeks after attending the inauguration of Minsaengdan on February 15, 1932, Pak left Kando for Xinqing. In July of that year, Minsaengdan dissolved due to the lack of cooperation of both the Manchukuo government and the Government-General of Korea. Two years later, the Kando Organization for Cooperation was set up by the Government-General, and it began to plant Korean agents in Manchuria in order to subvert the activities of the communist guerillas, initiating what later became known as the "anti-Minsaengdan struggle." The communist guerilla army consisted of Chinese and Korean fighters, and during the struggle, the Chinese tried to purge all Koreans, guilty or not. The Koreans, too, liquidated those who disagreed with them, based on unfounded charges of spying for the Japanese. By the end of the anti-Minsaengdan struggle, more than 500 Koreans had been sacrificed.

Pak was unaware that Minsaengdan, which he had organized two years before, only for it to be disbanded a few months later, had provided a possible cause for the anti-Minsaengdan struggle. He left Kando immediately after its inauguration and, over the next five or six years, he went on different diplomatic missions in Europe, China, and the United States. By the time he returned to Manchukuo as Counselor of Foreign

Affairs, many years had passed.

Kim's memoir *With the Century* appears to make room for Pak's situation in this regard. Pak is referred to as the "midwife" of Minsaengdan, whereas Kim Tong-han, the head of the Kando Organization for Cooperation, is referred to as "a field agent" of the Minsaengdan operations. In his testimony, discussed in Kim's memoir, I read Pak's true motive.

> ... Pak Sŏk-yun testified in court that he had believed in Korean self-rule under the Japanese monarchy, following the examples of the Commonwealth of Canada and the Commonwealth of South Africa under the British monarchy, and in the context of this belief, he nurtured his friendship with Governor-General Saito and admired Ishihara, one of the most notable proponents of hegemony and the spiritual leader of the East Asian Alliance.
>
> In addition, he vehemently denied that the aim of Minsaengdan had been to destroy the communists and partisans and that, in fact, its aim was to promote "the right of livelihood" of the Koreans. He said that it was only after he left Kando that it degenerated into a spy agency under Japanese direction, and that he was quite shocked to learn about the cruelties perpetrated during the anti-Minsaengdan struggle....

To me, the statement Pak gave in his final testimony rings true. Kim Il Sung's pronouncement on Pak's testimony demands attention:

> How much truth there is in Pak's testimony, only history will tell.

True, only history will tell. I realize that it is not possible to view historical events or actions solely through the motivations of the historical figures involved. It is up to the historian, free of the inclinations and deflections of his or her own time, to view facts as they are and evaluate their influence and outcomes over the course of history.

The crux of the charge for which Pak was tried in North Korea is that the anti-Minsaengdan struggle, not Minsaengdan itself, had resulted in the murder of 500 innocent Koreans. *With the Century* needed to hold up that truth. I believe that everything Pak did during the Japanese rule and in North Korea was done for his country and his countrymen. What I have witnessed in Korea in the ensuing 60 years reinforces this belief.

Pak received his death sentence in 1948, but his death occurred two years later, on October 20, 1950. For some reason, Kim Il Sung had kept him alive. October 19, 1950 was the day the South Korean Army entered Pyongyang, and Pak was killed the very next day. It is possible that he was executed just before the North Korean Army withdrew from Pyongyang, or that he was killed during the bombing by United Nations troops. There had been a week-long battle in the streets of the city. In the end, Yŏ Un-hyŏng had been assassinated in South Korea, and Pak Sŏk-yun executed in North Korea. With the political capabilities of these two men out of the picture, national division was perhaps inevitable. The "tragedy" of the nation, it seems, has yet come to its conclusion.

What happened to Pak's family after his death? I would like to recount here the story of one of his daughters. Pak had two daughters, Yŏng-hi and Su-hi, and one son, Hyo-wŏn. He had another out-of-wedlock daughter, Yŏng-ae, who, I surmised, was born of a Japanese woman. My great-aunt, a large-hearted woman, raised Yŏng-ae as her own. While Yŏng-hi was attending Kyunggi Girls' High School, she had introduced my father, her favorite cousin, to my mother, who was attending the same school. Being bright and beautiful, Yŏng-hi was sought after by many eligible young men. She married Pak In-sik who, while attending Tokyo Imperial University, had become good friends with my third uncle, Han-gŏm.

During the war years, Pak In-sik held a teaching position at Korea University as professor of economics, and during this time the Korean police arrested him for his involvement in the "Association of Journalists" incident, and he was executed without a trial. After her husband's death, Yŏng-hi went to Pusan and eked out a living by running a tearoom with her half-sister, Yŏng-ae. I remember visiting her tearoom with my father.

When the war was over, she did not return to Seoul. She obtained secret passage to Japan, where she learned the details of her father's death. A short time afterwards, she committed suicide in a hotel room in Tokyo. Her husband had been executed by Syngman Rhee of South Korea, and her father, by Kim Il Sung of North Korea. For her there was no longer a country she could call her own. This is the story of how a Korean woman of great beauty, intelligence, and ambition ended her life in a foreign country.

The tragedy of his youngest sister's family affected Grandfather deeply. On learning the death of his beloved niece, he remained immobile in his sickbed for several days.

Chapter 3

The Ui-dong Period and the Korean War

The countless tragedies that occurred before, during, and after the Korean War were not limited to individual persons or families. For Grandfather, one tragedy came on the heels of another. Apart from the Anti-National Japanese Collaborator Trial he endured in 1949, he saw his youngest son, in frail health, repeatedly incarcerated and tortured in Sŏdaemun prison as a "Red," his eldest daughter, mother of six children, brutally murdered by the North Korean Army, and his son-in-law abducted to the North. When the war ended, his eldest daughter-in-law (my mother) was detained by the South Korean police and persecuted. During the years when the family lived as refugees, one of his grandsons drowned in shallow waters, and his eldest son (my father), his greatest love and hope, died a sudden death.

His suffering was even keener because all these tragedies had occurred, not under Japanese rule, but in his newly liberated independent country, after he had dedicated his entire life to achieving that liberation. I am almost 70 now. Grandfather died when he was 68, so I have lived about the same number of years. *What would I have done, how would I have coped if such unspeakable tragedies happened to me?* Up to his last moments, Grandfather remained resolute. *What sustained him, propped him up, and kept him from collapsing?* In this book, I am going to tell the story of just how Grandfather survived and rose above the tragedies that besieged him.

1. The Sowŏn Memories

In the spring of 1944, Grandfather moved from Hyoje-dong to Ui-dong, where I have some of my earliest memories. The year before, as the Pacific War raged on, my father had taken my mother and me to my maternal grandmother's house in Puan to escape possible American bombings. Upon the Liberation in 1945, we returned to Ui-dong.

Among the memories I have of Ui-dong, the first thing that comes to mind is the inner room that Grandmother occupied. At the north end of the room, there was a wardrobe, and in the fall, Grandmother spread chestnuts in front of it for them to dry. I remember being puzzled by the way the chestnuts were dried. I wondered why Grandmother put them in a dark corner of the room instead of in the sun outside. Grandmother explained to me that chestnuts dried in the shade were easier to peel when they dried. This is my first memory of Grandmother.

Across a spacious hall was another room where I remember another "grandmother" sitting by the window. I learned later that she was the second wife of my great-grandfather, who had married a much younger woman after his first wife died. My great-grandmother, Yong'gang Paeng-ssi (woman with the surname of Paeng from Yong'gang), was still alive at that time. She spoiled me, the *chongson* of the Ch'oe family, to no end, and passed away during the war. Upon receiving the news of her death in Pusan, Grandfather composed a sijo in her memory, which was later anthologized in volume five of *The Complete Works of Yuktang Ch'oe Nam-sŏn*.

On our return to Ui-dong from my maternal grandmother's house in Puan, we moved into a building that was detached from the main house. It had previously been used as Grandfather's quarters. My father was then a gastroenterologist at Seoul National University Hospital.

While practicing, he also gave lectures. In addition, he taught a course on the history of natural sciences at the College of Arts and Sciences. Combining practice and teaching, he thrived on his busy schedule. During the week, he stayed at Myŏng'yun-dong near the university, and on Sundays he came to join us in Ui-dong and spent time mingling with the tenant farmers. To my recollection, he was a generous man with a common touch.

Compared to the tiny Japanese-style two-story house in Puan, the typical Korean-style house in Ui-dong was huge, or seemed so to me. Next to the house was an expanse of rice paddies and a smaller area where vegetables grew. The feature that stands out in my memory is the library building, which was separated from the main house. It was almost as large as the main house, but built on a raised foundation, with a higher floor level. Peering inside through the door, I could see Grandfather's books piled from floor to ceiling.

Between the main house and the library, there were several well-tended trees about my height at the time, and a big well. There was a thick wooden slab to cover the opening, and over the wooden cover, there was a roof. A lone bucket hung from the roof. I was mystified as to why there was a roof over the cover, and asked Grandfather. He answered, "The roof is there to keep the rain water from falling into the well, and the cover is there to keep the neighborhood children from falling into it. That's why the cover is thick and heavy." *Grandfather knows everything!* That was my first impression of him.

The open rice fields of Ui-dong stand out in my memory. The rural scene impressed me with its stark contrast to the city scene of Puan where my father had a practice in the center of town. Everything in Ui-dong seemed so different.

For some reason that is now lost to me, I caught a fish in the stream at the back of the main house and dropped it into the well in front of the library. A big uproar ensued in the household, and my mother was very upset with me. Grandfather happened to walk by and said, "Standing water needs to be stirred now and then, so don't worry. The fish will eat the little bugs in the water and make it clean." Having rescued me from my mother's displeasure, he sauntered away. That is my second memory of Ui-dong, and I must have been five or six years old then.

As I got a little older, I began to wonder why the well was so big. The huge library building that housed Grandfather's books was behind the well. The library had been built at a distance from the main house in order to safeguard it in case of fire, and a large well had been dug in front of it. All this planning notwithstanding, ten years later, an American bomber dropped a napalm bomb on Grandfather's library, obliterating it in a second, along with the well. *After all, Grandfather did* not *know everything*. He could not have known everything the tumultuous times would mete out to him.

Another memory of mine from Ui-dong is that Grandfather had a small thatch-roofed house about 200 meters from the main house. The family referred to it as the "little house," and it provided Grandfather with a quiet place to work and receive guests, away from the comings and goings of the household servants and tenant farmers. I ran errands from the main house to this little house, sometimes to let Grandfather know that a certain guest had arrived.

The path that led from the main house to the little house was on a raised bank between the rice paddies and a shallow stream called Uichŏn. On the bank stood a line of chestnut trees and cherry trees that alternated at about every ten meters. There were about 20 trees all together. In the early spring I ate cherries from the trees and in the fall, chestnuts. The chestnuts fell mostly on the rice paddy side, and Grandfather would go down to the edge of the rice paddy to pick them up for me. Sometimes he would take off his rubber shoes and cotton socks to reach those that had fallen into the water.

Strangely enough, Grandfather never picked the ripened cherries in the early summer. I needed Grandfather's height to reach the cherries, but I could sense that he was very reluctant about picking them. He said that if he stained his white shirt while picking the cherries, Grandmother would not be very happy. He told me, "I don't want to make your grandmother unhappy by picking cherries." I thought to myself then, *So Grandmother must be higher than Grandfather!* Actually, my perception was accurate, at least within the four walls of the house.

Still another memory of Ui-dong has to do with the fact that my father came only on the weekends. I remember this clearly because without his visiting, I didn't get the comic books that I had waited for all week. Unlike today, Ui-dong was not easily accessible at the time. People coming from Seoul had to get off at the last stop of the streetcar, Tonam-dong, then cross the Miari Pass, and from there walk two hours before reaching Ui-dong. It was the same trek returning to Seoul, and nobody ventured to undertake it after dark. My memories of Grandfather begin from the Ui-dong of that time.

2. The Anti-National Law and Grandfather's "Open Letter"

After the Japanese attack on Pearl Harbor in December of 1941, Grandfather told the Korean and Chinese students at the National University of Manchuria that the attack had been a mistake on the part of Japan and predicted Japan's eventual defeat. He stressed that the students should prepare themselves for this eventuality. In order to prepare the young people of Korea for the oncoming new era, he felt that it was important for them to have a good understanding of their own history. He hastily returned to Seoul and set about writing a book on the history of Korean culture, *Kosatong* (故事通: A Collection of Ancient Stories). Even with the manuscript completed, it took a whole year for the book to get published. The delay in publication, as well as the curious title for a history book, was the result of the convoluted censorship procedures required by the Government-General.

Thanks to his friends in the media, Grandfather was apprised of the content of the Cairo Conference held in November of 1943. Around this time, he again predicted the inevitable demise of the Japanese Empire, if not the details of when or how. The following spring, he moved to Ui-dong. Away from the noise of the war, he wanted to concentrate on his lifelong project, the *Encyclopedia of Korean History*.

On August 12, 1945, three days before Japan's official announcement, Grandfather heard the news of the Japanese decision to surrender from his journalist friend Sim U-sŏp. He responded, "I'm so glad that it came much sooner than I had expected." While he was staying with Sim, he was visited by Yŏ Un-Hyŏng in the early morning of the fifteenth. After giving a brief explanation of the transfer of power from the Government-General, which had already begun to take place, Yŏ asked Grandfather to participate in the work of the Committee for the

Grandmother's *hwan'gap* (Ui-dong, October 1947). Grandfather and Grandmother are flanked by their grandchildren. I stand at the far left.

Preparation of Korean Independence. Grandfather declined, and after advising Yŏ to contact Pak Sŏk-yun, his brother-in-law, Grandfather returned home to Ui-dong. Following Grandfather's advice, Yŏ, with Pak as the chief negotiator, continued to work with the Government-General.

Two years after the Liberation, Grandmother celebrated her *hwan'gap* on October 27th. I was seven years old then. In the photograph taken on that day, my grandparents' usual gentle smiles are nowhere to be seen, and the four grandchildren stand around with solemn faces. Third Uncle (Han-gŏm, then age 26) could not be there for the photograph because he was in prison for his activities as a socialist theorist for Yŏ Un-Hyŏng's Democratic Labor Party. On that day, Grandmother was probably more preoccupied with her youngest son's being in prison than with her birthday celebrations. Shortly afterwards, he was released on bail, and the events following his release form a major portion of my memories of Ui-dong.

On August 15, 1948, the Democratic Republic of Korea was established. It was that winter that the Anti-National Law was enacted. The following spring, Grandfather was imprisoned for the third time in his life. The first time had been at the end of the Chosŏn dynasty when he was 16 years old; the second time when Korea was under Japanese rule, at the age 30; and the third time when the Korea of his dreams enacted a special retroactive law to punish "pro-Japanese collaborators." Grandfather was 60 years old then.

In February of 1949, incarcerated in Sŏdaemun prison, Grandfather wrote this sijo.

The fifty-nine years of my wobbly, immature steps
I recount in my childish voice, kneeling before you.
I long to hear you say, "Son, get up and receive the rod!"

On April 7, he wrote another sijo when he was released from prison.

I was once given a welcome respite from my exhaustion.
Now, weary of too much rest, I'm let go to work again.
Everything is in God's hand; mine is not to reason why.

Two days later, on returning to Ui-dong, he wrote yet another sijo.

I wondered about the buds that show this time of the year.
With the cold lingering on, they've just begun blooming.
Perhaps they've waited to let me see my country's spring.

It was in the spring of 2007, almost 60 years after Grandfather's imprisonment, that my cousin Kook-ju (Second Uncle's son), who lived in Seoul, received a letter from the Committee for the Inquiry into Pro-Japanese Anti-National Activities, requesting him to explain "Ch'oe Nam-sŏn's pro-Japanese activities." Kook-ju forwarded the letter to me in New York. Until that time, I had never read the "Chayŏlsŏ" (Open Letter) Grandfather wrote in prison, so I looked it up in *The Complete Works of Yuktang Ch'oe Nam-sŏn*. I had majored in natural sciences, but I had no trouble understanding it.

I was mystified by the Committee's request. I presumed that the members of the committee were mostly academics in the field of humanities, and here they were asking for an explanation of what had already been explained more than half a century ago. *What more was there to explain?* What Grandfather stated in his Open Letter was quite clear and entirely factual, and I had nothing to add or subtract, that is, except for one point. Grandfather had written the following:

> While it is true that I have occasionally changed my clothing during my rounds at the Commission for the Compilation of Chosŏn History, the Advisory Board of the Government-General, and the National University of Manchuria, here I unequivocally declare that I have never once veered away from my main pursuit—the study of the Korean national origin and the establishment of Korean history.

Personally, I have never known Grandfather to change his "clothing." As far as I can remember, Grandfather had only one Korean outfit: a white jacket, a pair of white trousers, white cotton socks, white rubber shoes, and a light grey outer coat with short ties. That was the one outfit he wore. He had the outfit washed and mended, and he wore it again and again. To the end of life, he had remained steadfast in his pursuit of true Korean identity.

After his release from prison in 1949, Grandfather lived another eight years, until his death in 1957. During those eight years, I ate with him and fell asleep next to him. The book I am writing now recounts the conversation Grandfather and I had during those eight years.

3. Third Uncle Goes North

It must have been 1950, since I was in third grade. Grandfather was working on the fifth printing of his book *A History of Chosŏn for the Korean People* (國民朝鮮歷史, Tongmyŏng Publishing Company, 1947), the first book in his life that he had written without being subjected to colonial censorship.

On New Year's, my father was practicing his figure skating on the ice that had formed from the water poured into the rice paddy. Music played on the RCA Victor gramophone. When the music began to slow down, Grandfather manually rewound the gramophone. With a switch in my hand, I was playing with my top nearby. When the tiny metal ball at the bottom of my top got loose, Grandfather pushed it back in with his fingers. Then he made another switch for himself, and we took turns lashing at the top to keep it spinning. He taught his other grandchildren, who had come from Seoul to pay their respects, how to play chach'igi (Korean cricket). He also pushed them around in a homemade sled, once falling on the ice with a big thud.

When it got a little warmer, my father and my cousins returned to Seoul. Now and then, Third Uncle came for short visits. I was only ten years old, but I began to learn, in bits and pieces gleaned from the grownups' conversations, that the frequent visits from the local police were related to Third Uncle's leftist underground activities. Third Uncle spent more time in prison than he did at home. Because of his frail health, he came home now and then on bail. He had a chronic cough, so I didn't get to spend too much time with him, but we managed to go through the primer *The Thousand Chinese Characters* together.

On the days the police did not come, Uncle would take me on a hike along the Ansan Mountain range that led to Obong Valley and then

Photograph of the guests who attended Grandfather's *hwan'gap* in April of 1950. Among the guests were Yi Sang-hyŏp, Cho Yong-man, and many other intellectuals of the day. Two months later, when the Korean War broke out, each of them had to make a choice, voluntarily or otherwise, between the South and the North.

to Wŏntong Temple. I showed him where Paek'undae, Insubong, and Man'kyŏngdae were located, and led him to Hwagyesa Valley, where we could take a cool drink from the mountain spring. Then, he was again taken back to Sŏdaemun prison, and my mother busied herself delivering food and warm clothing for her incarcerated brother-in-law. During each of my mother's trips, Grandfather and Grandmother waited anxiously for news of their son. The excruciating tension they felt was shared with everyone else in the family as well—most of all, by me.

On one of my mother's visits to the prison, Uncle told her that he had a confession to make about something he could no longer keep to himself. He said that while he should be concentrating on the revolution, an image of a girl had taken hold of him, and, even as he lay on the cold cement floor, he was consumed by thoughts of her. Her name was Yi Chŏng-ja. He had met her during his involvement with the movement against the nationalization of Seoul University, in which she led a group of students from the Pharmaceutical College.

On her return from that prison visit, my mother promptly relayed Uncle's predicament to Grandfather and Grandmother, and with their consent, she journeyed to Ulsan, the girl's hometown. Years later, my mother talked to me about the obstacles she faced.

> Everybody knows about our family, but what family in the world would give their daughter in marriage to a man who lies bloodied on the prison floor?

My mother told the girl's family everything about Uncle, and following the girl's wishes, they accepted the marriage proposal. On April 26 of that year, there was a brief marriage ceremony in Ui-dong. I found out from the guests who had come from Seoul that this day was also Grandfather's *hwan'gap*.

Earlier that spring, friends and family had begun making plans for the celebration of his *hwan'gap*, but Grandfather put a stop to it by saying, "How could I celebrate when I am being charged with pro-Japanese activities in the name of the Korean people?" So the family had to be satisfied with sending out invitations to a few of his close friends under the pretext of Third Uncle's wedding. At the insistence of his friends, many of whom had come from a great distance, Grandfather reluctantly consented to an abbreviated version of a *hwan'gap* feast.

The photograph taken that day hangs in my study in New York. In a pair of shorts, showing bare knees, I am standing next to Grandfather. My standing height and his sitting height are about the same. That day, one of the guests, Ko Hŭi-dong (a prominent Korean painter), made a

The marriage of Third Uncle, Han-gŏm, in April of 1950. The groom stands at the center of the back row and the bride, to the far right. Grandfather sits in the front row, and I stand to his right.

brush painting of Sowŏn and presented it to Grandfather. His study is shown, with Uichŏn stream in the foreground and Ansan Mountain in the background. To this day, whenever I look at the photograph, a whiff of Grandfather's scent, emanating from his long grey coat jacket, lingers in my nose.

It was on this day, at the joint celebration of Grandfather's *hwan'gap* and Third Uncle's marriage, that I saw my aunt for the first time. As a young bride, she was much prettier than Grandmother or mother, and taller, and she was very affectionate, taking my not-so-clean hands in her own without hesitation. She drew pictures for me on drawing paper, and showed me how to hold the paper properly, saying that if I wanted to draw a really good picture, it is more important to learn how to hold the

Brush painting of Ui-dong that Ch'un-gok Ko Hŭi-dong, famed painter, presented to Grandfather on his *hwan'gap* (45cm × 51cm). The inscription in the upper right-hand corner reads:

> *With the wind calm, the lotus fragrance spreads afar.*
> *With the stream deep, it is cool under the thatched roof.*

paper than how to hold the crayon.

Two months after Third Uncle got married, Yuggio broke out. He immediately left Ui-dong for Seoul. We learned later that he was working at the Communist Party headquarters in the city. For several days, Third Aunt waited quietly in Ui-dong. Then, one day, as jet aircraft shrieked over Ui-dong, she changed into a pair of loose-fitting pants and set out to Seoul to see her husband. Three months later, when Seoul was recaptured, Uncle went to the North. As a notable figure in the communist organization, he probably withdrew with the North Korean

People's Army.

Third Aunt walked all the way to Pyongyang, embedded as a nurse in the People's Army, and as the Army was moving toward Sunchŏn, north of Pyongyang, she was taken prisoner by an Australian parachute unit. She was in civilian clothes, and, in halting English, told the Australian soldiers, "I am not a soldier. I am a woman... a refugee." Under their protection, she was escorted back to the South.

When the Chinese Red Army intervened, the Korean Army with the United Nations forces was forced to withdraw on January 4, 1951. Everyone in the family fled south to Pusan, with the exception of Third Aunt and Grandmother. Third Aunt stayed on in Myo-dong in Seoul under the pretext of taking care of Grandmother, whose health was not good enough to withstand the hardships of the flight. In fact, she probably stayed in Seoul to wait for her husband. That year, spring returned to Seoul, but he did not.

The next time the family heard from Third Uncle was in October of 1957, when Grandfather passed away. All we had heard of him until that point was that he had given a radio broadcast on the North Korean radio station, and therefore we knew he was still alive. The day after Grandfather died, two of Third Uncle's Japanese friends from his Tokyo University days visited Myo-dong to offer their condolences. They gave the family news of their friend, Han-gŏm, along with a letter from him.

According to his letter, which was read aloud to the entire family after the visitors left, Third Uncle had remarried and had two children, a son and a daughter. The son's name was Tŏk-ju, sharing the same last character with me. He said that both children were healthy and doing well. It was evident that Third Uncle was in a position where the news of his father's death could reach him. The first thing Third Aunt heard about her husband after seven long years of waiting was that he had married again and had two children. As she sat in the corner, repeatedly dabbing her eyes, I could not take my eyes off her. Years later, my mother told me what Third Aunt had said to her that evening: "He must be in good health to have had two children."

Third Aunt never remarried. The entire family urged her to do so, but she was adamant about remaining single. She put her energy into her pharmacy business, contributing her free time and resources to the good works of the Catholic nuns she knew. When I came home on leave from military service duties, she took me to movies and concerts. On these occasions, she often asked me about her husband. She said that I knew a lot more about her husband than she ever did, and asked me many questions about him.

Many years later, when I was living in the United States, I heard that Third Uncle had been pushed out of the central communist party and to Ch'ŏngjin, at the northern tip of Korea. During the mid-1990s when North Korea was hit with a serious food shortage due to a severe famine, he crossed the Tumen River in search of food in Yanji, a small city in China across the river. A distant relative of Grandmother's who had settled there sent word about Third Uncle's plight. It is my guess that, on a few occasions, Third Aunt, who was doing moderately well with her business, sent money to Yanji. She once told me, "I hear your uncle in North Korea already has four children," as if she were talking about a complete stranger.

In the mid-1990s, I got a call from Third Aunt in Seoul. She said that Third Uncle would be in Yanji in a few days and asked if I wanted to contact him. Then she gave me the number where he could be reached. At the time, phone calls between China and the United States had

Third Uncle Ch'oe Han-gŏm (199?). As an earnest young man, he hoped that his choosing philosophy as his college major would later help him effect improvement in his country.

become quite routine, so I was able to make the connection without difficulty. Third Uncle and I talked for several hours over the next two days.

We talked about how I grew up under Grandfather's care, how incredibly sad he felt when my father died, how the rice-and-red-bean balls that my mother gave him sustained him during the retreat of September 28, and how I couldn't possibly imagine how good they had tasted. He went on to talk about my mother, his elder sister, his mother, and the house in Ui-dong. He said he now had two sons, two daughters, two sons-in-law, and many grandchildren.

I interrupted him to ask, "What do you do for work now, Uncle?" He replied that he was working as a translator. During all our calls, we didn't say a word about politics—or about Third Aunt, for that matter. Several months after the phone calls, the relative in Yanji sent me a recent photograph of Third Uncle. He was no longer the young genius of Cheil High School, with a pale face full of existential anguish. My civics teacher in high school, Sŏ Chang-sŏk, who was a year behind Third Uncle at the same high school, once told me that, along with Yu Chin-o (constitutional scholar) and Yi Hyo-sŏk (writer of "modern" novels), Ch'oe Han-gŏm was one of the three true geniuses he had ever known.

In the photograph, Third Uncle had a darkish tan, and his left hand resting on his cheek looked big and strong, but his eyes still had that same penetrating look. In his advanced age, he bore more resemblance to his mother than to his father. *Uncle, what if you had listened to your father? If only you'd chosen to become a medical doctor, wouldn't life have been so much easier on you?* Third Aunt died a few years ago of a heart attack. My cousins in Korea buried her in a Catholic cemetery near her father-in-law, Ch'oe Nam-sŏn.

4. North Korean Soldiers Visit Ui-dong

In May of 1950, we moved to Samsŏn'gyo, where my father had already settled in. He was then teaching at the Seoul National University Hospital. I had been attending a subsidiary of Miari Elementary School, located in Ui-dong. It was a one-room school where a teacher named Chu taught first and second graders. Because I had to walk, beginning in third grade, 20 *ri* (5 mi.) to the main school, my family moved to Samsŏn'gyo.

My grandparents stayed on at Ui-dong with the newly married couple, and my sister and I transferred to Kyo-dong Elementary School, she as a first grader and I as a third grader. There was a little distance between Kyo-dong and Samsŏn'gyo, but with the help of my aunt, who was then the president of the Parents' Association at Kyo-dong Elementary School, we had been accepted at the beginning of the summer.

June 25th was a Sunday, so there was no school. When I woke up, I heard the grownups whispering that a war had broken out along the 38th Parallel. My father left hurriedly for the hospital. Two weeks passed before he could return. He said he couldn't leave the injured patients at the hospital and that there were too few doctors for too many patients.

My mother, unable to decide whether she should flee or stay put, remained for two days at Samsŏn'gyo, waiting for my father's return. But when she saw the Korean soldiers setting up machine guns on the castle wall behind our house, she packed a small bundle for each of us and led us through Naksan path along the castle wall, then to Tongdaemun, and finally to my aunt's house in Iksŏn-dong. We stayed there for the night.

The next day we watched as the North Korean People's Army tanks rolled though the streets of Chong'no. My mother gave up the idea of fleeing, and we returned to our house in Samsŏn'gyo. After waiting again for a few days for my father, we decided to head for Ui-dong.

Clutching our little bundles, my sister and I followed my mother, crossing the Miari Pass, heading toward Ŭijŏngbu. On the sides of the streets, we saw demolished tanks, half-burned trucks, and corpses covered with straw mats. My mother told us not to dawdle and hurried us along. She tried to shield my little sister by lifting one end of her long skirt. I just walked, thinking to myself, *maybe this is what war is like*. I didn't feel scared.

Everything was quiet at Ui-dong. No tanks, no corpses. It was exactly the same as when I had left it two months before. Nothing in my room had changed either. There was my folded bedding, my low desk, my comic books, my copy of *The Thousand Chinese Characters*, a wall clock, a top, a box of cards, a bag of marbles–everything was there. Outside, I saw the sled, the slightly deflated soccer ball, my shepherd dog Meri, and a few clucking brown, white, and black chickens. Everything was there.

One thing that was different was that Third Uncle and Third Aunt were nowhere to be seen. I was especially disappointed at not seeing Third Aunt, whom I liked very much for her open, outgoing nature. I wanted to brag to her about the multiplication table I had just memorized at my new school, but she wasn't there. Disappointed, I told my mother that I wanted to go back to our house in Samsŏn'gyo.

Then it happened midsummer that year. Bored out of my mind, I didn't know what to do with myself. I remember it was a hot and muggy day.

In the shade, I am playing with Meri under the front steps. Through the open windows, I hear the boisterous laughter of women ironing bed sheets with charcoal-filled irons. All of a sudden, the laughter stops. I look up, and see five or six North Korean People's Army soldiers stepping into the front yard through the open gate. My mother emerges from the inner room, and after hurriedly slipping into her shoes on the stone step, goes down to the yard and stands in front of the soldiers. My dog Meri tries to pull away and jump on the soldiers, but I hold her back, pulling on her leash and collar with all my strength.

My mother inquires in a quiet voice on what business they have come. The soldier in charge doesn't answer. Instead, he orders everyone present to step down to the front yard. My mother explains in a still quieter voice that there are only two elderly parents in the inner room. The soldier is insistent and threatens to enter the room himself unless everyone comes out promptly. Then, with his boots still on, he jumps onto the hall floor.

At that very moment, we hear Grandmother's voice from the inner room: "Just a moment, dear, I'll be out shortly." Everyone stays still, including the soldiers. The only movement comes from Meri who still struggles to get free of my hold. One of the soldiers gives Meri a threatening look and begins to take his rifle down from his shoulder. I get up quickly, trying harder to hold on to Meri. Everyone–my mother, the women who had been ironing, the soldiers–turns towards me.

I tell Grandmother, who has just come out of inner room, "Grandma, I'll go get Grandpa,"

Grandmother says, "Yes, go get Grandpa, dear."

I know Grandfather is at the little house. Getting up, I again pull hard at Meri, but she pulls back harder. I give her a kick, shouting that we have to go to Grandfather quickly. Meri doesn't listen, and I begin to sweat. I know she will calm down once we pass the rear gate—but then I see Grandfather entering by it. Someone must have alerted him already.

Everyone is standing in a row between the *changtokdae* (a raised area in the yard where large jars of food are kept) and the low trees. Red peppers are drying on a large straw mat in the yard. I begin to worry that the soldiers will trample on the mat with their dirty boots. With her tongue hanging out in the summer heat, Meri has now quieted down a little. One of the soldiers, who looks a little brighter than the others, starts to examine everyone's hands. First he looks at the backs of our hands and then turns them over to examine the palms. He doesn't say anything while doing this. After the second in line, the rest voluntarily show the soldier both sides of their hands.

Grandfather is standing at the end of the row. Now it is his turn. As the soldier examines his hands, he suddenly palpates Grandfather's palms with his own fingers. With a disapproving look, he shouts at Grandfather, "YOU, comrade, are a reactionary!"

Grandfather seems a little taken aback and responds, "Huh...?"

Everyone is familiar with the word *reactionary*, but no one seems to know what it means exactly. Grandfather must have known, but he simply puts his hands down to his sides and looks at the soldier without saying anything. The soldier doesn't say anything either. Then he looks away and asks for water. He orders his men to rest in the shade. One of the women brings the soldiers water, and offers to fix the buttons that have almost fallen off their uniforms. The soldiers smile. Another woman offers to mend their torn arm bands, telling them that she could do a better job if they would take off their jackets. The soldiers happily take off their jackets, feeling relief from the summer heat.

Grandfather and I head back to the little house. On the way, I ask, "What is a 'reactionary,' Grandpa?"

Grandfather doesn't seem to have a ready answer. ". . . I have no idea."

This is what I remember of the day when the soldiers of the North Korean People's Army visited our house in Ui-dong.

That summer, Ui-dong was unusually quiet. By September, American bombers were flying over Ui-dong, but they left it alone. The children my age sang "Changbaeksan" (the North Korean anthem) instead of "Tonghaemul" (the South Korean anthem), oblivious to what was happening in Seoul. Our food was running low, and we often had gruel instead of rice. Grandfather was happy that we had a good harvest of potatoes that summer. In mid-September, my mother, my sister, and I returned to Samsŏn'gyo, and were relieved to find some food left in the house. On September 29, the news of Seoul's repatriation reached us.

5. Grandfather Escapes Abduction to the North

During Yuggio, many prominent public figures, such as Yi Kwang-su, Chŏng In-bo, and An Chae-hong, were abducted to the North, but Grandfather escaped abduction. Some have theorized that Grandfather's escape was possible due to the consideration shown by Hong Myŏng-hi, who was then a high-ranking member of the Military Committee of the Chosŏn Labor Party in North Korea. I know this is not the case because neither Yi Kwang-su, whom Hong had held in high regard, nor Chŏng In-bo, who was Hong's in-law, went to the North voluntarily. Others surmised that Grandfather eluded abduction because his son, Han-gŏm, held a relatively high position in the City Labor Party in Seoul at that time. I know this is not the case, either.

About a week after the visit by the North Korean soldiers, one of whom called Grandfather a "reactionary," my father came to Ui-dong from Seoul. It was around the middle of July.

As in countless villages across South Korea, many things were happening in my village. My house was the only house in the village with a tile roof, and most of the villagers were tenant farmers attached to Grandfather's estate. Many of them were illiterate, totally unaware of what was happening in the outside world. It was they who chose my father as president of the village's People's Committee.

My father was a big-hearted, sociable man. He joked effortlessly with the villagers, and often drank *makkolli* (rice wine) with the tenant farmers. It was these farmers, along with Kyŏngman, the son of the village shaman; An, the warehouse truck driver; and Chŏng, owner of the village general store, who banded together and decided that my father, "a man of education," should be the president. As vice-president, they chose Chu, who was then a teacher at the Ui-dong subsidiary of Miari

Elementary School.

About a month later, my father and a young man named Won were sent away to join the Righteous Volunteer Army led by the North Korean Army. At the time, a fierce battle was raging near the Nakdong River perimeter near Pusan, and every able man under the age of 35 was mobilized. My father was 36 at the time, but because he looked younger than his years, he had to go, too. I remember going to the open field at Tonam Elementary School with my mother to give him some money and rice balls before he left.

The day before his departure, my father had asked Chu to take care of Grandfather. Chu had promised that he would gladly take care of the "family of Ch'oe Nam-sŏn." Chu, though his family origin could be characterized as *petit bourgeoisie,* had a strong commitment to the rural movement. Although it is not clear whether he had any communist leanings, his choice of a teaching career in a rural area was indicative of his deep social consciousness.

Chu's wife graduated from Kyunggi Girls' High School in the same year as my mother. My mother was aware of the family's financial difficulties, and quietly helped them in any way she could. One day, Chu's wife came to see my mother and warned her that the People's Committee had been discussing "the Ch'oe Nam-sŏn question," so he should flee immediately. Taking the house servant Yi with him, Grandfather escaped to a nearby mountain where he stayed in a tiny cottage owned by the village shaman. He had with him only a bag of potatoes and a Buddhist sutra he had been reading. When the soldiers from the People's Committee came for him the next day, my mother told them that he had gone to a temple to attend a service. Chu and his wife had kept their promise to my father and saved Grandfather from abduction.

6. My Aunt Is Murdered and My Mother Is Beaten

With the Repatriation of September 28, 1950, members of the Korean Youth Corps, under the pretext of national security, appeared in Ui-dong, just as they did in other villages throughout Korea. The head of the Ui-dong Youth Corps, who had been running for a National Assembly seat prior to Yuggio, accused Chu and his wife of being "Reds" for several reasons: one having to do with the whereabouts of my father, the former president of the People's Committee; another reason related to Third Uncle's going to the North with the retreating North Korean Army.

As the investigation progressed, one of the police officers who had kept Third Uncle under watch before the war was found murdered. The Youth Corps accused Chu of being the killer, and he, along with his wife and three children, were openly executed near a stream in the village. The men who pulled the triggers had been Chu's students. His only "crime" was that he had been chosen by the uneducated villagers as vice-president of the People's Committee. If he had been a true "Red," he would have gone North, just as Third Uncle had. The three murdered children were even younger than I was at the time. I still remember the oldest girl, with her large pretty eyes.

Sam-ung, my best friend in Ui-dong, witnessed the execution. Afterwards, he told me, "They had to kill the children because Mrs. Chu was trying to cover them with her body."

As if Sam-ung had anything to do with the killings, I screamed at him, "WHY DID THEY HAVE TO KILL MRS. CHU?!"

Yuggio was like that. Children, barely ten years old, talked about killing and dying as if they were mundane events. Grownups with guns and rifles acted like children, and children fought like the grownups.

My father, who had been president of the People's Committee, was put under arrest. The Korean Youth Corps believed that the reason Grandfather had not been abducted was because Third Uncle had used his influence as an important member of the City Labor Party. There were many unfounded theories flying about. Grandfather went to Seoul and stayed at the house of Sim U-sŏp's daughter, waiting for things to quiet down.

Then one day the Korean Youth Corps came to the house and arrested my mother. I was arrested too, but was let go because of my young age. My mother was detained for over a month and beaten for information about the whereabouts of her husband, her brother-in-law, and her father-in-law. Grandfather, on learning of his daughter-in-law's plight, immediately paid a visit to Cho Byŏng-ok, then Minister of Interior, and demanded her prompt release. My mother was released after a month-long detainment in Tongdaemun police headquarters on charges of "sheltering collaborators."

Grandfather's tragedy didn't end there. His eldest daughter, Han-ok, the mother of six of his grandchildren, was murdered in Seoul by the retreating North Korean soldiers, and her husband, Kang Kŏn-ha, was abducted to the North. Han-ok, who had graduated from Tokyo Teachers' College, was a mother and housewife, living a quiet life, with little interest in public affairs. Three months after the breakout of Yuggio, Grandfather had no information on the whereabouts of any of his three sons, and knew not even whether they were alive or dead.

Grandfather was relentlessly pelted with ordeals that might have tested the prophets of the Old Testament. On the death of his eldest daughter in September of 1950, he tried to contain his uncontainable grief by composing this sijo:

For forty-two years you lived a life of beauty and purity.
Your six children whom you loved so much are still here,
But you, who held them under your wings, are here no more.

The poisonous arrow has found you as its mark.
As if aware that stains show up better against white,
The sign of evil times has chosen you as its target.

Grief does not end the way tear marks dry.
I'll weep to my heart's content, beating on my chest.
Silencing a father's love, can one act as if reason has returned?

On June 25, 1951, the first anniversary of the breakout of Yuggio, he wrote this sijo:

Who is right or who is wrong, it's nothing but idle chatter.
After a year's fighting, all we've left is our land destroyed.
Look at it with your left eye or right eye–it's the same.

Which hill, which valley, the war did not discriminate.
The land won with spilt blood, the land where corpses rotted,
And the land now green with grass–they are one and the same.

7. The Burning of Grandfather's Library

In December of 1950, Grandfather fled to Taegu, the hometown of his second daughter-in-law, Han-ung's wife. The following year, with the invasion of the Chinese Army on January 4th, he had to flee even further south to Pusan. He traveled on a military truck arranged by Sin Sŏk-u, a childhood friend who was then Korean Ambassador to China. Even in Pusan, the family tragedies had not come to an end. His grandson Sŏng-ju (the eldest son of Han-ung), died by drowning while playing in a shallow stream. Already beset with tragic losses, he again turned to sijo to express his grief:

Having endured so many things lost or destroyed,
I'd hoped at least to keep the remaining family intact.
Oh, where have you gone, leaving me with such a void?

In Pusan, Grandfather, as adviser to the Committee for the Compilation of Korean Naval History, was deeply involved in the commemoration project for Admiral Yi Sun-sin. After the repatriation of Seoul in May of 1951, he asked my father to get the books he needed for the project from his Ui-dong library. With the assistance of the Commander-in-Chief of the Korean Navy, my father was able to reach Ui-dong by way of Inchŏn. On arrival, he saw that Grandfather's library, with its collection of 170,000 books, had burned to the ground. A month before, during the Chinese Spring Offensive in April, the American bombers had napalmed Ui-dong.

Grandfather valued all books. He treasured not only books but any piece of paper with writing on it. He prohibited newspapers from being used as toilet paper, and he once upbraided a family member on his way to the toilet with a torn piece of newspaper in his hand. Many of the books that he had collected during the half century of his life were of "national treasure" caliber. He had spent his entire life accumulating a collection that neared 170,000 books.

Mesmerized by the books piled high in the bookstores when he first went to Japan, he bought every book he could find on modern history. For 12 years after founding Kwangmunhoe, he collected ancient Korean texts that had been scattered all over Korea. When Yi Si-yŏng left Korea for his Manchurian exile, he left his family's book collection to Grandfather, making him the caretaker of tens of thousands of books and documents. In 1916, Kim Kyo-hŏn, founder of Taejong'gyo (an indigenous Korean religion characterized by Tan'gun worship), also gave Grandfather his book collection before he went into exile in Manchuria. In 1928, when Grandfather entered the Commission for the Compilation of Chosŏn History, he was able to collect the materials published by the Government-General. When he went in 1939 to teach at the National University of Manchuria, he collected more books while traveling throughout Manchuria, Mongolia, and Beijing.

After Yuggio, he reminisced about his book collection:

> Thinking that our culture should be preserved even as our nation could not be saved, I founded Kwangmunhoe and set about collecting extant books in Korea. I did not even ask about the subject matter. I tried to collect every book containing material that might have something to do with Korean culture.
>
> Few people being aware, at the time, of the importance or the value of this endeavor, the book collection progressed without much difficulty. Over the span of 12 years, it grew to several tens

of thousands. In addition, the family library of Yi Si-yŏng (future Vice-President of Korea), which he had left in my care before moving to West Kando, was a major catalyst in this project. The Yi collection contained hundreds of rare books on the post-Sino-Japanese War years.

As time passed and my collection became significant in size and language variety, I became known in Korea and abroad as "Korea's book collector." My intent was not simply to become a collector of books, but to search for the light of Korean culture hidden within them. The large number of books in my collection was only a byproduct of this search.

A time of hardship ensued, and the Commission for the Compi-lation of Chosŏn History came into existence. Also, museums and libraries and many academic institutions sprang up. I began to develop relationships, both direct and indirect, with these organizations, and they played a large role in augmenting my collection. For example, at the time of the founding of the National University of Manchuria and my subsequent appointment as a professor, ostensibly representing the Korean people, I was given the serendipitous opportunity to collect a great number of Chinese books, as I was able to travel for several years through Manchuria, Mongolia, and northern China.

Grandfather took great pains to safeguard the collection. To him, it was not a personal possession, but a repository of Korea's cultural heritage for which he was a mere caretaker. The reason he moved out to rural Ui-dong was that he felt the location would provide a safe haven from the destructive powers unleashed by the Pacific War. But Ui-dong had turned out to be no haven after all; instead, it became his library's burial ground. On hearing that his book collection had burnt to the ground, he wrote a long piece of sijo, probably the longest as well as the most heart-rending in his entire collection. Here are some excerpts:

……

Ten years ago I tried my best to hide it from harm,
Only to prepare its burial ground ten years later.
I can but chuckle at how my toils have all been for naught.

In lieu of wine and flowers, you were my constant companion.
With you I took refuge from my sorrows and shared my joys.
Together we had many good times, so let's see how we fare apart.

……

Both the bailiffs and communists came to claim it.
Funny how they thought to claim it as their own.
Now the true owner has shown itself, the napalm bomb.

One ordeal arrives right on the heels of another.
Mercilessly scorched by the flaming train of ordeals,
I learn to endure, remembering the old tale of Job.

Every piece of paper, every letter, I gathered with my soul.
Now they're all gone up in flames, but their spirits remain.
Each one lives on, untouched, in my memory.

……

A hundred ingredients I gathered to make one terrific soup.
Before I could drop them in the pot, they've turned to ash.
Alas! I've dreamt a long dream that lasted all my life.

8. The Return to Seoul and My Father's Death

In the spring of 1952, Grandfather, then living in Taegu, sent a letter to Grandmother telling her that he would soon be returning to Seoul. Here is the letter, which Grandmother gave me many years later.

> I hope you and the entire family are well. I am doing well and the children here are all healthy. The family in Pusan seems to be doing a lot better now that they have moved to a new house. I'm particularly happy about the birth of our new grandchild–a baby boy. Inson will be visiting you in a while. You must be pleased about Hyŏk and Jinson's entering middle school. I have asked Ung to give them a gift of 300,000 won each.
>
> Buying an ox might be a good idea, but I'm not sure. I regret that there are just so many expenses. I'm going on a trip in a few days to Ulsan with Mr. Kwŏn, and will be in Seoul around the 20th, in time for the cherry blossoms. My medication is all gone, so please have Inson bring me about 100 capsules. I've also misplaced my glasses, so if you can find a pair lying around (one of my brother's would do, too) and send it with Inson, that would come in very handy.
>
> I hope the mill business is growing. Our new grandson, according to Ki-ju, has a longish face and apparently takes after his father. Please remember to lock the door to the guest quarters.
>
> P.S. Let's wait a little on buying the ox. I might manage to come up with the money once I am in Seoul.

Grandfather returned to Seoul at the end of May, and I wrote to Grandmother from Pusan. I was 12 years old, a fifth grader at an elementary school for refugees. I found this letter several decades later in Grandfather's black notebook, *Chasŏngrok*. Grandfather must have forgotten to write me back.

Dear Grandma,

I'm so glad you and Grandpa are well. Here, all of us–Mommy, Daddy, Dong-ju, and me–are doing great. Only, I miss you so much! I'm sure you miss me just as much. Dong-ju and I go to school every day, and we do a lot of things here that we haven't done in Seoul.

I'm so very sad about Sŏng-ju. How I wish he could come visit me again in Ui-dong so we could play together in the fields! Whenever I think of how Grandpa used to gather chestnuts for us to share, I really miss Ui-dong.

I thought about you a lot on my birthday, Grandma. I didn't even get to bow to you, and I felt sad about that. Please take good care of yourself, and promise me you will write back.

Your grandson, Hak Joo

In June of the same year, we moved to Myo-dong to live with Grandfather and Grandmother, and we waited for my father to join us after tying up loose ends in Pusan. Then one afternoon, the postman came and handed me a telegram, which I gave to Grandfather, who was then conversing with some guests. After reading the telegram, he told the guests, "Forgive me, but I need to take care of some family matter." When the guests had left, he turned to me and said softly, "Dear, go get Mommy."

Once the family had gathered and taken their seats, Grandfather told Grandmother, "It looks like something has happened to In." That was all he said. Grandmother and my mother must have understood, but my sister and I didn't know what those words meant. Soon Grandmother broke into loud cries, and my mother gathered my sister and me into her arms. I saw tears in my mother's eyes. My father had suffered a cardiac arrest and died that morning in Pusan. Handing my mother the telegram, Grandfather said, "You'll need to go to Pusan."

For Grandfather, the string of tragedies that Yuggio unleashed had not yet ended. On July 31, 1952, he wrote this sijo in his black notebook:

For a glorious stroll down life's wide road,
He had everything, seeming to lack nothing.
Who'd have thought it would be so short?

Once again, Heaven raises his sharp whip.
I, a ne'er-do-well, have little use for you,
Why, why do you test me with such bitter trials?

After my father's death, Grandfather recited the Buddhist Prayer to the Goddess of Mercy for two to three hours every day for 49 days. One year later, on the first anniversary of his son's death, he published a sijo in *Seoul Sinmun*. In it, he described the scene in which his wife and daughter-in-law prepare food for the first *chesa* (rite for the dead) for his son. At the end of his sijo, he mourned his beloved son and what he might have been.

As if the bustle of preparing food would lessen their grief,
His mother pounds the rice dough, and his wife grills the beef.
In the midsummer heat, droplets of sweat fall from their brows.

The ice that falls and the fish that gets away seem big,
So goes the saying, but now I find much truth in it.
I know not what to do should this grief persist.

My eldest son, Han-in, had exceptional inborn talent and extraordinary spirit. I loved him with all my heart. He passed away a year ago in Pusan, where he lived an unsettled life during Yuggio. His life dreams are but flowers that fell before their full bloom. Han-in not only excelled in athletics such as figure skating and volleyball, but was also an outstanding medical doctor.

9. Grandfather's Stroke and His Conversion to Catholicism

It was late spring in the year of 1954. I was a first-year student in middle school. When I came home from school one day, I was told that Grandfather was taking a rest because he was feeling very tired. I was then totally ignorant of what a stroke was, but judging by the expressions on the faces of the doctors who frequented the house, I began to realize the seriousness of Grandfather's condition.

A couple of weeks later, I began to take his dictations. The following sijo is the first one he dictated after his stroke:

Unexpectedly, I am given a good fortune of leisure.
Nailed to my bed, facing the ceiling, unable to think and talk,
I wonder if this is the kind of leisure I had in mind.

I had much to do when my body was whole.
Heaven decrees that there's more yet for me to do,
So I thank Heaven for sparing me half my body.

A year after the stroke, Grandfather became a Catholic, baptized with the name Peter. He published an article titled "Life and Religion" in *Han'guk Ilbo*.

> On November 17, 1955, leaving behind all my religious seekings of the last 50 years, I was baptized a Catholic. From a personal point of view, this baptism represents my quest for salvation, and from a national point of view, it represents my ardent wish for my country as it advances toward the new and reforms the old....

At the end of the article, he added that, with his embrace of the Catholic faith, he hoped to be unburdened of the legacy left behind by the earlier Korean philosophers and thinkers whose sole concern had been for the good of their country. Grandfather had felt that for Korea to be a fully modernized country, there was still much work to be done for the full establishment of the *Sirhak* (a branch of learning that emphasizes practical knowledge). He firmly believed that the spiritual framework of Catholicism would help advance the cause of the country's modernization. To his last breath, his main concern was the salvation of his country.

10. One Year after Grandfather's Death

Grandfather passed away at his Myo-dong residence on October 10, 1957. Grandmother and I, Second Uncle, his life-long friend Chin Hak-mun, Reverend Yun Hyŏng-jung, and Mother Dolorosa were at his bedside. Five days later, a mass was held at Myŏng-dong Catholic Church, officiated by Bishop No Ki-nam. That day, carrying a photograph of Grandfather in my arms, I led the funeral procession. I was 17 years old, a first-year high school student. That night I wrote in my diary, "Pity for my grandfather and his encyclopedia of Korean history. Shame on you, Koreans!"

One year later, on the first anniversary of Grandfather's death, I was asked by Hong Sŭng-myŏn, the editor-in-chief of *Han'guk Ilbo*, to write a piece about Grandfather. My eulogy, titled "A Grandson Remembers Yuktang: My Grandfather and Me," appeared in *Han'guk Ilbo* on October 13, 1958. I was a second-year student in high school then.

> At Ui-dong, there is the main house and then there is Grandfather's study, where he sometimes spends the night as well. On my way to the study, I pass rice paddies and vegetable patches, and on one side there is a narrow bank where cherry trees alternate with chestnut trees. Across the stream that flows along the bank, I see Ansan Mountain. When the morning sun rises above Ansan Mountain and begins to shine on Paek'undae on the west, it is breakfast time. Just before the breakfast tray leaves the kitchen, I run to Grandfather's study, feeling the cold on my ankles from the dew that the morning sun has yet to warm.
>
> With my calves scraped pink by the wet grass and my rubber shoes squishy with dew, I arrive at Grandfather's study. I step up

Grandfather's funeral mass at Myŏng-dong Catholic Church in Seoul, October of 1957. Grandmother was 71, and Second Uncle, 41. I was 17, a first-year student in high school.

to the hall and make my morning bow to Grandfather. He takes off his thick glasses, marks the page he has been reading, and together we head back to the main house. I follow, trying to keep up with his big steps. In the fall, when he spots chestnuts on the ground and hands them to me, I am elated.

When I return home from school, I first stop by at Grandfather's study to let him know I'm back. Then, if Grandfather has no guest, I sit on the rocking chair and rock myself back and forth. On some days, Grandfather gives me roasted chestnuts and, on other days, sweet and sour candy. I so love that purple-colored hard candy.

Every year, when the midsection of Paek'undae turns yellow, Grandfather and I go to the burial site in Ssang'geri to pay respects to our ancestors. Because my father and uncle are usually busy with work, Grandfather takes only me, even on *hansik* (the 105th day after winter solstice) and *chusŏk* (Korean Thanksgiving). From Ui-dong, it is a short walk to Ch'ang-dong, but our ancestral burial site in Ssang'gyeri is 10 *ri* further along Sŏrak Mountain.

On the way, we have to cross the Hanchŏn stream, which, at that time of the year, is quite deep and has strong currents. Over it is a narrow bridge made of old railroad tracks. As I start to walk over it with hesitant steps, Grandfather scoops me up, and, with me in his arms, walks over it with big strides. He puts me down on the sand on the other side of the bridge. We wash our hands in the cold stream, and as I walk along holding onto his warm fingers, I love watching the large and small footprints we make together in the sand.

I think Grandfather preferred walking to riding in cars. After the Repatriation, while living in Myo-dong, he used to take a walk every morning and evening. He would walk to the bookstores on the way to Pagoda Park, or to Donhwamun or Ch'ŏng'gyech'ŏn. On Sundays, he would take my sister and me, to our pure delight.

One Sunday we went to Pagoda Park. Wearing a brand new pair of sneakers, I was in high spirits. To tease us, he tried to hide under a bush, but in doing so, he ripped his clothes against a metal screen nearby. We were laughing so hard we left the park in stitches. But then, just outside the park gate, I fell into a ditch. Grandfather quickly tried to catch me, but I still ended up smelling pretty bad, not to mention the condition of my new sneakers.

When snow or heavy rain barred him from his daily walks, Grandfather would play *chang'gi* with me. Even in the heat of summer, he always had a cup of piping-hot green tea next to him. To start, he would play only half the board, then progress to giving me two handicap points, then one handicap point. To tell the truth, I let him give me handicap points only because he wouldn't play with me unless I let him. When I lost, I would make a deep bow to him on the floor, and when I won, I was offered a cup of the green tea.

Sometimes when my sister and I got too noisy, Grandfather would roll his eyes above his glasses and gently tell us to be quiet, but sometimes he would play jumprope with my little sister. Watching him play with her, I remember thinking that he understood little children. Until I entered middle school, Grandfather played with me and was tolerant of my childish ways, but after I entered middle school, he became stricter with me. The gentle smile never left his face, though.

Half an hour after each meal, Grandfather always went back to his reading. On the floor he would spread open the book pages and, with his upper body gently swaying, would recite the lines in a loud ringing voice. A silence would descend on the entire household as surely as the silence of schoolchildren after the bell rings. This would naturally make me turn to my own books.

There were two things that posed a challenge for me when I was with Grandfather. One was when we ate our meals at the same table. I think my mother wanted me to learn good table manners from Grandfather, but my food seemed somewhat tasteless during these meals. The other was when he dictated his sijo to me. After his stroke, he would dictate his writings to Second Uncle, to me, and sometimes to writers or reporters who came to visit him. It was mostly sijo, but lacking fluency in Chinese characters, I would constantly have to look them up in the dictionary. I felt sorry for slowing his progress, and even sorrier when Grandfather commented that my school didn't seem to be doing a good job at teaching Chinese characters. Moreover, when he would look over my dictation for errors, I got literally parched. With the dictation over, he would reward me with fruit or a piece of cake, but my dry tongue couldn't appreciate its sweetness.

One thing that I found intriguing about Grandfather's habits was that he viewed all papers as things of great value. He saved newspapers, magazines, notebooks, and every last piece of paper as long as it had writing on it. To this day, clumps or batches of paper can be found all over the house.

Grandfather let my sister and me play next to his sickbed whenever we wanted, in spite of my mother's concerns about us bothering him. Occasionally, when his illness weighed him down, he would call out to me and say, "Hak-joo-ya, help me get up." When I did, he would sit, wordless, looking out toward the front yard.

The white winter has passed now, as has the pink spring, the green summer, and the yellow fall, but the image of Grandfather in that pose grows more distinct in my mind. I feel blessed to be his grandson, to be able to draw strength from his life and his words. One year after his passing, I deeply honor the memory of my grandfather.

PART TWO

Building a Foundation and Making a Path for Korean Modernity

Chapter 1

The Discovery of *Minjok*

1. Sinmun'gwan (The Institute for New Learning): Opening the Doors to Modernity

It was the summer of 1955, when I was a second-year student in middle school. I vividly remember the conversation I had with Grandfather because of the deep embarrassment I felt about what had just transpired. Grandfather had been confined to his bed for about a year then, and I was taking dictation from him for his article, "The Fundamental Spirit of Learning." There were many Chinese characters that I was not familiar with. When I could not write *"hak-i-si-sŭp-chi"* (學而時習之: learn and master), the first line of the Chinese classic, *Analects of Confucius,* Grandfather said, "It worries me that your school is neglecting to teach Chinese characters, trying to follow the 'han'gŭl only' policy." At my middle school, I had one hour of Chinese characters a week, so I had not considered myself totally illiterate when it came to Chinese characters.

I remember asking Grandfather that day what the difference between Sinmun'gwan (新文舘: The Institute for New Learning) and Kwangmunhoe (光文會: The Institute for the Illumination of Culture) was. For his young grandson, he had a simple answer: One was where you prepared for what you were going to learn, and the other where you tried to master what you had already learned. He further explained that at Sinmun'gwan, exposure to "new writing" made later study easier, and that at Kwangmunhoe, the study of "old writing" promoted further study. He ended his explanation by saying that study, in its true sense, is an endeavor in which one learns the wisdom of those who had gone before in order to transmit it to those who will follow.

Was that all Kwangmunhoe did, actually? It was only much later that I realized that Grandfather hadn't told me everything about the organization he had founded. I guess he felt I was too young and not quite ready for additional information.

Twice Grandfather went to Japan to study, but on both occasions he came back before finishing. The first time he went, in 1904 as a 15-year-old, he had been chosen as one of the Royal scholarship students to attend First Tokyo Middle School in Tokyo, but he returned to Seoul within a few weeks. The second time, he was accepted to the department of geography and history at Waseda University in 1906, but again he left shortly afterwards when the university held a mock Diet in which the Japanese students denigrated the Korean king.

During these brief stays in Tokyo, however, Grandfather was deeply impressed with Japan's rapid modernization, and began to feel that he should put Korea's enlightenment before his own education. He thought that the only way to save his country, which was then precariously hanging by a thread, was to transform its people into modern citizens. As a 17-year-old, he was convinced that the most effective way to bring about this transformation was through publishing. When he went to his father, Ch'oe Hŏn-gyu, to ask for financial support for his publishing ventures, his father readily assented. The failure of the Kapsin Coup in 1884 had been rankling him ever since it happened.

On more than one occasion, Grandfather told me that Korea had lost its sovereignty due to the failure of the Kapsin Coup. I once asked him what Yu Tae-ch'i and his supporters had hoped to achieve with the Kapsin Coup. Grandfather answered, "With Japan's influence, they wanted to push China out of Korea, and with Russia's influence, to reclaim Manchuria, and, finally, to establish a brand new country with young people at its center." But the Kapsin Coup had totally failed. Grandfather once explained to me the reason for the failure:

> The Kapsin Coup failed mainly due to the weakness of Korean leadership, not just the perfidy of Japan or the meddling of China. That is the reason Ch'oe Hŏn-gyu, my father, entrusted me with his entire fortune so that I could play a role in strengthening Korean leadership.

Rain-stained calligraphy sign that hung in front of Sinmun'gwan (27cm × 66.6cm).

Ch'oe Hŏn-gyu hoped that the experience of the Kapsin failure would not be repeated if he could help his son succeed in strengthening Korean leadership through his enlightenment endeavors. The main objective of all of Grandfather's enlightenment and cultural projects, made possible with the support of Ch'oe Hŏn-gyu, was to overcome the Kapsin failure.

With his father's money, Grandfather went to Japan and bought a printing press and returned to Korea, bringing two Japanese printing technicians with him. Then he set up a printing factory in one of his father's houses, and in another of his houses, he set up a general office

Tosan An Ch'ang-ho, educator and enlightenment activist.

on the first floor and an editorial space on the second floor.

Sinmun'gwan opened its doors during the summer of 1907. The entire Ch'oe family was involved in the enterprise. Ch'oe Ch'ang-sŏn, Nam-sŏn's elder brother, managed its finances, and Ch'oe Hŏn-gyu, Nam-sŏn's father, began to pour money into its money-losing activities, as he would continue to do for the next 16 years.

The following year, in 1908, Sinmun'gwan published *Sonyŏn* (少年: Boys), the first general-interest magazine in Korea. The name did not refer to "boys" with today's meaning, but to "youths," young people with new ideas and aspirations for a new age. *Sonyŏn,* which continued for about four years, carried more than just general-interest articles introducing modern knowledge to its readers. Had it done only that, it may not have been banned in May of 1911. *Sonyŏn* had turned into an organ of the Youth Student Association, which was founded by An Ch'ang-ho and Grandfather.

Grandfather first met An in Tokyo in 1907. Three years before his death, Grandfather wrote about his first meeting with An, and the subsequent formation of the Youth Student Association, in his article "The Spirit of Truth":

> The historical background for the founding of the Youth Student Association was Korea's becoming a protectorate of Japan. Korea was on the cusp of its demise. The Association's aim was to regain

> national independence through the awakening of true national spirit. The "Youth Italy" movement was the model that gave us impetus. With a similar purpose and ideal in mind, we met with An Ch'ang-ho, who had just returned to Tokyo from the United States, and discussed our course of action under his leadership.

As early as 1907, Grandfather had been involved in the foundation of the Youth Student Association. An returned to Korea, and together with Yun Ch'i-ho, Yi Sang-chae, and Yang Ki-tak, he founded Sinminhoe, the New People's Association. 1907 was also the year Grandfather founded Sinmun'gwan, the Institute for New Learning. "New Learning" and "New People" were both working toward the same goal.

Although a secret organization, Sinminhoe performed its activities quite openly. The goal of these activities was to promote education, commerce, and the youth movement in Korea. The Youth Student Association focused on organizing the youth movement. The founding members consisted of 12 men, including Yun Ch'i-ho, Chang Ŭng-jin, Ch'a Ri-sŏk, Yi Sŭng-hun, An Tae-kuk, and Grandfather. Grandfather was much younger than the others, but An chose him to write the mission statement for the Association. In "The Spirit of Truth," the article cited above, Grandfather also wrote in detail about An's philosophy, as well as his own subsequent involvement with the Association:

> At the time, An was staying at a small house opposite Severance Hospital, and we met every day, morning and evening. During one of these meetings, he asked me to compose a mission statement for the youth movement. He said, "The fundamental reason for our national decline is the absence of true awakening, the absence of social consciousness and a sense of national his-

> tory. True, there is an anti-Japanese movement, but it is often no more than blind anger, devoid of a true sense of responsibility. Therefore, the national youth movement we are about to launch should put the emphasis on 'truth.' We should stress action over words, content over style; in short, *musilyŏkhaeng* (務實力行: Do your utmost with the task at hand). We should strengthen our physical and mental abilities in order to reach our objectives in a responsible manner." With these words, An asked me to draft the mission statement.
>
> As the Association's chief manager, I spent two months traveling to Kaesŏng, Anak, Pyongyang, Anju, Sŏnchŏn, Kwaksan, Yongsŏng, and Ŭiju, conducting business inspections and giving lectures. *Musilyŏkhaeng* was a motto created by An, which rejected empty, pleasing words and promoted the responsible execution of productive work. Instead of using high-flown language, he summed up his idea of *musilyŏkhaeng* simply as "not telling lies." He stressed that, as individuals and as a nation, we should never tell lies.

With the succinct motto of *musilyŏkhaeng*, An hoped to transform Koreans into modern citizens through a youth-led movement. Grandfather spread the Association's motto, along with its general principles, purpose, and plans, through his magazine *Sonyŏn*. During their countrywide lecture tours, An introduced Grandfather to the audience at each stop, praising him as a "20-year-old youth who, with the publication of his magazine, is giving his utmost to the enlightenment of his people and the creation of a new culture." With An's high praise during the lecture circuit, Grandfather became "a Sonyŏn celebrity" throughout Korea.

Along with fame, however, came serious difficulties.

Before long, the Japanese authorities began to look unfavorably upon Sinminhoe and the Youth Student Association, as well as *Sonyŏn*. At the beginning of 1911, fabricating an assassination conspiracy supposedly targeting Governor-General Terauchi Masatake, the authorities began to investigate those whom they suspected of involvement in Sinminhoe activities. In September of the same year, in the aftermath of the "105 incident," the majority of Sinminhoe members either fled overseas or were arrested. Along with Sinminhoe, the Youth Student Association was dissolved, and *Sonyŏn* was banned from publication.

An fled to the United States in 1911. He returned 20 years later as a suspect in another political case. Accused of inciting the Yun Pong-kil Uprising in Shanghai, he was arrested there in 1932 and forcibly returned to Korea. After his release from prison, Grandfather visited him often at the hotel where he was staying in Myŏng-dong. When An was hospitalized with cancer at Kyŏngsŏng University Hospital, he told his two sons and son-in-law, who were all working then as doctors at the hospital, to take special care of him. Throughout his life, Grandfather held An in the highest esteem. He once said, "I have never regarded anyone as my teacher, except for Tosan An Ch'ang-ho."

After the discontinuation of *Sonyŏn*, Grandfather began publishing two more magazines, *Pulgŭn Chŏgori* (붉은 저고리: Red Jacket) and *Aidŭl Boi* (아이들보이: A Reader for Children), specifically for children. In 1914, he started yet another magazine, *Ch'ŏngch'un* (靑春: Youth), this one, for older readers. For the first time, many writers, such as Yi Kwang-su, Hong Myŏng-hi, Hyŏn Sang-yun, Kwon Sang-ro, Yi Sang-hyŏp, Chin Hak-mun, and Min Tae-wŏn, had a magazine in which to publish their works. Many of these quintessential Korean writers began their careers in *Ch'ŏngch'un*, the only literary magazine at the time in Korea.

The era of *Sonyŏn* and *Ch'ŏngch'un* became synonymous with the "literary era of Yuktang and Ch'unwŏn." (the pen names of Ch'oe Nam-sŏn and Yi Kwang-su) A year after the publication of *Sonyŏn*, Grandfather had met Yi in Tokyo through a mutual friend, Hong Myŏng-hi. Yi began submitting his works to *Sonyŏn* from Tokyo. On his return to Seoul, he taught at the Osan School in Chŏngju, and whenever he visited Seoul, he stayed at Sinmun'gwan. During this period, Yi contributed many of his works to *Sonyŏn* and also served as a part-time editor of the magazine. Grandfather thought highly of Yi's literary talent and urged him to return to Japan for further study. Grandfather's long-time friend, Kim Sŏng-su, gave Yi financial support for his study in Japan.

Along with publishing, Grandfather put his efforts into the modernization of the Korean writing system. Although King Sejong invented the Korean alphabet, later named *han'gŭl*, nearly 500 years ago, Chinese remained the main literary medium during the Chosŏn dynasty. The result of this was that the written language of Korea was completely different from the spoken language. This issue had been raised when the Korean alphabet was first invented, but it remained unresolved until the end of the dynasty. Grandfather felt that Korea's modernization would be possible only through the establishment of a written language that was accessible to the common people.

Grandfather believed that han'gŭl should be the main writing system, with Chinese characters used in a subsidiary role. Because the Korean language had adopted many words of Chinese origin, it was not possible to do away with Chinese characters altogether, but han'gŭl had to be central. He also believed that spoken language should take precedence over written language. With these two core beliefs, he started his "new writing movement" with the publication of *Sonyŏn*, and this effort continued with the publication of his subsequent magazines.

In *Sonyŏn*, he also introduced his own "new style" of poetry, and urged his readers to submit manuscripts written in the new style. In poetry submissions, he required that the poems be written in Korean, with Chinese characters appended only when necessary for clarification. He did all this at a time when the use of Chinese characters was thought to be a badge of superior erudition. Grandfather thought otherwise; he felt that writing should be simple and earnest, and to achieve this end, people should try to use plain everyday language in their writing.

Grandfather's revolutionary ideas about writing gained their full momentum with his publication of *Aidŭl Boi* in 1913. The magazine used Korean exclusively, and all submissions were required to be written in Korean only. He replaced words written in Chinese characters with han'gŭl. For example, he substituted *ch'aek kŏjuk* (책 거죽: book cover) for *pyoji* (表紙), *namu saegim* (나무 새김: wood block) for *mokpan* (木版), and so on.

On the last page of the magazine, he showed Korean letters with the vowel letters and consonant letters arranged horizontally, as are the letters in English words. For example, he showed 한글 as ㅎ ㅏ ㄴ ㄱ ㅡ ㄹ. This way of writing Korean letters never caught on, but it provided the basis for the system that was used on Korean typewriters half a century later.

In addition, Grandfather coined the word *ŏrini* (어린이) for "child." In 1914, he published a poem titled "A Child's Dream," using the word *ŏrini*, predating Pang Chŏng-hwan's "A Child's Song" by six years. At around the same time, he also used the word *nim* (님) in his poems to

Sheet music for the children's song "A Child's Dream" that Grandfather wrote. It was published in the first issue of *Ch'ŏngch'un* (Youth) in October of 1914. In this song, Grandfather introduced the word *ŏrini*, a respectful term for "child."

refer to "beloved," and his readers knew that he was referring to his lost country. Although he searched for pure Korean words and promoted their use, Grandfather was opposed to doing away with Chinese characters altogether. He felt that they had become, with their long history of usage in Korea, an integral part of the Korean language.

From its foundation in 1907 to its closing in 1922, Sinmun'gwan served as a launching pad for many of Grandfather's publishing projects. Banned continually by the colonial censors, he kept on publishing his magazines, one after another. He translated and published books from the West, such as *Gulliver's Travels* and *Robinson Crusoe*, to introduce and promote new progressive ideas. His publication of countless books on Korean history and geography show how much he wanted his readers to know more about their country as it related to the world at large. During the 16 years of his publishing career, he had one thing in mind: the transformation of Koreans into enlightened modern citizens.

With the annexation of Korea by Japan in 1910, the word *kukka* (國家: nation) suddenly came to mean "Japan," and the word *kukmin* (國民: nationals), "Japanese." Bereft of his country, Grandfather substituted the word *minjok* (民族: people) for *kukmin*. For him, the discovery of *min-*

Grandfather(right) in August of 1910, the year of "national shame." He lost his country, but resolved to reestablish its identity. He was 21 years old.

jok and the establishment of its identity constituted the two important tasks he needed to undertake for the citizenry of his country, a country that, he was sure, would one day be free.

2. Chosŏn Kwangmunhoe (The Institute for the Illumination of Chosŏn Culture): Laying the Groundwork for Chosŏn Study

It was in February of 1910, "the year of national shame," (the year Korea was annexed by Japan) that Grandfather moved to the guest quarters of his father's house in Samgak-dong and set up the Chosŏn Kwangmunhoe on the second floor. He moved Sinmun'gwan to the first floor.

I still remember this structure, which once stood on the south side of Kwang'gyo Bridge over Ch'ŏng'gech'ŏn. Bluish tiles covered its roof. After the repatriation of Seoul, I would pass by the building when Grandfather sent me on an errand to the office of *Dong-a Ilbo* or *Chosŏn Ilbo*. I remember seeing signs that said, "Notary Public" and "Law Office." It wasn't a big building, but it had miraculously survived Yuggio without a scratch.

Now the building is long gone, but it was there that Grandfather worked on numerous cultural projects with his contemporary intellectuals. Together with Hyŏn Ch'ae, Pak Ŭn-sik, Chang Chi-yŏn, Yu Kŭn, Yi In-sŭng, and Kim Kyo-hŏn, he collected and published ancient Korean texts that were in danger of extinction. Along with Chu Si-gyŏng, Kwŏn Tŏk-kyu, Kim Tu-bong, and Im Kyu, he started compiling a dictionary of the Korean language. In addition, he founded the Youth Student Association with An Ch'ang-ho, Yun Ch'i-ho, Ch'oe Kwang-ok, and Ok Kwan-bin. With Yi Kwang-su, Chin Hak-mun, Sim U-sŏp, and Yi Sang-hyŏp, he promoted journalism and other activities that would "save the nation through letters." With Pak Han-yŏng, he debated the state of Korean Buddhism. With Ch'oe Rin and Song Chin-u, Hyŏn Sang-yun, and others, he planned the March First Uprising, which ignited the Korean independence movement.

Why did Grandfather found Kwangmunhoe just four years after he founded Sinmun'gwan? At first glance, Kwangmunhoe, with its stated objective of preserving ancient Korean texts, stood at the opposite pole of Sinmun'gwan, which purported to introduce new culture to Korea. Grandfather thought that, as much as Korea was in need of enlightenment, this enlightenment should be firmly based on Korea's indigenous learning and culture. To incorporate new culture in a meaningful way, Korea needed first to preserve and transmit its own culture.

At the time, ancient Korean texts were in critical condition, neglected by Koreans and taken out of the country by the Japanese. Since the opening of Korea's ports, the Japanese, who had long had a greedy eye for Korean artifacts, began to lay their hands on them in whatever way possible: buying them at dirt-cheap prices, confiscating them, or simply stealing them. The ancient texts, because of their small size and volume, were easy prey.

At that time, the Institute of Chosŏn Study, which was run by Japanese scholars in Seoul, began to publish ancient Korean texts. They were supported by the Government-General of Korea, which provided the Japanese scholars with materials taken from the Royal Library. Deploring the situation, Grandfather took it upon himself to preserve ancient Korean texts by founding the Chosŏn Kwangmunhoe.

Among the family memorabilia in my possession, I have the original founding document of Kwangmunhoe that Grandfather composed, now yellowed with age. Here is an excerpt:

> Each day, our ancient texts are disappearing, the essence of Chosŏn is rapidly deteriorating, and the brilliant achievements of the sages and philosophers of the last 5,000 years are fast fading, losing their influence. As a result, the spring from which the descendants draw their spiritual strength is being dried up, the well from which they draw their serious thoughts and inspiration

The Kwangmunhoe building prior to its demolition in 1969. After the loss of Korean sovereignty, Kwangmunhoe became the birthplace of Korean Studies, the Korean Language Movement, and the March First Independence Movement(1919).

is being blocked, and the true face of ancient Chosŏn and the wisdom of its highly talented people are about to be buried for all eternity. This is an unbearable tragedy not only for the Chosŏn people who, in their deep sincerity, are wont to look far ahead into the future, but also a great loss for the scholars of the entire world. Truly, this is a critical situation that neither a principled lay person nor a serious scholar could idly sit by and watch.

Though fully aware of our meager abilities, we will try our utmost to accomplish what many deem impossible, for we feel that both our past and our future demand it. Here we announce to the world the titles of the ancient texts we plan to publish, and respectfully request the kind support of those scholars and lay persons who appreciate the challenges of our endeavor. It will surely be a great boon not only for the ancient Chosŏn civilization but also for the entire academic world.

In the document, Grandfather lamented the disappearance of Korea's ancient texts, which would result in the deterioration of the Korean spirit and, ultimately, the burial of the true Korea. Listing 200 titles of ancient texts, he asked for assistance in locating their originals. With the success of this undertaking, he felt that the study of Korea would turn a new chapter. He continued, "Once the mission of Kwangmunhoe is accomplished, the ancient texts will no longer be 'rare,' and their publication will begin a new chapter for Chosŏn Study."

In Grandfather's words, I read great ambition and high hopes. However, the publication project did not proceed as smoothly as he had hoped. The countrywide search for these texts required a great deal of money, and many other obstacles intervened. Yet, Kwangmunhoe managed to publish 35 titles (59 volumes), 24 (46 volumes) of which were ancient classics, such as *Tongkuk Byŏng'gam* (東國兵鑑), *Tongkuk Sesigi* (東國歲時記), *Tongkuk Tong'gam* (東國通鑑), *Yŏlha Ilgi*(熱河日記), *Taekliji* (擇里誌), and *Samguksagi* (三國史記: The History of the Three Kingdoms). At present, there is no way of knowing how many more "rare" texts remained to be located and published.

Along with the publication of ancient texts, Kwangmunhoe initiated the compilation of a Korean dictionary. Grandfather simply could not tolerate the possibility that the Japanese might compile a Korean dictionary before the Koreans themselves did. First, he began working on a dictionary of Chinese characters. Chinese characters had become an inseparable part of the Korean language, and thus the compiling of a dictionary of Chinese characters was a preliminary step necessary for the compilation of a Korean dictionary. In 1915, the *New Dictionary of Chinese Characters* was completed, with Chu Si-gyŏng and Kim Tu-bong providing the Korean annotations.

Chu Si-gyŏng, who had been planning to compile a Korean dictionary for some time, initiated the Malmoi (word collecting) project with the help of his students, Kim Tu-bong, Kwon Tŏk-kyu, and Yi Kyu-yŏng. Four years into the project, however, Chu died in 1914 at the early age of 38; Grandfather was incarcerated for his independence activities in March of 1919; Kim Tu-bong fled to Shanghai in April of the same year; and, in 1920, Yi Kyu-yŏng also died. The Malmoi project was interrupted for a few years.

Then, in 1925, Grandfather handed the unfinished manuscript over to the Kyemyŏng Club (an organization for nationalist intellectuals) so that its members could continue the project. After many twists and turns, Ŭlyu Publishing Company, in 1957, published the finished manuscript in six volumes, with assistance from the Rockefeller Foundation. It had been 47 long years since Kwangmunhoe first launched the project.

During the Korean language movement, there was much debate as to what to call the Korean alphabet. Theories abound as to who first coined the name *han'gŭl*, but I believe that it was Grandfather. In 1913, he used it for the first time in the October issue of *Aidŭl Boi* and, as far as I know, this is the first documentation of its use. Grandfather himself retraced the genesis of the name *han'gŭl* in his book *Questions and Answers on Common Knowledge About Chosŏn* (朝鮮常識問答).

The Korean alphabet had been called by a variety of names, such as "our letters," "national letters," "vulgar letters," "incomplete letters," "Chosŏn letters," "common people's letters," and "correct sounds." The scholars at Kwangmunhoe decided to give it a new name that everyone could agree to. Grandfather suggested "han'gŭl," whose first letter, *han*, has the double meaning of "great" and "the origin of Korea." This new name was unanimously approved, and when Grandfather became president of the Korean Language Association after Chu's death, he disseminated the name through his publications.

Cover of the second issue of *Aidŭl Boi*(October 1913). In this issue, the term *han'gŭl* was officially launched to refer to the Korean alphabet. In *Common Knowledge About Chosŏn*, Grandfather stated that the scholars at Kwangmunhoe had agreed to the term.

To promote the correct use of Korean language among the people, Grandfather published a series of "yuk-chŏn novels" at Kwangmunhoe. The yuk-chŏn novels were traditional novels that were edited, published, and sold at a very affordable price of six chŏn (60 cents in US currency). Taking such popular novels as *Ch'unhyang-chŏn* (The Story of Ch'unhyang), *Hŭngbu-Nolbu-chŏn* (The Story of Hŭngbu and Nolbu), *Simch'ŏng-chŏn* (The Story of Simch'ŏng), *Changhwa Hong'ryŏn-chŏn* (The Story of Changhwa and Hong'ryŏn), and *Cho'ung-chŏn* (The Story of Cho'ung), he excised salacious elements, revised the language of the text to conform to the correct usage, and sold them countrywide. While publishing these novels, Grandfather, in concert with other Korean linguists, also worked on the standardization of Korean language, as well as the codification of Korean grammar.

Five years after the founding of Kwangmunhoe, Grandfather officially declared its three objectives: the first was the establishment of Korea's history through the publication of its ancient texts; the second, the standardization of Korean language through the compilation of a Korean dictionary and the codification of Korean grammar; and the third, the establishment of the field of Korean Studies. The activities at Kwangmunhoe had all been geared toward the establishment of Korean Studies.

Kwangmunhoe, however, was not simply a place to quietly pursue scholarly studies of Korea. More importantly, it was the birthplace of the Korean independence movement. During the militaristic Japanese rule of the 1910s, the only place where Korean leaders and intellectuals in various fields could gather legally was Kwangmunhoe. It was a haven where they could come to obtain and exchange information. The older generation of patriots, such as Chang Chi-yŏn, Yu Kŭn, Yang Ki-tak, and Yi Sŭng-hun, as well as the younger nationalists, such as Kim Sŏng-su and Song Chin-u, met here to discuss the future of their country. Chŏson Kwangmunhoe was veritably the *académie* of Korea, where debates of national importance took place and their results were often translated into action.

Chŏson Kwangmunhoe was also the birthplace of Kim Sŏng-su's "save-the-nation" education projects. Since his Waseda University days, Kim had had his heart set on educating Koreans, and on returning to Seoul after the completion of his studies, he went to Kwangmunhoe to discuss his plans. Grandfather advised him to take over an existing school, since it was next to impossible to obtain a permit from the Government-General for a new school. Following his advice, Kim bought Paeksan School, then in financial straits, and changed its name to Chung'ang School. Its administration consisted of Yu Kŭn as principal and An Chae-hong as superintendent, both of whom Kim had met through Kwangmunhoe.

The national movement to buy domestically produced goods also started at Kwangmunhoe. In 1915, it initiated the Korean Industrialization Movement to mobilize national sentiment in support of indigenous industry. Among its leaders were Grandfather, Ch'oe Ch'ang-sŏn (his elder brother), Yu Kŭn, Kim Tu-bong, and Yi Kyu-yŏng, as well as the graduates who had just returned from Japanese universities, such as Kim Sŏng-su, An Chae-hong, and Chang Chi-yŏng. The nationalist movement that had been dispersed since the dissolution of Sinminhoe in 1911 was revitalized by Chosŏn Kwangmunhoe, as it stood at the forefront of many national endeavors. These endeavors culminated in the March First Movement in 1919.

The information that Grandfather refrained from telling his young grandson was that the Chosŏn Kwangmunhoe was involved in a *de facto* resistance movement against Japanese colonialism. That it represented a resistance movement was a matter of common knowledge among his family members, scholars and nationalists who frequented Kwangmunhoe, and intellectuals throughout Korea. The Japanese Government-General of Korea, with its secret police apparatus, also knew the true face of Kwangmunhoe. This is a historical fact that cannot be hidden, even among the broken pieces of the blue tile from the roof of the Kwangmunhoe building, torn down some 40 years ago.

3. "The Declaration of Independence": Realizing the Idea of *Minjok*

I distinctly remember the day when I became interested in the March First Independence Movement. I was in middle school. In my Korean language class, I came across the text of the "Declaration of Independence" in my textbook. My teacher, who was struggling to decipher the meaning of the Chinese characters in the text, claimed that its author, Ch'oe Nam-sŏn, was a *ch'inilpa*, a pro-Japanese collaborator.

I came across the same text again in high school. It was in World History class, taught by a young history teacher who said that the May Fourth Movement in China and the Nonviolent Resistance Movement in India were both influenced by the March First Movement in Korea. He said that he based this claim on the "Declaration of Independence" written by Ch'oe Nam-sŏn.

How can both claims be true? I wondered. That was around the time when I had moved my desk to my Grandfather's sickroom, sharing my meals with him and sleeping next to him. I wanted to ask him directly whether he was a pro-Japanese collaborator or a Korean patriot, and whether his efforts had been scholarly or political in nature, but I never got up the courage to do so. My questions remain unanswered for me, and now they are shared by other Koreans as well. Looking back at the past 90 years, I begin to wonder if Grandfather had been predicting the future of Korea, China, and Japan when he wrote the Declaration. It appears to me that today's Northeast Asia, with its conflicts still festering, is not that different from the Northeast Asia of Grandfather's time.

In the summer of 1918, *Asahi Shinbun* in Tokyo ran a story about the upcoming Versailles Peace Conference, which was going to be held in Paris to discuss geopolitical affairs after World War I. The newspaper also reported on President Wilson's principle of self-determination

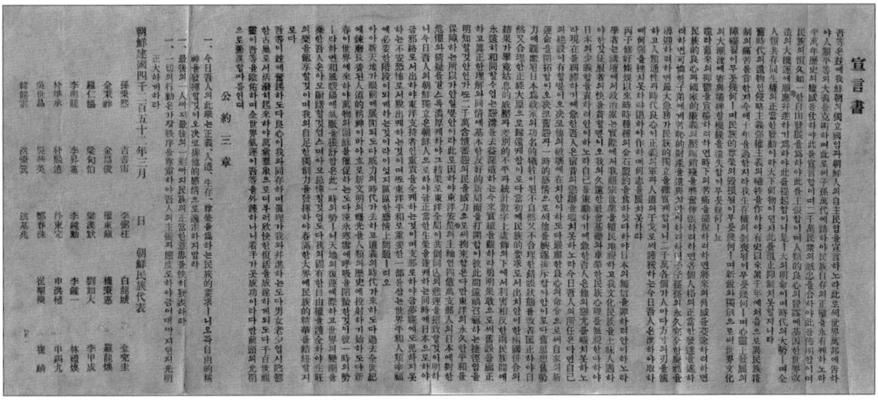
宣言書

公約三章

朝鮮建國四千二百五十二年三月 日 朝鮮民族代表

"The Declaration of Independence" as distributed on March 1, 1919(20.5cm × 38.5cm). Throughout the Japanese colonial rule, my father kept this document inserted between the pages of his diary.

for all peoples. That fall, Grandfather heard about the activities of the Korean exiles in the United States, such as An Ch'ang-ho and Syngman Rhee, and of the Korean exile Kim Kyu-sik in China. Together, these three men were planning to present themselves at the Versailles Conference. On learning of this plan, Grandfather began to work with the nationalists who frequented Kwangmunhoe to plan a domestic movement for Korea's independence.

In January of 1919, Grandfather, Song Chin-u, and Hyŏn Sang-yun met at Ch'oe Rin's house, and by February, the plan began to take shape. The four men decided to persuade the elder politicians to assume leadership. Then they decided to call on religious organizations to join the movement, because they had the ability to rally their members under existing leadership. They also decided that the movement would be limited to peaceful demonstrations. This was a time when the Japanese colonial government did not allow Koreans to own even a single gun or sword.

In order to obtain the commitment of the elder politicians, the four men planned to meet with Pak Yŏng-hyo, Yun Yong-ku, Han Kyu-sŏl, Kim Yun-sik, and Yun Ch'i-ho. Ch'oe Rin visited Pak Yŏng-hyo, Song Chin-u visited Han Kyu-sŏl, and Grandfather visited Yun Yong-ku and Kim Yun-sik, all urging the elder politicians to assume leadership roles in the movement.

Grandfather hoped that Kim Yun-sik would readily agree to participate in the movement because of their long-standing relationship. Kim, who was then widely known as a great scholar, had recognized Grandfather as a young man of great potential and had befriended him, giving him many books. He also gave his full support to Kwangmunhoe. In early February, Grandfather paid him a visit and asked him to join the leadership of the movement. Kim replied that he would discuss the matter with his colleagues. They failed to arrive at a decision, however. The other elder politicians also hesitated to come forward and assume leadership.

Grandfather, Song Chin-u, Hyŏn Sang-yun, and Ch'oe Rin conferred again and decided to contact Son Pyŏng-hi, then leader of Ch'ŏndogyo (Religion of the Heavenly Way, an indigenous Korean religion), as well as Christian and Buddhist leaders. Son readily assented to become one of the people's representatives of the movement, leaving all practical matters to Ch'oe Rin. Ch'oe Rin, who was an important member of Ch'ondogyo, was a close friend of both Grandfather and Song Chin-u. Ch'oe Rin asked Grandfather to draft the necessary documents for the movement: the Declaration of Independence, a letter of announcement to the Government-General of Korea and the Japanese government and Diet in Tokyo, a letter of appeal to President Wilson of the United States, and a message to the Versailles Peace Conference.

At night, Grandfather secluded himself in the house of Kosawa, wife of Im Kyu, and composed the "Declaration of Independence." During the day, he made necessary contacts for the movement. He was able to persuade Yi Sŭng-hun, the founder of the Osan School and the leader of the Christian Church, to come on board. Yi had just been released from prison for his involvement in the "105 incident," but when Grandfather sent Kim To-tae to make the case for his participation, Yi readily gave his assent despite his poor health. With Han Yong-un of the Buddhist faith joining the movement, the four men had succeeded in rallying all three major religious sectors in Korea.

As the plan reached its final stages, former emperor Kojong died. The country was rife with the rumor that he had been poisoned. The representatives of the movement accelerated their schedule. Instead of March 3, the day of the Emperor's funeral, they chose March 1 for the movement to commence. Then they secretly spread the word that the *mansei* (Long live Korea) demonstrations would take place simultaneously in Seoul, Pyongyang, Pusan, Taegu, Kwangju, and other major cities of Korea.

At 2:00 p.m. on March 1, 1919, all 33 representatives gathered at Taehwa'gwan, a restaurant in downtown Seoul, for a formal reading of the Declaration. With their chant of *mansei!* the movement began. The resounding cries of *mansei* from the streets reached Grandfather's ears in his Kwangmunhoe office. After having supper with his family, he went to rest at Kosawa's house, where he had composed the documents for the movement. The next day, he moved to the summer home of a Japanese admirer, Akaoki. When the Japanese police came, Akaoki had them wait outside all night long, and, the next morning after breakfast, informed Grandfather of their presence outside.

Grandfather at Sŏdaemun prison(1920), prisoner number "757." During his incarceration, he sought to reestablish Korean identity, as well as to discover the origin of Northeast Asian civilization.

Grandfather was arrested, and on his arrival at the police station, he learned that his wife had been detained as a hostage. In the living quarters at Sinmun'gwan, his elderly parents were taking care of their young grandsons, Han-in (my father, then age 5) and Han-ung (my uncle, then age 3). Grandmother was soon released. He was detained for a year, and, on February 6, 1920, sentenced to two years and six months of imprisonment.

For the record, I would like to recount here some of the conversations I had with Grandfather about the details of the March First Movement:

- *The time and place Grandfather wrote the documents needed for the Movement*
  In mid-February Grandfather stayed for about two weeks at a Japanese woman's house in Ŭlchiro. At night, he wrote the documents needed for the movement, and during the day, he was busy making the necessary contacts. The name of the Japanese woman was Kosawa, and she was the wife of Im Kyu, a linguist who worked at Kwangmunhoe.

- *The decisive factor for the success of the Movement*
  Grandfather believed that the money Kim Sŏng-su gave to Yi Sŭng-

hun, the representative of the Christian Church, was crucial for the success of the movement. He added that, without the money, the kind of success the movement achieved would not have been possible. Kim Sŏng-su himself declined to take the credit.

- *Grandfather's frame of mind as he was preparing for the Movement*
  At the end of February, Chin Hak-mun visited Grandfather at his home in Samgak-dong to bid him good-bye before he left for Tokyo. According to Chin's recollection, Grandfather, who was normally "unflappable," told him, "At this moment, my mind is pinpoint sharp and can concentrate on only one thing.... Study hard from now on.... try to find solace in books about religion."

- *The document Grandfather sent to the Japanese government announcing the independence of Korea*
  On February 27, Grandfather checked Im Kyu's Japanese translation of the document he had composed and sent Im on his way to Tokyo. On March 1, Im handed it directly to the Japanese government.

- *The original "Declaration" distributed on the streets on March 1*
  Grandfather wrote the entire text. After attaching the names of the 33 signatories, he personally set it in type and corrected typos. He then brought the original over to Posŏng Printing at Ch'ŏndogyo Church to have it printed. On the 27th and 28th, tens of thousands of copies were printed and distributed all over the country, as well as overseas. Because he was working under

extreme pressure, Grandfather missed the transposition of the characters in the first line of the document: instead of "cho-sŏn," he had set "sŏn-cho." In a great hurry, he also did not have the time to get rid of the traces of the typesetting spacers that appeared on the original.

- *Where the Declaration was formally read and who signed the document*
  The event had been scheduled to take place at 2:00 p.m. at Pagoda Park. However, some of the representatives expressed concern that the ensuing chaos might bring harm to the high school students who would gather, and they changed the location to a less public place. The representatives also decided not to include the names of Ch'oe Nam-sŏn, Song Chin-u, and Hyŏn Sang-yun, because they felt that the younger leaders of the movement must be spared imprisonment for the sake of its future.

- *The historical accuracy of the details surrounding the Movement*
  Grandfather once said that the accounts given by some people, as well as the claims made by some others decades after the event, were less reliable than the official record published by the Japanese Government-General of Korea, "A Collection of Court Documents: Preliminary Hearings and Final Decisions of Important Trials."

In 1955, a year after his stroke, Grandfather submitted an article entitled, "The Declaration as I Wrote It," to be printed in the third issue of the magazine *Saebyŏk* (Daybreak). In it, he briefly stated his role in the movement:

> The March First Movement was the natural outgrowth of our national spirit of independence. It would not be accurate to say that any single person planned it, directed it, or propelled it. Rather, it was a movement of the entire nation acting as one. That said, a small number of people did have a direct hand in its start-up in Korea. Among those, the two who made the final preparations were Ch'oe Rin of Ch'ŏndogyo and myself. I was responsible for communications between Ch'ŏndogyo and the Christian Church, as well as for the strategies to be adopted by the movement. I was also responsible for the composition of all the documents announcing its intentions.

Grandfather said that, with no precedent for such a document in the world, he had to create it from scratch, both in form and content. In the article, he listed the four points he wanted to present to the world:

1. The movement originates from the spirit of independence and from the conscience and natural right of the people. Among the leaders of the movement, many entertained the notion of returning to Korea's long-standing suzerainty status with China. I categorically rejected it. The first paragraph of the Declaration was specifically intended as a warning against this notion.

2. Next in importance, the independence movement is not rooted in enmity, or simple anti-Japanese feelings, but in Korea's need to claim its rightful place in the world, which will guarantee its survival and progress....

3. The movement does not originate from selfish reasons, but from its importance for the peace of all of Asia. It is a movement that is aligned with the existing trend of the world. The annexation of Korea creates a sense of imminent danger among the Chinese, and this will lead to the breakdown of peace in Asia. The annexation leaves a stain on human progress as it moves from a world ruled by power to one ruled by morality. This was somewhat prescient of the actual events that transpired. . . .

4. The Korean independence movement is not a short-term affair of fleeting emotions, but will continue until its goals are accomplished. . . .

For Grandfather, "independence" represented a natural, God-given right of the Korean people, not mere enmity toward another nation. Therefore, he made it very clear that it wasn't just Japan, but also China, that Korea needed to free itself from. He stressed that Korea should divest itself of its long-standing, subservient stance toward China as well. He also emphasized the importance of Korean independence, not just for Korea, but also for the crucial role it will play in bringing about stability in East Asia and ultimately peace in the world. Korean independence, Grandfather believed, represented a step forward in the progress of human history.

The March First Movement brought together all the elements of Korean society—people of different classes, people from different regions, the young and the old, men and women—creating a sense of oneness among Koreans. The movement had generated a momentum for the birth of a "nation" in the modern sense of the word. With this new sense of common identity as "Chosŏn minjok" (the nation of Chosŏn), Koreans were able to set the shared goal of eventual independence. In this sense, Grandfather felt that the movement had succeeded.

After the Movement, Grandfather worried that the newly gained sense of nationalism would encourage enmity toward people of other races on the part of Koreans, and he warned of the danger that a narrow nationalism would engender. This was the reason he set out to develop a sweeping, comprehensive ideological framework for his brand of nationalism. For him, the answer lay in the establishment of Chosŏn history with its origins in Tan'gun and the Purham Civilization, and also in the Chosŏn spirit as revealed in the Chosŏn land itself and its unique literary form, sijo. With this broad ideological framework, he suggested a way for Chosŏn nationalism to protect itself from potential exclusivism.

Once my children asked me whether I thought their great-grandfather, Ch'oe Nam-sŏn, who wrote the Declaration of Independence, is Korea's Thomas Jefferson. I was reminded of a similar comparison Syngman Rhee, as President of the Republic of Korea, made in his eulogy when Grandfather died in 1957. My children probably had come across the comparison in one of their history classes and wanted to verify its accuracy.

Is Ch'oe Nam-sŏn indeed the Thomas Jefferson of Korea? The answer is yes, I told my children, if one just views the two figures in terms of their authorship of historic documents that brought about major turning points in the course of their respective country's history. I also told them, however, that there were major differences in the particularities of the historical milieu in which these two men sought independence.

The goal of the American Revolution was to procure independence for a people who had never been independent, and their enemy was situated far across the Atlantic Ocean. In addition, the ideas of liberty and equality, the cornerstones of the new Republic, had already been firmly established in the minds of the American colonists, so it was not necessary to explain to them why independence was necessary. On the other hand, the "independence" that Ch'oe Nam-sŏm sought was to *regain* Korea's sovereignty and to put an end to the myriad divisions that tore at the society due to the incompetence of the Chosŏn dynasty: *yangban* (elite aristocrats) *vs. sangnom* (commoners), male *vs.* female, one region *vs.* another, seclusionists *vs.* enlightenment supporters, pro-Russian faction *vs.* pro-Japanese faction, conservatives *vs.* progressives, Christianity *vs.* Buddhism, Neo-Confucianism *vs.* Yangmyŏng ideology, and so on.

Unlike Thomas Jefferson's enemy, the enemy that Ch'oe Nam-sŏn fought against was close by, just beyond Tsushima Island, visible on a clear day. After World War I, Japan was a victorious country, acknowledged by all the superpowers of the world. Under these very difficult circumstances, Grandfather articulated the idea of "minjok" and gave it a modern national identity. What he achieved was nothing short of a miracle. That was why, I believe, Grandfather composed the Korean Declaration of Independence using an extraordinarily dignified and grand style. The success of the March First Movement provided Koreans with a center, bolstering their confidence in the possibility of their eventual independence.

For the above reasons, I told my children that their great-grandfather, Ch'oe Nam-sŏn, is not the Thomas Jefferson of Korea, just as Thomas Jefferson is not the Ch'oe Nam-sŏn of the United States.

Chapter 2

The Establishment of Chosŏn Identity

1. *Tongmyŏng* (東明) and *Sidae Ilbo* (時代日報): Establishing *Minjok*

After spending two years and eight months in prison for his involvement in the March First Movement, Grandfather was released in October of 1921. While in prison, he tried to re-start *Ch'ŏngch'un*, but could not obtain the necessary permit from the Government-General. In July of 1922, when permits were issued to current-affairs weekly magazines, Grandfather closed Sinmun'gwan after 16 years of operation, and founded Tongmyŏng Publishing Company, with the intention of starting a weekly magazine. He took the name of the company, "Tongmyŏng," from the founder of the Kokuryŏ dynasty. It was a name, he felt, that represented the aspirations of the Korean people, as well as the national consciousness heightened by the March First Movement. In his new publishing endeavor, Grandfather had the full support of his long-time friend Chin Hak-mun.

It was New Year's Day in 1967. I was soon to be off for Boston to pursue my graduate studies, and I visited Chin Hak-mun to do my *sebae* (formal bow to the elders on New Year's) and also to say good-bye. The weather had warmed up a little, and the icicles hanging from the eaves were dripping. I remember trudging up the narrow alleyway, trying to dodge the falling water drops.

Chin was living in a small Japanese-style house. When I rang the bell, he came to the door and opened it himself. He had been wrapping the small trees in his garden with straw. He wanted to finish the job before going into the house, so I offered help by holding the straws together around the trees while he secured them with pieces of string. I asked Chin why he undid the straws he had tied the previous fall, only to tie them again. He answered, "When the snow melts and the water gets in through the straws, it creates gaps between them, letting the cold air in."

Chin was just like that. Everything he did, he did with great care and meticulousness. He gave those around him the help they needed, large or small. He had two children with his Japanese wife, but they died when they were young. His wife, a woman of great refinement, was fluent in Korean and always wore a *hanbok* with impeccable taste. At the time, Chin was vice president of the National Association of Businessmen.

"Sir," I began, "I'm afraid you'll have to be generous with your *sebae-ton* (money the elders give to the young on New Year's in return for a respectful bow) today."

"You're hopeless, Hak-joo, that's only when you're a student! You should know by now that, once you have a job, you should give me *sebae-ton*."

"Yes, I know that, sir, but I'm about to be a student again. I plan to study in America for four or five years. In fact, I'll be leaving next week."

"Why? You've already done your military duty, right? Is it because you don't like your current job?"

"There're times when I'm not happy with what I'm doing. Sometimes it's hard to know what's right and what's wrong, so I've decided that the best thing for me now is to study some more."

At the time, I was working as an engineer at a consulting company run by the government. My job entailed preparing opinion papers on applications submitted by private businesses for government loans to develop new industrial technology.

When we went inside, Chin's wife prepared hot tea for us. After sipping it silently, Chin said, "You mother has had a tough time. Do you think your going abroad is a good idea?"

"Mother said four or five years would be okay with her, sir."

"I guess it'll be all right, then. Have you heard the old saying, 'Don't kill the ox trying to fix its horns'?"

"Yes, I think there's a similar saying in English, too—'Don't burn the house down to roast a pig.' I believe both sayings warn against paying too much attention to small things, and forgetting the main thing."

"It seems you'll be just fine, Hak-joo. Go, and come back home. I promise I'll live another four or five years."

That was my last encounter with Chin. He lived more than five years after I left Seoul, but when I heard the news of his passing, I was in New York. *Chosŏn Ilbo* carried an obituary, which included these words by Chin:

I have been the recipient of all your great love, and no small bother to all of you. I express my deepest gratitude. Today, I depart, before you, for another place.

Wishing you peace,
Chin Hak-mun

He had written his adieu before his death. It was the spring of 1974.

Chin Hak-mun was four years younger than Grandfather. I don't recall hearing about exactly when they first met. Grandmother once told me that Grandfather, Chin Hak-mun, and Sim U-sŏp became blood brothers: Ch'oe was the eldest, Sim, the middle one, and Chin, the youngest. Chin and Sim called my great-grandmother "Mother," and the Ch'oe men of my father's generation called Chin and Sim "Uncles."

Grandmother also said that Chin, a print journalist, and Sim, a broadcast journalist, were Grandfather's eyes and ears. Sim was then the head of Korean Broadcasts at Kyŏngsŏng Radio Station, and he later left an important legacy in the field of Korean broadcasting. Other media professionals in Korea were well aware of the collaborative work undertaken by these three men.

Grandfather's four friends: Chin Hak-mun, Sim U-sŏp, Yi Kwang-su, and Yi Sang-hyŏp (1918). All journalists, these men provided Grandfather with up-to-date news from around the world.

In a commemorative book published by Chin's followers, there is a copy of the letter written on August 2, 1920, by Chin to Grandfather, titled "I greet you, *hyŏng* (elder brother), who is now in prison," followed by "On leaving Kyŏngsŏng (present-day Seoul)." In the letter, Chin recounts the conversation he had with Grandfather on the eve of the March First Movement:

> I recall it was toward the end of February last year. Not your usual calm and unflappable self, you said in an excited, yet grave voice, "At this moment, my mind is pinpoint sharp and can only concentrate on one thing." When I heard you say this in the darkened street in front of your house in Samgak-dong, I was quite surprised and, at the same time, moved in an indescribable way.
>
> Then I put this question to you, "What manner of life should I lead in the future?" And you answered, "Study hard from now on. Also, knowing your present situation and state of mind, I urge you to try to find solace in books about religion."
>
> With this advice coming from you, whom I know not to be a religious person, you opened my future path. While I had previously tried to find comfort in religion and develop a strong life within it, I now sought stronger faith. I sought God. Since I had long known that He doesn't exist in a faraway place, but is hidden deep inside me, I struggled to open the dark shade in my heart that was blocking His light.

In Chin's words, I sense Grandfather's travails, caught in a life-and-death situation at age 30, and Chin's anguish, wrestling with his inner struggles as a passionate journalist at age 26. Above all, I read their friendship and deep concern for each other. At the time he wrote this, Chin was in charge of the politics and economics section at *Dong-a Ilbo*, which started publication in April of 1920. He went on to assume the manager position of its culture section and then became a columnist before leaving the newspaper six months later.

In the fall of 1921, while in Tokyo, Chin received a letter from Grandfather, which began, "This is the first letter I am writing since leaving prison. . . ." In the letter, he asked Chin to return to Seoul to work on an urgent project, along with Yi Kwang-su. The project Grandfather was referring to was the foundation of a newspaper, which Grandfather named *Sidae Ilbo* (時代日報: Times Daily).

During Grandfather's incarceration, Sinmun'gwan and Kwangmunhoe had slipped into a state of relative inactivity, and his father's money had reached its limit as well. Grandfather, no longer able to finance his projects himself, decided to form a corporation. After a series of meetings on the matter with Chin and his other colleagues, he decided to just go ahead and start the weekly magazine *Tongmyŏng* in September of 1922. He was the publisher, and Chin, the managing editor.

If the magazines published by Sinmun'gwan had been mainly geared toward Korean youths yearning for their country's independence, *Tongmyŏng* was geared toward the entire Korean population, which was now bound together by the March First Movement. Grandfather was greatly encouraged by the Movement's outcome, and began to entertain high expectations about the future of his country.

The following is excerpted from an article titled "The Policy of the Chosŏn People: From Quest to Discovery," which was published in the first issue of *Tongmyŏng*:

> Brethren! The most important task for us today is the establishment of a consistent *minsi* (民是: people's policy). We must determine where the focus of our people's spirit should lie and to what endeavor we should devote our capabilities. Needless to say, our circumstances at this moment are far from favorable, and our capabilities severely limited. In other words, we lack the ability to overcome the myriad challenges we face.
>
> Still, we can say with a modicum of confidence that the trend of the times is conducive, combined with our sincere efforts, to realizing our dream in the not-too-distant future. Looking at ourselves, however, I worry that we might fall into a terrible trap right in front of us unless we take the correct action. The "correctness" of an action, in turn, is dependent on the establishment of a unified policy that supports the regenerative efforts of the people. Today, the issues of whether we have an accurate understanding of where we stand, where we want to go, how we want to get there, and how we can correctly use our abilities, will determine our destiny.

Here, I note that Grandfather used the word *minsi*. This was a word that did not appear in *The Great Dictionary* that the linguists of the day, such as Chu Si-gyŏng, Pak Sŭng-bin, Im Kyu, and Yi Yun-chae, had spent years compiling since 1910. Grandfather would not have used a nonexistent word for no reason, and the readers of *Tongmyŏng*, living under the foreign yoke, had no problem understanding what Grandfather meant by *minsi*. To decipher its meaning, I tried substituting *kuk* (國: nation) for *min* (民: people) in *minsi*. I came up with *kuksi* (國是: national policy). The word *kuksi*, according to a modern Korean dictionary, means "ideas and policies that are consistent with the spirit of the nation."

In the magazine article, Grandfather reminded the Korean people of the necessity of establishing a consistent "people's policy." He stressed the need to decide on the focus point of "the people's spirit," because he had been concerned that the recent advent of socialism would blur the direction of the nationalist movement's progress since the March First Movement. At the time he published the article cited above, Grandfather believed that modernization could take place concurrently with the recovery of sovereignty, and rejected the notion that one had to come after the other. Instead of worrying about the independence for which people were not yet quite prepared, he concentrated on the "full discovery of *minjok*." Because the socialist movement and the nationalist movement shared the same goal, he felt that they should stand side by side, not in opposition.

In *Tongmyŏng*, I read not only his quest as a nationalist, but also his striving for the establishment of the study of Chosŏn that would help establish its identity. Beginning in the third issue, he published "A Treatise on Chosŏn History" in 20 installments, listing the topics to be studied. In the treatise, he proclaimed that Korean history should be written by Koreans:

> We need independence of spirit. We will gain independence with ideas and scholarship. We will realize absolute liberty and complete independence, with the spirit of self-preservation, self-expression, and self-study. With our own hands, we will establish "Chosŏn Studies." Through our efforts, we will create Chosŏn texts through which our own blood courses.... With our own two hands, we will beat the drum of our liberty.

From his efforts of the 1910s to disseminate modern knowledge in order to enlighten Koreans, Grandfather had moved on to the establishment of Korean Studies through the study of Korean history and culture. He believed that independence of ideas, studies, and spirit would clear the pathway to liberation.

Reality did not sustain his optimism, however. Although the first issue of *Tongmyŏng* sold 20,000 copies within two or three days of its publication, subsequent issues were banned repeatedly by the Government-General, just as its predecessors, *Sonyŏn* and *Ch'ŏngch'un*, had been. The Government-General also put up roadblocks to the process of setting up a corporation. With the financial repercussions of these colonial obstructions, Grandfather was forced to discontinue the magazine within a year of its inception. In the final issue of the magazine, he expressed his frustration and outrage in these words:

> People of Chosŏn! If you have the courage, say "Yes!" It is not the people of Chosŏn that deserve pity, but Chosŏn itself—its mountains and rivers. It is the spirit of Chosŏn that resides in its mountains and rivers.

His frustration and outrage notwithstanding, Grandfather persisted in his publishing efforts. He decided to start a newspaper, *Sidae Ilbo*. This time, he knew he could not do it singlehandedly. During the preparation stage of forming a corporation, he garnered enthusiastic public support, and many people promised to invest. Encouraged by the response, Grandfather started publishing *Sidae Ilbo* on March 31, 1924, with Chin Hak-mun as executive editor, An Chae-hong as head of the politics section, and Yŏm Sang-sŏp as head of the society section.

I have long mulled over why Grandfather was in such a hurry to start *Sidae Ilbo*. His father's money had all but dried up with his work at Sinmun'gwan and Kwangmunhoe, and Grandfather's reputation alone was not enough to raise the necessary funds. I have always felt that he should have started the newspaper with public funds, not his personal resources.

The reason for the haste, as I have come to understand later, was his wish to put a stop to the division that was beginning to fracture the nationalist movement. Since 1922, with the advent of socialism, the nationalist movement had showed signs of an internal rift between nationalists and socialists. This rift began to manifest itself in the two major newspapers of the day, *Dong-a Ilbo* and *Chosŏn Ilbo*. The former supported the gradualist approach to regaining sovereignty, and the latter, immediate and complete independence. Grandfather, convinced that a third newspaper could play a role in bridging the divide, had rushed into the publication of *Sidae Ilbo*.

By the time *Sidae Ilbo* published its first issue in 1924, the rift had deepened between the nationalist and the socialist factions. The division was based on where to put priority, on the nationalist issue or the class issue. To Grandfather, a division within the nationalist movement was simply not acceptable. Ever since the March First Movement, he had strived for "*minjok* unity" and through it, "completion of the *minjok*." To him, the class issue was not separate from the nationalist issue.

Sidae Ilbo's first and foremost mission was the unity and cooperation of the *minjok*. In its editorials, it addressed the class issue as an inseparable component of the nationalist movement, arguing against the socialist idea that it was not possible to resolve the issue of nation without first resolving the question of class. To counter this position, Grandfather had published *Sidae Ilbo* in haste, bringing in the socialist theorist An Chae-hong on his side. Due to internal disputes that arose during the initial public offering, the newspaper folded, but it represented a direct attempt on Grandfather's part to bring together the different factions of the nationalist movement.

A few years after *Sidae Ilbo* failed in its objective, Grandfather, along with Hong Myŏng-hi and Sin Sŏk-u, failed yet again to create a united front during the Sin'ganhoe movement. *How would Grandfather have felt when his efforts at bridging the factions failed time and again? Could he foresee the tragic division that would befall the nation 30 years later?* I did not have the chance to ask him these questions while he was still alive.

Sidae Ilbo had sold 20,000 copies, making it one of the three prominent Korean newspapers, the other two being *Chosŏn Ilbo* and *Dong-a Ilbo*. However, from the outset, it was bedeviled with management problems, and its initial public offering was marred by the "Poch'ŏn'gyo Incident." The 30,000 won the newspaper had received from Poch'ŏn'gyo, a pseudo-religious group, became a thorny issue, and it was forced to hand over its management to this group. A few of the journalists working at the newspaper opposed the handover. An Chae-hong resigned after writing an editorial that expressed concern over the prospect of the newspaper becoming the organ of a religious group. Soon, Chin Hak-mun, the executive editor, also resigned. Grandfather resigned from his position as president in September of 1924.

While *Sidae Ilbo* was enmeshed in its many problems, Grandfather himself experienced severe financial hardship. The money he had spent through the years, from the foundation of Sinmun'gwan to the start-up of *Sidae Ilbo*, amounted to 300,000 won (equivalent to 30 million dollars in today's US currency). The debt he owed to Siksan Bank alone exceeded 170,000 won. The interest mounted daily. In 1926, his brother Tu-sŏn returned from Germany, after completing his studies there. In order to pay off the debt, Tu-sŏn sold the printing press, along with the Sinmun'gwan building, and other pieces of real estate the family owned. Even with these drastic measures, a debt of 27,000 won still remained, to be paid off in installments over the next 20 years.

After leaving *Sidae Ilbo*, Chin Hak-mun emigrated to Brazil, but returned to Korea in 1928. On his return, he visited Grandfather at Yangsakkol and discovered that he had been living without electricity for some time because he couldn't pay the bills. In the 1930s, Chin went to Manchuria and worked as adviser at *Manchuria-Chosŏn Daily*, and after the Liberation, went to Japan to work in the business field. As soon as he learned of Grandfather's stroke in 1954, he returned to Korea. In the 1960s, at the beginning of the Park Chung Hee regime, Chin was heavily involved in its implementation of the Five-Year Economic Plan, as well as the resolution of Korea's property claim against Japan. During that time, I visited him to seek his advice on my future career. His vision of Korea's industrial development and globalization played a crucial role in my decision to study engineering in college.

2. The Theory of the Purham Civilization: Tan'gun, the Progenitor of Chosŏn

Grandfather's departure from *Sidae Ilbo* precipitated a major turning point in his life. Leaving behind his publishing and journalistic careers, he turned exclusively to scholarly pursuits. During the four-year period after he left *Sidae Ilbo*, he published numerous books and articles that later became his quintessential works. These include "Purham Munhwa ron" (不咸文化論, 1925), *Simch'un Sullye* (尋春巡禮, 1925), "Tan'gun ron" (壇君論, 1926), "Asichosŏn" (兒時朝鮮, 1926), *Paektusan Kŭnch'amgi* (白頭山覲參記, 1926), *Paekpal Pŏn'noe* (百八煩惱, 1926), "Samguk'yusa Haeje" (三國遺事解題, 1927), "Salmangyo Ch'agi" (薩滿教箚記, 1927), *Sijo Yuch'i* (時調類聚, 1928), "Chosŏn Yuramga" (朝鮮遊覽歌, 1928), and "Tan'gun gwa Samhwang'oje" (壇君과 三皇五帝, 1928).

The central focus of his works during this time was his theory of the Purham Civilization, an ancient civilization of Northeast Asia that placed Tan'gun as its center. The existence and meaning of Tan'gun claimed all his scholarly passion. For Grandfather, the Purham Civilization and Tan'gun comprised the theoretical base for the Chosŏn identity, and he maintained this belief throughout his life.

In his article "Purham Munhwa ron" (不咸文化論: The Theory of the Purham Civilization), Grandfather approached the ancient culture of Korea from the broad angle of human civilization. The origin of the word *purham* is *park*, or "pak" (밝), which comes from an ancient Korean word meaning "god of light," "heaven," or "sun." Using this word as a starting point, Grandfather analyzed the names of places that spanned an area from the Black Sea in the west to Japan in the east. Based on his analysis, he envisioned this area as a site of a major world civilization. He named it the "Purham Civilization." The Purham

Civilization, to put it briefly, is an ancient "park"-worshipping Northern civilization, as opposed to the Southern civilization that included China, India, and other South Asian regions. Grandfather posited that the center of this Purham Civilization was Korea, with Japan at its periphery.

The theory of the Purham Civilization countered the claim advanced by the Japanese scholars that Korean history lacked cultural autonomy. Moreover, it suggested for the first time that Koreans, with their cultural creativity, had made significant contributions to human culture as a whole. In short, it was an audacious attempt on Grandfather's part to reframe Korea's role in the cultural history of humanity. Yet some Koreans criticized him for including Japan in the civilization at all and accused him of supporting the Japanese claim of *naesŏn ilch'e*, a slogan created by the Japanese to promote the idea that that Japan and Korea are "one body."

Before the Liberation, as well as after, Grandfather offered neither an explanation nor an apology for any criticism that came his way. However, on the question of the Purham Civilization, he gave a clear explanation in his "Chayŏlsŏ" (Open Letter), which he presented to the court of Anti-National Law for Japanese Collaborators in 1949:

> Many years ago, I published an article titled "The Theory of the Purham Civilization," in which I posited that Asian civilization has two branches, the North and the South. I also posited that the civilization in the North developed around the old capital of Tan'gun and that it constituted a major step forward in the development of world civilization, with Japan as its natural wing. Of course, this theory represented my scholarly viewpoint, but embedded in it was a sword that could be used in the long-term spiritual battle

against Japan.

A few people willfully misinterpreted my theory and directed their criticisms at me, and many others twisted the theory into a baseless accusation that I supported *naesŏn ilch'e*. However, anyone who has given the article a serious reading will understand that my theory suggests a bold idea: that the Tan'gun culture encompassed one half of world civilization, of which Japan was only a part.

Grandfather made it very clear that with his theory, he attempted to establish a vast civilization with Tan'gun at its center, Japan being only a part of this civilization. In fact, he included almost half of all ancient human civilizations in the Purham civilization, with Korea's national progenitor, Tan'gun, at its center. Grandfather believed that the Purham Civilization extended far beyond Korea, forming one of the major ancient civilizations of the world.

After the publication of "The Purham Civilization," he dedicated himself to the study of Tan'gun. He argued, point by point, against Japanese scholars' claim that Tan'gun had never existed. He proved the historical authenticity of *Samguk'yusa* (The History of the Three Kingdoms), the only historical document in which Tan'gun is discussed. He revealed the shamanistic character of Tan'gun, and also delved into mythological studies to understand the structure of Tan'gun myths.

In addition, in order to understand and interpret the religious aspects of Tan'gun worship, he went on a pilgrimage to Paektusan, the mountain where Tan'gun is popularly believed to have descended. He also made trips to various landmark regions of Korea where he believed the Chosŏn spirit resided. Grandfather, in short, devoted his life's passion to the study of Tan'gun. His life was indeed one of *kohaeng* (religious penance characterized by extreme hardship). In his "Open Letter," he said that he could brook all criticisms but those aimed at his work on Tan'gun:

> ...A few items listed above pertain solely to my actions in the personal sphere, so I will refrain from making any comments, even though I could provide my motivations, as well as relevant facts. However, for the items that pertain to the matter of national ancestry, since they relate to the fundamental issue of our national spirit, I am compelled to offer a clarification.
>
> The average person, looking back on the past half-century of my *kohaeng*, will agree that my consistent focus has been the study of Korean history and the establishment of Korean culture. Those in the know will not deny that, through my scholarship, I have attempted to revive the father of our nation, Tan'gun, who was in danger of being obliterated at the hands of frivolous academics, and to elucidate and affirm the national spirit emanating from him.

To Grandfather, Tan'gun was the source from which the spirit of Chosŏn flowed. When the Japanese scholars, the "frivolous academics," set out to expunge the very existence of Tan'gun, he presented scholarly arguments to expose their intent. From this point of view, Grandfather's study of history perhaps cannot be characterized as purely academic. The main goal of all his scholarly endeavors was inextricably tied to the furthering of the national spirit, as well as the establishment of Chosŏn identity, which he felt was necessary for the achievement of this goal.

Most of Grandfather's articles during this period were published in *Dong-a Ilbo*. After joining the newspaper as its writer-at-large in August of

1925, he contributed countless articles, columns, and travelogues, such as *Simch'un Sullye* (in installments), "Tan'gun ron," "Paektusan Kŭnch'amgi," and "Chosŏn Yuramga." Even after he left the newspaper in October of 1928, his works, such as "Tan'gun gwa Samhwang'oje" and "Chosŏn Yŏksakanghwa," continued to be published there in installments.

Grandfather's relationship with *Dong-a Ilbo* was both special and long-standing. Publisher Kim Sŏng-su, President Song Chin-u, and Grandfather all studied at Waseda University, and together they had led the March First Movement during the Kwangmunhoe days. Grandfather sent his younger brother, Tu-sŏn, to Kim after his graduation from Waseda University. Ch'oe Tu-sŏn played an indispensable role in Kim's involvement in education and journalism endeavors. Over the years, he worked in various capacities, such as registrar and principal of Chung'ang High School, president of Kyŏngsŏng Textile Company, director of Posŏng Institute, and finally, president of *Dong-a Ilbo*.

In the spring of 1957, I remember going to *Dong-a Ilbo* on an errand for Grandfather. At the time, my great-uncle, Ch'oe Tu-sŏn, was its president. The manuscript I was carrying that day was the poem that Grandfather had composed to commemorate Kim Sŏng-su on the second anniversary of his death. I distinctly remember the poem because I took the dictation. In the poem, published on February 19, 1957, Grandfather recalled his visit to Kim's father in Chŏng'ŭp to convince him to fund his son's decision to take over Posŏng Institute.

Grandfather once told me that, had Kim Sŏng-su not given Yi Sŭng-hun the needed money during the preparation stages of the March First Movement, it would not have succeeded to the extent that it did. He also said that Kim did not want people to know about his part in the Movement's success. Through some unspoken agreement, Grandfather and

Widang Chŏng In-bo, scholar of Chinese classics.

Kim understood, trusted, and cared for each other. They were indeed the two stalwart walls between which the current of Korea's modern history flowed. One resuscitated, through the study of history, the trampled pride of the Korean people. The other, through his commitment to education, journalism, and industrialization, made preparations for the recovery of Korea's sovereignty.

When considering Grandfather's relationship with *Dong-a Ilbo*, Chŏng In-bo comes to mind. Grandfather was quite impressed with Chŏng's erudition in the Chinese classics. During Grandfather's travels in Ch'ungch'ŏng Province, he visited Chŏng (then residing in Mokch'ŏn) and urged him to come to Seoul. Soon afterwards, Chŏng arrived in Seoul with his family, and Grandfather found a house for them near his house in Yangsakkol. As neighbors, they met almost every day and spent time together discussing history and literature.

According to Second Uncle's recollection, Chŏng was a quintessential Korean *sonbi*, a scholar well versed in the Confucian code of propriety. When he first arrived in Seoul, he was going through financial hardship, and Grandfather put in a word to Song Chin-u, then president of *Dong-a Ilbo*, who subsequently commissioned Chŏng to write articles for the newspaper. From this beginning, Chŏng went on to write numerous articles for the newspaper. His representative works, "Lectures on Yangmyŏng Study" and "The Five Thousand Years of Chosŏn Soul," both appeared first in *Dong-a Ilbo*.

In addition, Grandfather recommended Chŏng for a teaching position at Yŏnhi College (now Yonsei University) so that he could cultivate students of Korean history. Grandfather had a passing acquaintance with Rev. Horace Grant Underwood, the founder of the college. When Underwood was dying, he asked his son to invite Grandfather to teach at the college. Following his father's last wish, Rev. Horace Horton Underwood offered Grandfather a position as professor of Korean Studies, but Grandfather was hesitant about holding a salaried position at an institution run by foreign missionaries. However, feeling that Chŏng would be a good fit, Grandfather recommended him for the position. Grandfather had judged rightly that Chŏng In-bo would effectively promote Korean Studies at the college. During his 20-year teaching career at Yŏnhi College, Chŏng nurtured many promising young scholars in Korean Studies, thanks to his varied lectures on subjects including Korean literature, Chinese literature, and Korean history.

In 1940, as the Japanese military rule intensified, Chŏng left Seoul and settled in the quieter Ch'ang-dong. Hong Myŏng-hi did the same. Grandfather, who had been teaching at the National University of Manchuria, also returned to Seoul in 1942, and often visited his two good friends in Ch'ang-dong. At their urging, he sold his house in Hyoje-dong in 1944 and moved to Ui-dong, which was near Ch'ang-dong.

After the Liberation, when Grandfather, having been charged with anti-national pro-Japanese activities, was going through one of the most trying periods of his life, Chŏng, who was then the first Inspector-General of the Republic of Korea, immediately came to his defense. During Yuggio, when Chŏng was hiding in Nakwŏn-dong, he was said to have worried about Grandfather's welfare. Amidst the tumult of war, Chŏng was abducted and died during his passage to North Korea. Grandfather narrowly escaped abduction.

I once heard about a rumor that had spread concerning Grandfather and Chŏng In-bo. It was said that, when Grandfather joined the Commission for the Compilation of Chosŏn History in 1928, Chŏng had spread a *chesa* (symbolic meal for the dead) table for him and keened, "Ch'oe Nam-sŏn is dead!" Another version had Han Yong-un spreading the *chesa* table. When asked whether it was true that he had "received" Chŏng's *chesa* table, Grandfather replied, "A *sonbi* would never spread a *chesa* table for the living. Please do not insult Wi-dang (pen name of Chŏng In-bo)!" As Grandfather pointed out, this false rumor does great disservice to the memory of Chŏng In-bo, the quintessential Korean *sonbi*.

My own memory confirms the extraordinary friendship that the two men enjoyed in each other's company, and I wonder, *Who in the world would invent such a malicious rumor? Why?* It is my hope that the younger generation will honor the genuine friendship that existed between Grandfather and Widang Chŏng In-bo.

3. The Kyemyŏng Club and the Korean Dictionary: Clear Language Leads to Clear Thinking

It was summer vacation in 1956, when I was a third-year student in middle school. It had already been two years since I moved my desk into Grandfather's sickroom. A friend of my mother's from Kyunggi Girls' High School, class of 1935, wanted to gather a few of her classmates' children to give them Japanese lessons. Eager for a break from the serious atmosphere of the sickroom, I quickly signed up. Twice a week, I went to the home of my mother's friend, also my teacher now. In her parlor, a few of us children got together for the lessons, and also for some lighthearted fun.

Our teacher's name was Pak Sŏng-wŏn, and she had graduated from the Department of Japanese Literature at Tokyo Teachers' College for Women. She was the eldest daughter of Pak Sŭng-bin, a notable Korean linguist. Pak Sŏng-wŏn taught Korean at her alma mater, Kyunggi Girls' High School, and, later in her career, became a professor of Japanese Language and Literature at Hankuk University of Foreign Studies.

My friends and I belonged to the so-called "han'gŭl generation," but since we had one hour of Chinese characters a week at school, we could read the daily newspapers with basic competence. Japanese, with its liberal use of Chinese characters, was much easier to learn than English, and our lessons progressed quite rapidly. By the time winter vacation rolled around, we were reading, with the help of a Japanese-Korean dictionary, Ibsen's *A Doll's House* in Japanese translation.

During the lessons, Pak often talked about her father, Pak Sŭng-bin. She said that her father, who was originally a lawyer, felt that law books should be compiled in Korean for Korean people. In order to accom-

Hakbŏm Pak Sŭng-bin, lawyer and linguist.

plish this task, he began to study the Korean language. His goal was to devise a codified grammatical system for the Korean language, like those of Japanese, English, and German, the languages he had studied during his legal training.

One year before the March First Movement, Pak Sŭng-bin, along with Grandfather, O Se-ch'ang, and Yi Nŭng-hwa, formed the Hanyang Club. When a group of Koreans who strongly supported Korea becoming a part of Japan formed the Taejŏng Club (named for a Japanese imperial era) in 1921, the Hanyang Club changed its name to "Kyemyŏng Club" (*kyemyŏng* meaning "dawn") and continued with its study of Korean culture and language.

Beginning in 1925, when Grandfather became writer-at-large for *Dong-a Ilbo*, he attended many of the Kyemyŏng Club's meetings. The club published a periodical of the same name, *Kyemyŏng*, the only periodical at the time that published manuscripts on scholarly subjects. It published, for example, Grandfather's *Samguk'yusa Haeje* and *Salman'gyo Ch'agi*, Yi Nŭng-hwa's *Chosŏnmusokgo*, and O Se-ch'ang's *Kŭnyŏksŏhwajing*. One other important reason Grandfather frequented the Kyemyŏng Club was to continue the compilation of the Malmoi project that Chu Si-gyŏng had worked on before his death. Grandfather and Pak Sŭng-bin, who had enjoyed a close relationship since the Hanyang Club days, were both committed to the completion of the Korean dictionary.

Grandfather, who had depleted his family's wealth while publishing *Tongmyŏng* and *Sidae Ilbo*, could no longer personally fund the management of Kwangmunhoe, and as a result, the Malmoi project also had come to a halt. Along with the Malmoi manuscript, Grandfather sent Im Kyu and Yi Yun-chae to the Kyemyŏng Club, so that they could continue to work on the project. After the manuscript went through the hands of the Committee for the Compilation of a Korean Dictionary and the Korean Language Society, it saw its partial completion and went into its first printing in 1942. In October of that year, however, an incident occurred in which the Japanese Government-General arrested all the Society's members and confiscated tens of thousands of the index cards created for the Malmoi project.

The first edition of *The Great Dictionary*. On its publication in 1957, its publisher, Ŭlyu Publishing Company, presented Grandfather with a six-volume set.

Upon the Liberation, the Society's members, who had suffered extreme torture, were released, only to discover that the Malmoi manuscript had disappeared into thin air. The enormous effort that they had poured into the making of the Korean dictionary had come to naught. Then, one day, to everyone's incredulity, the manuscript turned up in a warehouse at Seoul Train Station. In 1947, Ŭlyu Publishing Company began to print this manuscript, under the title *The Great Dictionary of the Chosŏn Language*, only to be stopped again three years later by Yuggio. The manuscript that survived the war was finally published in

1957 in six volumes, under the title *The Great Dictionary*. It had been 47 long years since the Malmoi project was first launched at Kwangmunhoe.

Pak Sŭng-bin died before the Liberation, but he had said, according to his daughter, my Japanese teacher, "As long as Yuktang Ch'oe Namsŏn of Kwangmunhoe is alive, the Korean dictionary will see the light of day." The six-volume set of *The Great Dictionary*, which Ŭlyu Publishing Company presented to Grandfather on its publication, now sits in my study in New York.

It was not only during my Japanese lessons that I saw Pak Sŏng-wŏn. Because her father had been a close friend of Grandfather's, she regularly came to visit Grandfather during his illness, and I was able to listen in on their conversations about the Korean language movement her father and Grandfather had led together.

Her father, Pak Sŭng-bin, had been opposed to the "systemization of han'gŭl orthography" as promulgated by the Korean Language Society. Pak believed that instead of "systemizing" Korean orthography, Korean words should be written the way they were pronounced: for example, for the verb *to eat* "먹으니" (mŏk-ŭ-ni) should be written as "머그니" (mŏkŭni). He pointed out that this was the way Korean had been written since its invention 500 years ago. Pak founded the Korean Language Research Society and published the journal *Chŏng'ŭm* (Correct Sounds). The Korean Language Society had published a journal called *Han'gŭl*, in which it proposed a more formal system for Korean orthography.

Grandfather was in general agreement with Pak's school of thought on Korean orthography. Moreover, he was opposed to the "han'gŭl only" idea, because he was concerned about the possible negative consequences of the educational policy based on this idea. During the

unpaved roads.

In the outer guest room at Pŏbchusa, it was so cold that the only way we could fall asleep was to hold each other tight for body warmth. In the main hall at Kapsa, the door had flown away, and the only thing we could see were the candlesticks, with their huge congealed drippings. At Sudŏksa, Venerable Iryŏp (a famous female monk) sat in the sun warming herself and said nothing for a whole hour. At the time, I had a copy of *Simch'un Sullye* in my backpack.

The initial impact of the first line of *Simch'un Sullye* is still vivid in my memory for its audacity:

> Our national land of Chosŏn, with its rivers and mountains, embodies its history, philosophy, poetry, and spirit. . . .

When *Simch'un Sullye* was first published in 1925, the word *national* in the phrases "national language," "national residents," "national song," and "national flag," all meant "Japanese." Regardless of the degree of outrage Grandfather felt, it is a mystery how his bold declaration that his land was Chosŏn land managed to bypass the censorship of the Government-General. Reading between the lines of his writings, Korean people knew what he was referring to. They also knew the true identity of the "nim" (beloved) that Grandfather repeatedly invoked in his writings.

When the newspaper installments of *Simch'un Sullye* were collected and sold as a book, it became an immediate bestseller and went through several printings. This passage from its preface reads like a confession:

> Perhaps my faith in the land of my country borders on animism. The land looks upon me with tenderness and talks to me with

> words and smiles. Wherever I go, I hear its low whispers, sweet stories, and affecting appeals.

To me, the passage sounded much like a lover's confession. The published portion of *Simch'un Sullye* comprised only half of the entire manuscript he completed. In its last chapter, Grandfather wrote, "I will write another chapter on Chiri Mountain." What happened to that chapter is unknown. Whether the second half of his manuscript was confiscated by the Government-General or destroyed when Grandfather's library was bombed during Yuggio, I have no way of knowing.

Paektusan Kŭnch'amgi (白頭山覲參記: The Travels to Paektu Mountain)
In the summer of 1926, Grandfather again went on a tour with Venerable Pak Han-yŏng, this time to the sacred Paektu Mountain. After making a climb to its summit, he submitted his travel writings to *Dong-a Ilbo*, which serialized them in 89 installments. The following year, Hansŏng Book Company collected these installments into a book and published it, again to much acclaim.

A year before his ascent, his mother had died. The day he reached the mountaintop was the first anniversary of her death. Grandfather begins *Paektusan Kŭnch'amgi* with a heartfelt dedication to his mother:

> Mother, I offer my little book to you, who are now in heaven above. I think Paektu Mountain is the most fitting place to connect my deep, inexpressible love for you and your great love for me, which is beyond words.
>
> I believe that Paektu Father descended on me as you gave birth to me, and through you revealed his own great love for me. It

behooves me that I express my unending love for Paektu Father through you.

The day I saw the hallowed face of Paektu Mother at Ch'ŏnji Lake at the summit was the first anniversary of your passing. On the water's surface, I witnessed my two mothers become one, united in body and spirit. It was an experience that will forever be etched in my memory.

Grandfather continues, bewailing that he was "a beggar child who, after crossing many mountains and rivers, had come to get a glimpse of the gentle face of his merciful mother." Then, "wiping blood from my torn flesh," he cries out, "Great Father of Paektu Mountain, I have come to you empty-handed," but promises him that the *minjok* would survive, that he himself would make it so.

For Grandfather, Paektu Mountain represented "the origin of our ancestors, the source of our culture, the cornerstone of our land, the swaddling cloth of our history, and the nourishment of our life." In *Paektusan Kŭnch'amgi*, he personified it as his beloved mother.

The first time I read this book was in 1964. Seven years had passed since Grandfather's death. I was serving, after graduating from college, as an Army lieutenant in a suburb of Seoul. Twice a week, I was on night duty, so I had plenty of time to read. At first, I did not venture to open *Paektusan Kŭnch'amgi* because it appeared forbiddingly challenging. However, after reading the first few pages, I was pleasantly surprised that it was easier to understand than either *Simch'un Sullye* or *Kŭmgang Yech'an*. On every page of the book, I came face to face with Grandfather's beliefs, aspirations, and resolve. I felt that whoever could not understand *minjok* and the aim of *minjok chuŭi* (nationalism) while

Grandfather at the top of Paektu Mountain in July of 1926. Grandfather is at left and Buddhist scholar Pak Han-yŏng, in the middle.

reading this book was simply not a Korean.

The first time Grandfather used the word *minjok* was in 1907, when he wrote an article titled "The Kind of People the Modern Age Needs." It appeared in the March issue of *Korean Students Abroad*, a newsletter published by the Korean students living in Tokyo. In the article, Grandfather wrote, "with earnest prayers to heaven and earth, twenty million Chosŏn *minjok*, men and women, young and old, must contain our anger at this difficult juncture and demonstrate our national characteristics, as well as declare our earnest aspirations." He was barely 18 years old at the time.

Kŭmgang Yech'an (金剛禮讚: A Paean to Kŭmgang)

Kŭmgang Yech'an, which was published in 1928, has a richer and more refined appearance than the two books discussed above. The first edition in my possession has an overlay of dark blue silk on the cover, and the title is printed in gold, creating the sense of gravitas one feels when handling a Buddhist sutra.

As Grandfather stated in his preface, he had submitted the manuscript three years before, so the record of his travels in Kŭmgang Mountain, *Pung'ak Kiyu*, may well have been the forerunner of *Kŭmgang Yech'an*. The first time I read it, I was in the United States, so it must have been after 1967. Perhaps I had matured a little as a reader by then, but in this book, I could hear the voice of a serious historian, which was quite different from the emotional voice in *Simch'un Sullye*, or the impassioned voice in *Paektusan Kŭnch'amgi*. The voice I heard in *Kŭmgang Yech'an* was that of a dispassionate historian who had something of consequence to convey.

Grandfather had begun to work on the manuscript three years before, in 1925. His weekly magazine, *Tongmyŏng*, had closed down, and his newspaper, *Sidae Ilbo*, had passed on to a new owner. In the winter of that year, Grandfather went on a two-month tour of Kŭmgang Mountain, and on his return, began to submit his manuscript. It is not clear whether it actually took him three years to finalize the manuscript into book form, or whether the censorship procedures of the Government-General delayed its publication. In any case, the book was published in 1928, and it quickly went through several printings.

Chosŏn Yuramga (朝鮮遊覽歌: Songs About Travels Across Chosŏn)

Grandfather wanted to instill in Korean youths knowledge of and affection for Chosŏn by having them sing about its rivers and mountains. With this intention, he wrote, in 1908, tributes to the Korean landscape in the form of children's songs, and published such songs as "The Song of the Kyŏngbu Railroad" and "The Song of Hanyang." However, during the ensuing 20 years, unforeseen problems began to surface. As his songs spread among the people, the original meaning of the lyrics began to change, and sometimes the words themselves were replaced with unrelated coarse words. It got to a point where Grandfather deplored, "If only I could put an end to these songs, I would."

Beginning in June of 1928, he submitted his manuscript for *Chosŏn Yuramga* to *Dong-a Ilbo*, which published it in 10 installments. His words were set to music by Paek U-yong and Kim Yŏng-hwan. In his preface, he wrote about the goal he had in mind for the songs:

> Of late, I often hear children in kindergarten, elementary, middle, and high schools singing songs whose words I find disturbingly coarse in their sentiment. In addition, some of the more passable lyrics deal with subjects imported from foreign countries. On perusing school textbooks, I am troubled to see no evidence of Chosŏn spirit and little attempt to elucidate the meaning of important words and concepts. For this reason I decided, taking time out from my study of history, to create songs about Chosŏn. Here I present to you *Chosŏn Yuramga*, songs about the nature and culture of Chosŏn.

Grandfather worried about the debasement of the song lyrics and the failure of the existing textbooks to include and teach Chosŏn subject matter. In order to minimize the ill effects of the situation among

Korean youths, he created a new set of songs, *Chosŏn Yuramga*, that harmonized, as it were, the nature and culture of Chosŏn. He started with a song about Paektu Mountain, at the northern tip of Korea, and ended with a song about Mosŭlpo Harbor, at the southern tip of Cheju island. In his final song, he expressed his heart-thumping excitement as he looked out on the Pacific Ocean.

In reading the lyrics below, I feel Grandfather's unwavering love for the sea-facing Chosŏn, which he had previously expressed in his earlier poem "Hae egesŏ Sonyŏn ege" (From the Sea to Boys):

I long for my beloved's land, mysterious,
Flickering beyond the dancing white waves.
Look! Mirrored in the sea, I see her starry eyes
Burning with intensity. My heart leaps!

Paekpal Pŏn'noe (百八煩惱: One-Hundred-and-Eight Agonies) and *Sijo Yuch'i* (時調類聚: A Sijo Selection)

Sijo is one of the four genres of traditional Korean poetry. It consists of three lines: the first line states the theme, the second line elaborates on it, and the third line is a twist on the theme or resolution. Sijo developed into the *hyang'ga* form of the Silla dynasty, the *kayo* form of the Koryŏ dynasty, and reached its full glory during the Chosŏn dynasty. By the end of the dynasty, however, the sijo form had lapsed into empty wordplay.

Grandfather had an abiding interest in sijo. He wrote his first sijo at age 18, when he was a student in Tokyo, titled "Kukpungsasu" (國風四首: Four Sijo in Korean Style). They appeared in the first issue of *Korean Students Abroad* in 1907. As young as he was, he already

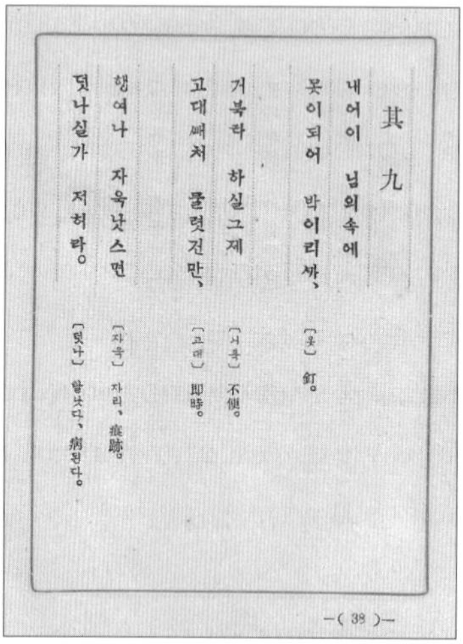

其九

내어이 님의속에

못이되어 박이리싸、 [못] 釘。

거북라 하실그제 [거북] 不便。

고대빼처 물렷건만、 [고대] 即時。

행여나 자욱낫스면 [자욱] 자리、痕跡。

덧나실가 저허라。 [덧나] 탈나다、病된다。

—(38)—

Grandfather's sijo from *One-Hundred-and-Eight Agonies*. Hong Myŏng-hi, in the postscript he wrote for the collection, averred that the word *nim* refers to Chosŏn.

had an understanding of sijo as a poetic form unique to Korean literature. Considering the fact that "Kukpungsasu" was published a year before he wrote his "free-verse" poem, "Hae egesŏ Sonyŏn ege," which is universally viewed as having opened the doors to modernity in Korean literature, it is clear that Grandfather, from early on, was engaged in the study of both traditional and new forms of Korean poetry.

Grandfather wanted to save the sijo form from frivolous wordplay, and he experimented with it in order to modernize and establish it as a major genre in modern national literature. In 1926, twenty years after the publication of "Kukpungsasu," he published *Paekpal Pŏn'noe*, the first collection of sijo in Korean literary history. In the preface, he reveals the book's objective:

> I am afraid the sijo themselves are unremarkable, but I would consider myself extremely fortunate if you could appreciate my sincere efforts to rescue sijo from the slough of wordplay and to remake it into a vessel for weighty thoughts.

It needs no mention here that the "weighty thoughts" Grandfather had in mind were those related to the spirit of Chosŏn. He used the word *nim* (beloved) to symbolize that spirit. For Grandfather, *nim* was the source of the fortitude that enabled him to forge ahead in the face of all hardships:

> Looking back, I have walked this beautiful world as if walking on a field of grainy sand. The only reason that, even after treading half of my life in the scorching, sand-burning sun, the light of spring did not leave my heart and my parched throat and painful legs did not get the better of me, is the existence of my sun goddess, *nim*.

The exact number of sijo in *Paekpal Pŏn'noe* is 111, not 108. The first sijo is titled "Kung'gŏ'wŏ" (Longing):

> *I wrap and rewrap the glass bead I treasure deeply.*
> *For its chips and stains, my beloved would never chide me,*
> *But when I present it to her, I would like it to be whole.*

Here, Grandfather promises to do his utmost to preserve "Chosŏn," and even though it has suffered minor damage, he will give it his all until it regains its independence. Etched in those three lines are Grandfather's constancy and resolve.

The book ends with postscripts written by Pak Han-yŏng, Hong Myŏng-hi, Yi Kwang-su, and Chŏng In-bo. Hong's postscript clarifies the meaning of *nim* as used by Grandfather:

> Who is Yuktang's *nim* exactly? Let me take a guess. The name of *nim* is Chosŏn. The name has never left his lips, but many readers don't know its identity for sure. In *Paekpal Pŏn'noe*, the frequent

> use of *nim* might raise questions, but the basic idea of Chosŏn as the beloved is no different from its usage in his other writings, such as "The Theory of Tan'gun," *Simch'un Sullye,* and *Paektusan Kŭnch'amgi. Nim,* used in this sense, appears throughout Yuktang's works.

Hong Myŏng-hi correctly pointed out that, like *Paekpal Pŏn'noe*, all of Grandfather's works, including his scholarly studies on Tan'gun and his travelogues of the Chosŏn land, were dedicated to Chosŏn, which Grandfather lovingly called *nim*. In his brief postscript, Hong showed keen insight as to what the aim of all of Grandfather's works had been, namely, the establishment of Chosŏn identity. Twelve years before the publication of *Paekpal Pŏn'noe*, Grandfather had, at age 25, "created" *nim* in his mind and revealed it to the world. In 1914, when he published a sijo titled "Nim" in the first issue of *Ch'ŏngch'un*, Korean readers all knew what the word referred to. Grandfather's "nim" was always and only Chosŏn.

Two years after the publication of *Paekpal Pŏn'noe*, Grandfather edited and published a collection of old sijo, *Sijo Yuch'i*. He collected all the sijo that had come down through Korean history in both written and oral form, and chose one thousand that he considered to be of superior quality. He then categorized them into 21 topics, such as "seasons," "plants and trees," "ideas," "pleasures," and so on. He had compiled the collection with students of Korean literature in mind, so he provided annotations for their ease of study.

For Grandfather, sijo was a vessel in which the heart and spirit of Chosŏn could be preserved. He viewed sijo as the literary form that best exemplified the spirit of Chosŏn. Extremely proud of its versatility, he pronounced that "there is nothing in the world that sijo cannot express." In the sense that he revived the neglected form of sijo and revitalized it, Grandfather is the father of modern sijo, as Chu Si-gyŏng is the father of modern Korean language.

5. Sin'ganhoe (新幹會: The New Korea Society): Forestalling the Division Among the Nationalists

Throughout my school years, I learned Korean history. In elementary school, the lessons began with Tan'gun, and continued on with King Tongmyŏng, Pakhyŏkgŏse, General Ch'oe Yŏng, King Sejong, Admiral Yi Sun-sin, and so on. In middle school, we had history classes, but by the end of the school year, we had only covered the Unification of the Three Kingdoms, the war against the Mongols, the Imjin War against Japan, the Pyŏngja War against the Manchu, Chŏng Yak-yong of the Sirhak Movement, and, if we were lucky, Taewŏn'gun's seclusionist rule.

In our history classes, most Koreans in my generation have never learned why the 500-year-old Chosŏn dynasty was so easily toppled by the Japanese Meiji Empire, which had just awakened from its sleep only a few decades earlier. We never had a chance to ask why our country fell, how we were liberated, and what really brought on the tragedy of Yuggio. We just crammed the dates of historical events the night before the exams.

My interest in modern Korean history bears little relation to the fact that Ch'oe Nam-sŏn is my grandfather. I really want to better understand that particular era in Korean history. In the absence of a solid understanding of the past, making plans for the future is meaningless. I hear that today, Korean history textbooks do not give even a cursory nod to the March First Movement.

To be honest, I myself was unaware that, around the time of the Japanese annexation of Korea in 1910, there had been a nationalist organization called Sinminhoe (the New People's Association), which secretly pursued "a republic form of government." Nor was I aware of Sin'ganhoe (the New Korea Society), which, after the March First Movement, pursued "political independence" for Korea. Because my history classes had omitted these historical facts, I remained ignorant of them until I was well into college. In view of the fact that almost all nationalists in modern Korean history had connections, either direct or indirect, to Sin'ganhoe, I began to wonder what we had learned from our history lessons, if anything. In order not to repeat the error of omission, I want to record here what I have learned about this important period in Korean history.

Sinminhoe was founded in 1907 by An Ch'ang-ho. Yun Ch'i-ho served as its first president, and its members included Pak Ŭn-sik (scholar), Yi Tong-hwi (general), Yi Sŭng-hun (businessman), Yi Hoe-yŏng, and his brother, Yi Si-yŏng (both scholars). Although a secret organization, Sinminhoe had more than 800 members. To promote national education, it founded and managed the Osan School in Chŏngju and Taesŏng School in Pyongyang. To promote industrial production, it founded and managed a porcelain factory in Pyongyang and a bookstore called Taegŭksŏgwan in Taegu.

The Youth Student Association, for which Grandfather served as director, was an auxiliary of Sinminhoe, which led the youth movement. Kwangmunhoe, which Grandfather founded, led the nationalist cultural movement. Grandfather's rise to fame began with his involvement with the Youth Student Association in his late teens. Through this connection, he also gained the acquaintance, as well as the expectations, of the older generation of Korean intellectuals. The "105 incident" in 1911 led to the exposure of Sinminhoe's leadership. As a result, Kim Ku, Sin Ch'ae-ho, and other leaders fled abroad and there began to prepare for an armed resistance. Those who stayed, such as Grandfather, Ch'oe Rin, and Song Chin-u, laid the foundation for the March First Movement of 1919.

With the March First Movement, the idea of *minjok* had solidified in the consciousness of the Korean people, giving impetus to the nationalist movement for independence. However, the movement soon began to splinter into two groups: those who wanted a gradual return to sovereignty in a state of autonomy and those who wanted immediate and complete independence as a republic. In 1927, in an attempt to create a united front for the movement, a group of nationalist intellectuals founded Sin'ganhoe. This organization opened its doors to all the existing factions of myriad ideological stripes that had sprung up since the March First Movement, including socialism and communism.

Unfortunately, Sin'ganhoe fell short of its objective and disbanded after four years. I regard Sin'ganhoe's failure as a watershed in modern Korean history. It signified the failure of Korean intellectuals to form a united front for their country, which resulted in its bifurcation after the Liberation, which, in turn, brought on the tragedy of Yuggio. It is a tragedy that is still acutely felt in every aspect of Korean life.

Through the foundation of *Sidae Ilbo*, Grandfather had tried, to little avail, to establish a unified nationalist movement that included the socialist wing. A couple of years after the failure of *Sidae Ilbo*, Grandfather felt that the formation of Sin'ganhoe was an absolute necessity for the country's future. Those within the nationalist movement expected him to assume a leadership role, and he himself probably felt he should assume some responsibility in deciding what direction the movement should take.

At this time, the Japanese had allowed, as part of their more "flexible" colonial policy, a small degree of political activity in Korea, albeit under their watchful eyes. The different factions of the nationalist movement began to form their own organizations. These factions, although sharing the same goal of regaining sovereignty, disagreed on the method for achieving this goal. The new and old wings of

Ch'ŏndogyo, *Chosŏn Ilbo* and *Dong-a Ilbo*, Hŭngsadan Suyangtong'uheo (led by An Ch'ang-ho) and the YMCA Hŭng'ŏp Club (led by Syngman Rhee), the Shanghai Provisional Government, the Shanghai Koryŏ Communist Party, and the Russo-Chosŏn Communist Party—all held widely divergent views on how to go about achieving their common goal: "the recovery of sovereignty and independence" for their country.

As different factions tried to narrow the divide in their approaches, Yi Kwang-su published an article titled "Minjok Kaejoron" (A Treatise on the Reconstruction of the People) in *Dong-a Ilbo* in January of 1924, igniting a debate on political autonomy among the nationalists. The following year, the debate intensified, with Ch'oe Rin leading the group that supported autonomy. Grandfather tried to restrain the shrill tone of the debate.

In January of 1925, *Dong-a Ilbo*, with its editor-in-chief, Hong Myŏng-hi, provided an open column titled "Socialist Movement and Nationalist Movement: Differences and Commonalities," and invited six of the major leading figures of the day—Grandfather, Han Yong-un, Chu Chong-gŏn, Kim Ch'an, Cho Pong-am, and Hyŏn Sang-yun—to contribute their opinions. In their articles, all agreed that their sole objective was national liberation and independence, an objective that differed significantly from that of supporters of an autonomous state under the Japanese monarchy.

While the nationalist movement was all but splintering into pieces, Grandfather published his sijo collection titled *One-Hundred-and-Eight Agonies. Surely, Grandfather must have had more than 108!*

At the end of 1926, Hong Myŏng-hi, who was then teaching at the Osan School, came to Seoul during the winter recess and visited Grandfather. He had written the postscript to Grandfather's sijo collection and wanted to offer his congratulations on its publication. Hong and Grandfather had known each other since their student days in Tokyo. Hong said that Grandfather's house had been the first house other than his own in which he stayed overnight and took his meals. Grandfather said that visiting Hong's home had first given him the occasion to travel to the northern section of Seoul.

When Hong paid a visit to Grandfather in the winter of 1926, the ostensible topic of their conversation was Grandfather's recently published sijo collection. However, the significance of this visit was more than their discussion of poetry. According to the record kept by the Government-General, their discussion centered on the founding of Sin'ganhoe.

> Toward the end of 1926, Hong Myŏng-hi, during the winter recess (he was teaching at the Osan School in Chŏngju, North Pyŏng'an Province), came to Seoul to visit Ch'oe Nam-sŏn. Ch'oe apprised Hong of their [the nationalists'] intent, and discussed the issue of autonomous self-rule far into the night. The next day Hong paid a visit to An Chae-hong and invited Sin Sŏk-u to join them to discuss the situation. Together they decided to create a nationalist organization. Also, with the agreement of Kwon Tong-jin, Pak Rae-hong, Pak Tong-wan, Han Yong-un, Ch'oe Ik-hwan, and a few others, Hong immediately got in touch with Sin Ch'ae-ho, who was then in Beijing, to invite him as a founding member. Hong also got in touch with Sin Sŏk-u, who had connections to the Government-General, and, with his approval, decided to name the organization "Sin'ganhoe."
>
> (Source: "*The Arrest of Koryŏ Communist Youths in Conjunction with the Chosŏn Communist Party, Top Secret #8036, Police Headquarters of Kyŏnggi Province, October 27, 1928*)

The official document above, published by the Government-General, indicates that it viewed Ch'oe Nam-sŏn as involved in the founding of Sin'ganhoe. In order to legitimize the organization, Sin'ganhoe needed a conduit to the Government-General. Sin Sŏk-u, then publisher of *Chosŏn Ilbo*, assumed that role and succeeded in procuring a permit from the Government-General. With the permit, Sin'ganhoe established itself as a legitimate entity that could engage in political activity, albeit within certain limits imposed by the Government-General. Its stated mission was "*minjok* liberation through a unified *minjok* party."

The chief architects of Sin'ganhoe were Hong Myŏng-hi and Sin Sŏk-u. Grandfather had a long-standing friendship with Sin as well. Although Grandfather's newspaper, *Sidae Ilbo*, ultimately had to close down, Sin had played a significant role during its founding stage. In addition, during the January Fourth Retreat of the Korean War, Grandfather was able to flee from Taegu to Pusan on a police vehicle provided by Sin, then Korean ambassador to China. Once in Pusan, Grandfather stayed at Sin's family residence for a couple of months.

I believe that Grandfather brought together Hong Myŏng-hi of the socialist wing and Sin Sŏk-u of the nationalist wing in order to forge a unified Sin'ganhoe. He believed that under their joint leadership, Sin'ganhoe would provide a meeting ground for all the existing factions. Twenty years earlier, Grandfather had had firsthand experience of bringing nationalists together through his involvement with the Youth Student Association, the auxiliary of Sinminhoe that had enjoyed the unanimous support of the nationalist intellectuals. Ten years later, at the end of the 1910s, as Grandfather worked at the forefront of the countrywide March First Movement, he had envisioned a national movement that would unite all the factions representing diverse ideological lines.

In February of 1927, Sin'ganhoe was inaugurated, with Yi Sang-chae as its first president. Hong Myŏng-hi declared that the line Sin'ganhoe should follow was "at the left of the nationalists, but at the center when viewed from the socialists." In short, Sin'ganhoe launched the first attempt at the bringing together of the "right" and the "left." The Sin'ganhoe membership increased rapidly. However, its internal division showed no signs of diminishing. Instead, the scramble for leadership intensified. The gradual nationalists who supported autonomy stepped up their activities as well.

Even after the inauguration of Sin'ganhoe, Grandfather and Hong Myŏng-hi continued their discussion of autonomy and the organization's role. Grandfather warned that, if the autonomy faction proved successful, half of Sin'ganhoe's members would support it, while the other half would split itself into nationalists and socialists. The executive members of Sin'ganhoe met repeatedly to discuss Grandfather's concerns. They all felt that in the event the autonomy faction prevailed, the other members, who had come from diverse backgrounds, would splinter, and that eventually the organization would disintegrate. However, the autonomy faction did not emerge as a major force.

The eventual rupturing of Sin'ganhoe occurred, neither as a result of the rift among the nationalists, nor by the opposition to the autonomy faction, but by the Chosŏn Communist Party's attempt to take over the leadership. In September of 1927 when Sin'ganhoe was inaugurated, the Chosŏn Communist Party had supported Han Yong-un, the head of the Kyŏngsŏng branch of Sin'ganhoe, in his attempt to take over the branch. Hong had urged Han to refrain from working with the Chosŏn Communist Party, but Han refused. In the end, Hong had to ask Han to resign from his position. Hong, as well as Grandfather, did not want

Sin'ganhoe to veer recklessly toward the far left.

During my middle-school years, anti-communism was the national policy. I remember when Grandfather pronounced in front of his guests that "Byŏk-ch'o (Hong Myŏng-hi's pseudonym) was *not* a communist." Everyone present was inwardly shocked, and, of course, the Korean police would have reacted adversely if they had heard this pronouncement. With it, Grandfather wanted to make it publicly clear that his lifelong friend Hong Myŏng-hi had not been a hardcore communist who supported a proletarian revolution. He believed that Hong's going to the North was at the urging of his son Hong Ki-mun, combined with the misinformed ignorance of the American Military Administration.

The dismantlement of Sin'ganhoe was not brought on by moderate socialists such as Hong Myŏng-hi, but by the radicalized Chosŏn Communist party. When a student movement erupted in Kwangju in 1929, Sin'ganhoe planned a popular countrywide demonstration, but the plan was crushed by the colonial government. The incident resulted in the imprisonment of various leaders, including Hong Myŏng-hi and Cho Byŏng-ok. The leadership of Sin'ganhoe, having suffered a great blow, had no choice but to change its course, for the sake of its continued existence, toward more moderate, legal activities.

However, the Chosŏn Communist Party, having received the "December Thesis" from the Comintern in December of 1929, began to bitterly criticize the moderate stance of the Sin'ganhoe leadership. Through its branches, the Communist Party pushed for the dissolution of Sin'ganhoe, and, during Sin'ganhoe's national convention in 1931, the members voted for its dissolution.

Just as I had many unanswered questions about Grandfather's role in *Sidae Ilbo*, I had as many about his role in Sin'ganhoe. I wondered why he, with no funds available, had rushed into the publication of the newspaper. I surmised that he took this action because he saw the nationalist movement splintering into moderate nationalists and socialists, as evidenced by *Dong-a Ilbo* and *Chosŏn Ilbo*, and he wanted to mitigate the ideological division between the two major factions.

After the failure of *Sidae Ilbo*, Grandfather again attempted to mend the rift by helping to form Sin'ganhoe. Grandfather refrained from taking sides while the myriad factions proliferated. He probably felt that if he, with his influence, took sides, it would only help to deepen the division. I believe that his restraint, or his nonaction, was a conscious decision on his part. However, even as he refrained from taking sides, Grandfather provided the critical link between Hong Myŏng-hi of the left and Song Chin-u of the right, a link that provided a decisive factor in the inauguration of Sin'ganhoe. In my mind, this explains Grandfather's action and nonaction during this intractable period of Korean history.

Still, questions remain. *Why was Grandfather helpless when the Chosŏn Communist Party took over the Kyŏngsŏng branch and maneuvered to dissolve Sin'ganhoe? Why did he keep his silence, taking no action?* Grandfather's attempt to bring the right and left together during the 1920s ended in failure in 1931 with Sin'ganhoe's demise, which, I believe, led to Yuggio and, ultimately, national division.

As I was growing up, I lived through many family tragedies brought on by the Korean War. I remember asking Grandfather once who was responsible for the country dividing into North and South. His reply was brief:

> It wasn't Japan, the United States, Russia, or the era, for that matter. It was the immaturity of the Korean people.

I did not ask Grandfather any more. I couldn't. All his life, he had lived with the agonies of his country at different times of its history, and now he was lying on his sickbed, unable to move. Yet, at times, I wondered if anything would have been different had he been a politician, rather than a scholar. The nature of the problem that time had assigned him, I felt, was inherently unsolvable by scholarship alone.

Chapter 3

The Globalization of Korean History

1. The Commission for the Compilation of Chosŏn History: Korean History as Part of World History

Grandfather's study of Tan'gun began with his desire to find a valid counterargument against the Japanese scholars who had denied Tan'gun's very existence. The Japanese academics, in support of their government's imperialistic political agenda, claimed that Tan'gun was a recent invention. In order to refute this claim, Grandfather conducted in-depth research into a variety of academic disciplines. The Japanese academics had made their claim utilizing modern research methods, so Grandfather set out to refute it using the same tools.

Grandfather's Tan'gun was not the Tan'gun of Chosŏn alone. He proposed that Tan'gun was at the center of all of Northeast Asia. To support this proposition, Grandfather established the theory of the Purham Civilization, a civilization that extended over all of Northeast Asia. Here I do not wish to enter a debate with scholars as to the existence of the ancient civilization in Northeast Asia. However, I would like to point out that the Commission for the Compilation of Chosŏn History could not simply ignore the theory of the ancient civilization as asserted by Grandfather because it had to answer to the world academic community. Chosŏn history, as maintained by Grandfather, was not a part of Japanese history, but a part of world history.

The year 1928 was a period of relative stability in Grandfather's life. Sin'ganhoe's efforts to unite the left and the right seemed to be bearing some fruit, and there was a general sense of growing political maturity in the country. On April 9, *Maeil Sinbo,* an organ of the Government-General, published an interview with Grandfather, titled "What to Expect of the New Policy: A New Path for Those Caught Between the Left and Right," in which he expressed cautious optimism for the country's future, and made a call to press forward toward eventual independence.

Grandfather's optimism, of course, proved wide of the mark, as Japan started to prepare for world war. From 1928 on, however, the identity of Korea as an independent country had taken root in the Korean consciousness. Grandfather, after retiring from political life altogether, began to devote his life to Korean history and its globalization. His conviction that the existence and identity of Korea was dependent on its history and that it should be established as a part of world history remained firm.

One of the convictions Grandfather held throughout his life was that everything about Korea–its people, its culture, and its history–should be viewed and interpreted as a part of world history. As early as in his late teens, he had been a citizen of the world. In 1909, at age 20, he published an article in *Sonyŏn*, titled "The Need for World Knowledge," in which he wrote eloquently about how every region of Chosŏn was connected to the world:

> The entire world unfolds before our very eyes. The waves that lap Chemulpo harbor are mixed with the salt of the Mediterranean Sea, the sounds that stir the air around Paektu Mountain spread the dry Siberian air, the Chong'no streets are coated with the fine sands that fall from the shoes of Saharan black men, and the trees on Namsan Mountain breathe in coal vapor from the European

> plain through the mouths of its people. The earth and sky that envelop the Chosŏn Peninsula are no longer purely Chosŏn.

Twenty years later, Grandfather summed up his zeal for modernization since the founding of Sinmun'gwan by stating that "my most urgent task was the development of civilization." For Grandfather, zeal for modernization was synonymous with zeal for the globalization of Korea.

As he immersed himself in the study of Korean history in his thirties, Grandfather continued to pursue its globalization. All of Grandfather's efforts were informed by his desire to advance the understanding of Korean history as a part of world history and, at the same time, the understanding of world history as an extension of Korean history. Under colonial rule, the narrative of Korean history had already been "semi-Japanized." Grandfather, in an effort to stand against the colonial version of Korean history, tried to establish Korean history as a part of world history.

In October of 1928, when it became known that Grandfather had decided to enter the Commission for the Compilation of Chosŏn History, some critics accused him of "betrayal." However, people in the know readily understood his motive, namely, the establishment of Chosŏn's Tan'gun as a historical fact and as a part of world history. Witnessing Korean history pulled up by the roots by Japanese colonial scholars, Grandfather decided that the only way he could combat the situation was to take on the Commission itself. As a scholar of Korean history, it was an inevitable choice.

Grandfather did what the time required him to do as a Korean historian. No apology or explanation was necessary on his part because he had stood his ground against the Japanese scholars. Grandfather's position was clear, as recorded in his son's diary entry of April 2, 1934. I wonder how many of Grandfather's critics knew that Grandfather had engaged in a "battle for truth" against Imanishi, Inaba, and Kuroida, the leading Japanese scholars at the Commission, who had insisted on the erasure of Tan'gun from Korean history.

The meeting minutes of the Commission provide incontrovertible evidence of these battles. In 1932, the Commission held its sixth meeting since the publication of the first three volumes of *The History of Chosŏn*. At this meeting, Grandfather, after first discussing the methodological issues in dating events in antiquity, brought up the subject of Tan'gun. He pointed out that among the records on King Tongmyŏng in *Samguk'yusa*, "Sŏk'yu Hwankuk"(昔有桓國: "Once upon a time there was country called Hwankuk....") had been changed to "Sŏk'yu Hwanin" (昔有桓因: "Once upon a time there was a man named Hwanin....") by the "careless brush of an ignoble man." The phrase was an indirect attack on Imanishi, who had engaged in deliberate misinformation, substituting *in* (man) for *kuk* (country).

Imanishi was a leading Japanese scholar on the subject of Tan'gun, who had asserted that Tan'gun was a mere fabrication, created toward the end of the Koryŏ dynasty. Imanishi had made the substitution in *Samguk'yusa*, when it was published by the Kyoto University Press.

At the Commission, Grandfather and Imanishi represented Chosŏn and Japan respectively. Grandfather had already published "The Theory of Tan'gun," in which he argued, point by point, against Imanishi's theory that Tan'gun was a product of fabrication, without historical basis. Grandfather knew otherwise, because he had worked on *Samguk'yusa* since his Kwangmunhoe days and, in 1926, had seen it to publication through the Kyemyŏng Club. At the official meeting of the

Commission, Grandfather decried the deliberate distortion of history by the Japanese scholar.

Two years later, in 1934, the eighth meeting of the Commission took place. Inaba, then executive secretary, announced that, instead of the planned 30 volumes, *The History of Chosŏn* would now be published in 35 volumes. He also announced that the ancient history would be abbreviated and that the Koryŏ and Chosŏn dynasties would be given more extensive coverage. The stated reason for this change of plan was that there was more material to cover for the two dynasties, but the real reason was that the Commission wanted to keep the coverage of Korea's ancient history to a minimum. Grandfather, objecting to this change, strongly argued for the inclusion of Tan'gun in *The History of Chosŏn*.

According to the meeting minutes of the Commission, Grandfather continued to speak out on the issue of Tan'gun and Kija (founder of Kija Chosŏn, 1122 BC–104 AD), making it the central focus of the meeting. Pointing out that it is preposterous to exclude Tan'gun from Chosŏn history, Grandfather made his demands:

> Despite the fact that Tan'gun and Kija are the two most important figures in Chosŏn history, this Commission refuses to include them in the first volume of *The History of Chosŏn*. The historical facts surrounding Tan'gun and Kija should be inserted in either the main text or as a supplement during the final editorial stage.

Kuroida replied that, since it was the editorial policy of the Commission to compile Chosŏn history in chronological order, Tan'gun could not be included. Feeling that this explanation was a ruse, Grandfather retorted, stating that the inclusion of Tan'gun was merely a technical problem with an easy solution. He maintained that Tan'gun should be viewed beyond the simplistic framework of historical dates, stressing the need for ideological and mythological approaches. Grandfather ended his response by requesting that the findings of these approaches be reviewed and published in a special edition. Kuroida rebutted Grandfather's argument by repeating the claim that Tan'gun was unquestionably a mythological figure, not a historical one. Grandfather responded that, to the Chosŏn people, Tan'gun *was* a historical figure:

> Whether Tan'gun and Kija are historical or mythological figures is a subject for scholarly inquiry. However, the Chosŏn people have always regarded them as figures of history. For this reason alone, as a Korean, I believe that the decision of this Commission not to include them in Chosŏn history is highly regrettable. This exclusion is the reason that *The History of Chosŏn* has not been read by many Koreans.

The meeting ended with the Japanese scholars promising that they would try to find an appropriate way to accommodate Grandfather's request, but in the end they did what they had set out to do. By participating in the Commission, Grandfather had risked his good name in an attempt to protect Tan'gun and Chosŏn history from the political spin of the Japanese scholars. Having failed to achieve his goal at the Commission, he now wanted to present his views of Korean history to the world academic community. With this objective, he decided, at age 43, to go to France.

In the fall of 1957 Grandfather died, and the following spring, my family moved to Samsŏn'gyo. As we were going through the cardboard boxes, we came upon a small wooden box containing some old family photographs. There were photographs of my great-grandfather's *hwan'gap* (1917), my parents' wedding (1936), my *paek'il* (hundredth day after birth, 1942), Grandmother's *hwan'gap* (1947), and Grandfather's *hwan'gap* (1950). The photographs showed Grandfather at different stages of his life, from ages 28 to 60. He was always dressed in Korean clothes, his hair closely cropped, and without a moustache. The photographs showed him as a slightly heavyset man.

In all the pictures, Grandfather looked not very different from my memory of him in his sixties, but there was one picture that instantly caught my eye. It had been taken in front of the broken windows at his home in Yangsakkol, showing Grandfather, Grandmother, their four children, and their son-in-law, all looking rather solemn. In that picture, Grandfather wore the familiar dark grey coat, but I could see a parting in his hair, and under his nose I could see he had grown a moustache. Based on the school uniforms his sons were wearing, I could infer that the picture was taken around 1932.

Looking at the photograph, Grandmother explained that Grandfather, at that time, had "caught wind and wanted to fly to Pulguk (France)." In preparation for the trip, he had let his hair and moustache grow. According to Grandmother, he had bought a Western-style suit and a pair of leather shoes as well. He had the family photograph taken so that he could take it with him on his trip. Grandmother added that she was very relieved when Grandfather's "wind had finally subsided," and he decided not to go to France after all.

Some elderly family members suggested that Grandfather had planned to go to France to pursue his studies. Some of Grandfather's close acquaintances suggested that he had planned to go to Shanghai to join the Korean independence movement there. However, I make an alternate inference. I think he actually did plan to go to France. A few years before, his thesis, "The Theory of the Purham Civilization," had been partially translated into French and introduced to the world academic community, and he wanted to participate directly in discussions of his thesis among world scholars. However, he missed the chance because his father, Ch'oe Hŏn-gyu, had suddenly taken seriously ill. Ch'oe Hŏn-gyu died the following year.

The unusual photograph of Grandfather with longer hair and a moustache, together with Grandmother's recollection of him at that time, prompted me to look up and read "The Theory of the Purham Civilization." I was then a third-year high school student who should have been busy preparing for my college entrance examination. In the

Grandfather and family in 1932. This is the only photograph that shows Grandfather with longish hair. At the time this photograph was taken, he was making preparations to leave for France, where he wanted to present to the world academic community his theory of the Purham civilization. With his theory, he hoped to repudiate the colonial views of Japanese academics.

summer of 1959, Hong Il-sik (later president of Korea University) had published his doctoral thesis, "The Study of Yuktang," which included "The Theory of the Purham Civilization" translated into more accessible modern Korean. Soon afterwards, I read other related writings by Grandfather, such as "Tan'gun ron," (1926), "Salmangyo Ch'agi" (1927), "Tan'gun Kogijŏnsŏk" (1954), and "Kyegoch'ajon" (1918). I spent the summer vacation of that year in the company of Grandfather's writings about the origin of Korean history.

2. *Songmak'yŏnunrok* (松漠燕雲錄) and Ancient Korean History: Korean History Is at the Center of Northeast Asia's History

A few years ago, a controversy arose between Korea and China about their histories. China wanted to include all events that took place within its current borders as its history. Its attempt to include the histories of Koguryŏ (old Korean kingdom, 37 BC-668 AD) and Parhae (old Korean kingdom, 698-926) in its history angered many Koreans. The unresolved questions of ancient history remain a thorny issue in diplomatic relations between China and Korea.

In 2005, a conference was held at Harvard University on the topic of Koguryŏ history and its historical remains. Scholars from eight countries–South Korea, China, Japan, the United States, Great Britain, France, Australia, and North Korea–participated, with North Korea only submitting papers. Because of the ongoing controversy between Korea and China regarding Koguryŏ history, I was very interested in attending the conference.

Harvard's Korea Institute, which sponsored the week-long conference, kindly invited my wife and me, and, as part of the audience, we listened to a variety of presentations on Koguryŏ's historical records, archeological findings, and ethnological debates. About a hundred students and professors of Korean history from various universities all over the United States attended, as well as a few scholars from abroad. Instead of breaking into smaller groups in separate rooms, all the speakers presented their papers in a lecture hall, their presentations being simultaneously translated into five languages.

Nearly all the presentations at the conference impressed me greatly. In addition, I was pleasantly surprised that in every field of inquiry, Grandfather's name, Ch'oe Nam-sŏn, kept cropping up. Every time the presenters made a reference to his name or his work, I was again reminded of the vast range of Grandfather's work. I couldn't help noticing, however, that, unlike the presenters from other countries, the presenters from South Korea made hardly any mention of Ch'oe Nam-sŏn's work on ancient Korean history. In particular, this impression was pronounced during their discussion of Koguryŏ remains discovered in the Liaoning region of China. This experience at the conference prompted me, on my return home, to reread Grandfather's travelogues of his trip through Manchuria, titled *Songmak'yŏnunrok*.

In 1937, at the invitation of Ninomiya, chairman of Sŏnman Development Company, Grandfather had the opportunity to make a tour of the farms cultivated by Korean immigrants in Kando. The year before, Ninomiya had hosted a discussion in Seoul about the problem of Korean farmers who had emigrated to Manchuria. At the time, Manchukuo viewed the soldiers of the Korean resistance movement as a huge headache, calling them "undesirables." At this discussion, Grandfather pointed out, to everyone's shock, that if Japan wanted to hold up its professed ideal of "harmony among the five races," it should listen to the demands of the Koreans, instead of treating them as "undesirables." Ninomiya, impressed with Grandfather's directness, had sent him an invitation to visit Manchuria.

From October of 1937 to April of 1938, *Songmak'yŏnunrok* was serialized in *Maeil Sinbo* in 84 installments. These installments were collected and included in volume six of *The Complete Works of Yuktang Ch'oe Nam-sŏn,* published by Korea University in 1973. The travelogues in this volume represent Grandfather's writings that were completed before his official stay in Manchuria in 1937 as an adviser to *Manmong*

Ilbo (Manchu-Mongol Daily).

In *Songmak'yŏnunrok*, as indicated by the title itself, Grandfather wanted to write about the ancient land of Korea, with its histories of Koguryŏ and Parhae. The character "song" in the title refers to the part of Manchuria near the Song'hwa River; "mak," to Mongolia; "yŏn," to Beijing; and "un," to the Shanxi region. The title notwithstanding, Grandfather's travels actually covered only Manchuria, in the northeastern part of China.

Grandfather started out from Hoeryŏng in Korea and traveled to Kando, stopping by at Yongjeong, Yanji, and Hunchun. He then went to Ningan, the eastern capital of Parhae, and from there, went north to Harbin. From Harbin, he traveled to Xinqing, and then, south to Jilin, stopping by at Shenyang and Liaoyang. Next, he traveled to Dalian. From there, he took a boat back to Korea.

As Grandfather explored these different regions, he wrote about the history, geography, indigenous customs, and religious practices of each region. He wanted to communicate to the readers of *Maeil Sinbo*, namely Koreans, that these regions were parts of Korea. It is a mystery to me now how these articles eluded the rigid censorship of the Government-General at the time. As I read Grandfather's articles, I was struck by the sense of urgency with which he wanted to convey to the Korean people the vestiges of Chosŏn breaths he felt so palpably at each of his stops during his travels.

Some 70 years later, as I read Grandfather's writing, which is so full of passion and romantic fervor, I could easily understand where his dreams and aspirations lay. The following passage is an excerpt from the 36th installment, in which Grandfather, at age 48, wrote about the area along the Song'hwa River:

> Just as the record of the Yellow River is the history of ancient China and the record of the Nile, the history of ancient Egypt, the record of the Song'hwa River is the history of our ancestors in Manchuria. The Song'hwa valley leading to Jilin, along with all of Northeast Asia, is the birthplace of the Purham civilization, one of the oldest civilizations in the world. The Song'hwa River, which flows around Jilin castle, carries within itself the shadow of a great secret of Asian history.
>
> Nobody knows for sure if the waves on its surface and the sounds of its shallows tell a long story about the time. Is it possible that we, poor of eyesight and weak of hearing, can't see or hear the story? Who can tell for sure that the rounded mounds and pointed rocks along its banks are not the time's pyramids and obelisks?

With Korea's sovereignty lost, Grandfather had placed his dreams and aspirations in an obscure spot along the Song'hwa River under Paektu Mountain.

After I finished reading *Songmak'yŏnunrok*, a conversation I had had with Grandfather resurfaced in my memory. After reading a book on ancient Korean history, I had asked him some questions about this particular period. My first question was whether the Koguryŏ (37 BC–668 AD) and Silla (57 BC–936 AD) people used the same language. For example, when Kim Ch'un-ch'u (later king of Silla) went to visit Yŏn'gaesomun (a general of Kokuryŏ), did he need a translator to communicate? I wondered if the three kingdoms used different languages, and if so, to what extent they were different. Were they as different as Korean is from Japanese?

Now, a half century later, I don't remember the exact words of either my questions or Grandfather's answers, but I do remember the gist of our conversation quite well. Risking the possible inaccuracies of my long-term memory, I reconstruct here, in a question-and-answer format, the conversation Grandfather and I had more than 50 years ago:

- *Did Silla people and Kokuryŏ people regard each other as members of a foreign race?*
  No. Pyongyang fell due to internal division, and during the subsequent Silla-T'ang War that lasted seven years, Silla made an alliance with Koguryŏ refugees. Because a portion of Kokuryŏ land had originally belonged to Silla, its redistribution of the land south of Taedong River did not discriminate against the Malgal (a Tungusic tribe that was a part of Koguyrŏ) and Paekche people.

- *Did Silla people believe in the idea of* Ilt'ongsamhan (一統三韓), *the unity of the three kingdoms? Or was it an idea created by Kim Pu-sik (premier historian) during the Koryŏ dynasty in order to establish its legitimacy?*
  The former is correct. The Chinese history recorded during the T'ang dynasty also refers to Paekche as Mahan ("region inhabited by Korean people"). The three Han kingdoms during the T'ang dynasty refer to all the land occupied by the three kingdoms. And that the Kim dynasty of Silla came to rule the three kingdoms is a historical fact.

- *With the unification of the three kingdoms, Silla gained its legitimacy, but did Koguryŏ lose its identity?*
  No, there are numerous historical examples of a single race form-

ing from more than one country. After the fall of Pyongyang, its people formed Parhae, inheriting the Koguryŏ identity, and Koguryŏ figures such as Ko Sŏn-ji and Yi Chŏng-gi contributed to the establishment of the T'ang Empire. Paekche's Hŭkchisangchi participated as well. The identity of a *minjok* is determined by the collective memory and culture of its members. The countries that Chosŏn minjok established or participated in during its development are not limited to the Chosŏn Peninsula.

- *Is the history of Parhae a part of the history of Chosŏn?*
  Without a doubt. To begin with, "Parhae" is a misnomer. The correct name of the country that the Koguryŏ refugees built north of the Apnok (Yalu) River is "Chin" (震). Parhae is just a name of the region. Chin became Kŭm (金), which then became Ch'ing (清). The fact that the ancestors of Ch'ing were ruled by Chin does not mean that Chin's history is a part of China's history.

- *Chin and Silla co-existed in Northeast Asia for more than 200 years. Why aren't those years defined as Korea's "North-South Period"?*
  This is because Koryŏ, although it inherited South Chosŏn Silla, did not regain North Chosŏn Manchuria. It is also related to the Yi dynasty's political subservience to China during the compilation of *The History of Koryŏ*. Its compiler, Chŏng In-ji (the premier historian of the Yi dynasty), was a politician, not a historian.

On looking back on our conversation, I realize that all my questions had centered around one thing: I wanted to know if all the kingdoms of Korean ancient history–Koguryŏ, Paekche, Silla, Unified Silla, and Parhae–were composed of one minjok, despite their existence as separate kingdoms. The answers Grandfather gave me helped me understand that, even as far back as the era of the Three Kingdoms, its peoples had a sense of belonging to one minjok. Because Silla had subscribed to the idea of "the unity of the three kingdoms," it was justified in waging war to unify them.

Grandfather pointed out that the name of Parhae, commonly used to this day, was a misnomer all along. He pointed out to me that the accurate name for the kingdom is "Chin," as it was named by the Koguryŏ people who had founded it. The T'ang Empire, seeing that the kingdom of Chin was gaining strength, started calling it by its regional name in an attempt to turn the kingdom into its suzerainty. Grandfather believed that the identity of a minjok was determined by the collective memory and culture of its members. The countries established by the Chosŏn minjok, as well as the countries in which Chosŏn minjok played an important role in developing, were all part of the history of Chosŏn minjok. To Grandfather, Parhae was, without a doubt, a part of Chosŏn.

3. *Kosatong* (故事通), *Yŏksa Ilgam* (歷史日鑑), and *Chosŏn Sangsik Mundap* (朝鮮常識問答): Keeping the Embers of Korean History Alive

Some critics have suggested that Grandfather should have "broken his brush in half" and waited out the dark times in self-imposed retirement. However, that was not his *modus operandi. How could he be hiding somewhere when there were pressing things to do?* Koreans, if they were to be ready for their eventual independence, needed to keep their Korean spirit alive.

The 1930s began with the Manchurian War of 1931. The colonial rule of the 1930s was radically different from the so called "cultural rule" (or "divide and conquer" policy of manipulation, depending on one's perspective) of the 1920s. Japan set out for the complete eradication of Korean language and history. Beginning in 1930, Koreans were not even allowed to utter the words "Korean history." The first history of Korea ever written, *The History of Chosŏn,* written by Grandfather, was banned from publication in 1931.

Under these circumstances, Grandfather had to find alternative ways he could educate Korean people about their history. Unable to use the word *history* or to write history books at all, he thought long and hard about ways to break through these impossible restrictions. Soon he came up with three unconventional formats: the "daily" format, the "thousand characters" format, and the "question-and-answer" format.

At this time, Grandfather was working very closely with Yi Sang-hyŏp (1893-1957), a journalist of great renown. Yi had worked at *Maeil Sinbo*, but after the March First Movement, he joined the nationalist paper *Dong-a Ilbo* and served as its first editor-in-chief. Grandfather had known Yi since the Sinmun'gwan days, and when Grandfather started *Tongmyŏng*, he secured a permit for the magazine from the

Government-General. After Grandfather resigned from *Sidae Ilbo*, Yi took over the newspaper in 1926, changed its name to *Chung'oe Ilbo*, and published it until 1931.

Grandfather started to submit his writing to *Chung'oe Ilbo*, and the newspaper began to serialize his work under the column title of "Daily History," using a format similar to the "Today's History" feature in today's newspapers. In his "Daily History" column, Grandfather wrote about historical events that occurred on that day. However, with the closing of *Chung'oe Ilbo*, Grandfather's column also came to an end. In 1933, Yi suggested Grandfather write for *Maeil Sinbo*, and, when Yi became its vice president the following year, Grandfather began writing under the column title "Daily News" on April 16, 1934, a column which continued for 365 days, until April 15, 1935. Five years later, in 1939, Grandfather revised these writings under a new title, "Past Events of Today," and *Maeil Sinbo* serialized them from February 19 to October 1.

After the Liberation, his columns, "Daily History," "Daily News," and "Past Events of Today," were collected into two volumes and published under the title *Yŏksa Ilgam* (Daily History). In its preface, Grandfather wrote about the difficulties he had faced in writing about Korean history:

> As the Japanese colonial techniques employed to destroy Korean history gathered intensity to the point where it became impossible to publish Korean history in any conventional format, I racked my brains to come up with other ways I could write about it and have it published. Hoping that ancient history presented in a random fashion might be able to evade the censors' net, I began to write history books in which historical events were arranged in monthly or daily formats.

Apart from the fact that *Yŏksa Ilgam* was written in a daily format, another of its distinctive feature was that it discussed world history alongside Korean history. The pages of *Yŏksa Ilgam* were divided into two sections: one section was arranged by the lunar calendar; the other section, by the solar calendar. In the lunar-calendar section, Grandfather listed the events of Korean history on that date, arranged by period. When a notable historical figure died on that day, he wrote about the person's life and achievements. In the solar-calendar section, he wrote about the history of Korea since it began to use the solar calendar (namely, after the Kabo Reform) and also about relevant events in world history. In short, *Yŏksa Ilgam* was at once Korean history and world history written in a daily format. Grandfather's aim was to build consciousness among the Korean people that Korean history was a part of world history, not a part of Japanese history.

The "Kosa Chŏnja" format (ancient history arranged by a thousand Chinese characters) represented another original idea for writing history devised by Grandfather. Starting from the first letter, "ch'ŏn" (天), he collected historical events or concepts that included that Chinese character (for example, "bi-kyŏk-chin-ch'ŏn-roe" 飛擊震天雷) and appended an explanation ("a kind of missile weapon invented by Koreans during the Imjin War of 1592") pertinent to the event or concept. Starting from June 29, 1935, Grandfather continued to submit his writings to *Maeil Sinbo*, which serialized them in 365 installments, until December 31, 1936.

The "Chosŏn Sangsik" was yet another creative idea Grandfather utilized to write about Korean history. Under the cover of the word *sangsik*, meaning "common knowledge," he wrote about the religion, culture, and institutions of Korea. From January 10, 1937, to September

30 of the same year, *Maeil Sinbo* serialized his writings in 160 installments. These were later collected and published as a book titled *Chosŏn Sangsik Mundap* (朝鮮常識問答: Questions and Answers on Common Knowledge About Chosŏn).

Even after he went to Manchuria, Grandfather continued to submit his articles to *Maeil Sinbo* under the column head "Past Events of Today." This meant that from 1934 to 1939, Grandfather had, using unconventional formats, continuously written about Korean history. Had he not found ways to continue writing about Korean history and published his writing during these years, the generation of Koreans born during the Japanese colonial period would have been either completely ignorant of Korean history, or would have known their history merely as a collection of historical romances or legends. Grandfather had continually stoked the "Chosŏn" fire so that it wouldn't completely go out, as the Japanese had hoped it would.

The publication of Chosŏn history continued even after Grandfather returned from his four-year stay in Manchuria. The task of "writing Chosŏn history for Chosŏn people" had become all but impossible in the throes of the Pacific War, but Samchungdang published Grandfather's *Kosatong* (A Collection of Ancient Stories) in 1943. It immediately sold 30,000 copies. *Kosatong* was a book about Korean history, with emphasis on Korean culture. At a time when Korean history books were nowhere to be found, *Kosatong* was the sole book that served to keep the historical consciousness of the younger Korean generation alive.

I remember what a few of my high school teachers told me. They said that, as college students, they taught themselves Korean history by reading Grandfather's *Kosatong*. They also said that, as they listened to

Grandfather's speech encouraging them to join the Japanese army, they could hear his unshaken belief in the future of their country and also his conviction that Korea needed to acquire military skills to be ready for its future independence. These particular teachers, who decided to become teachers of Korean language, Civics, History, and English, had made the personal choice not to join the Japanese army, but many others of their generation decided to join, acquiring the basics of military science that their independent country would need in the future.

4. The Sojourn in Manchuria and "Manmong Munhwa" (滿蒙文化): Koreans Need to Study Military Science

As I got a little older, I began to question Grandfather's stay in Manchuria. *Why did he go by himself, leaving his family behind? What did he do at the National University of Manchuria, besides teach? Why did he return to Seoul after only three years?* I couldn't get any clear answers from anyone, so these questions linger in my mind to this day.

As far as I know, Grandfather was not a person who would have been happy away from Korea. A long-time friend of Grandfather's, Ham Sŏk-hŏn (1901–1989), who was a student of Yu Yŏng-mo (1890–1981), once said that that "it was God's will that Yuktang was born in Korea, and it was also God's will that Yuktang spent his entire life in an embrace with Chosŏn." Ham understood that Chosŏn was Ch'oe Nam-sŏn's body and soul. Grandfather and Chosŏn were inseparable, even for a brief moment.

As someone who has lived more than 40 years as a Korean outside the Korean Peninsula, I can perhaps venture to say this about Grandfather's sojourn in Manchuria: I think Grandfather understood Korea as defined by a people, rather than a territory. For him, Chosŏn was wherever Chosŏn had its ancestors and wherever its culture flourished.

In the spring of 1938, when Grandfather arrived in Xinqing, there were about a million Koreans living in Manchuria. It was the time when Grandfather was making his scholarly inquiries into the boundaries of Korean culture within world history, along with his study of Korean history within Korea.

The country of Manchukuo had recently been founded on the two principles of "harmony among the five races" (Japanese, Korean, Chinese, Russian, and Mongolian) and the "Royal Road to Prosperity."

As part of an attempt to realize these principles, the National University of Manchuria was founded to educate the country's youth. In 1936, when the new university was being planned, Ishihara Ganji, chief of staff of the Kwantung Army, had suggested the name "University of Asia." In 1937, he began to recruit its teaching staff. To represent the Korean race, Grandfather was contacted by Tsuji of the Kwantung Army, who had played a leading role in the founding of the university. He later personally paid a visit to Grandfather to extend an offer of professorship at the university.

Surrounding this appointment, there is a fact still unknown to most people who were critical of Grandfather's involvement with the university: the Government-General of Korea was vehemently opposed to his appointment. The ostensible reason was that Grandfather had been one of the leaders of "the March First Banzai (Mansei) Disturbance," and was therefore a person with a criminal record. However, the real reason, I suspect, was its concern over the possibility that Grandfather would use his stay in Manchuria as an opportunity to try to expand the boundaries of Chosŏn culture. Officials in the Government-General were concerned that, as a professor at the National University of Manchuria, Grandfather would consolidate his theory about Chosŏn cultural territory covering Manchuria, Mongolia, and the area north of the Yellow River to Beijing.

Because of the disagreement between the Government-General and the Kwantung Army, it took two years for Grandfather's appointment to become official in 1939. At the university, he taught the history of Manchuria to students from China, Japan, Korea, and Mongolia. He also wrote theses on this subject at the university's research institute. The central idea of his lectures and theses was that Chosŏn was the originator of Northeast Asian culture, an idea he had consistently advanced since the publication of "The Theory of the Purham Civilization."

Grandfather's emphasis on the importance of Chosŏn culture soon rankled the university management, and, after only one semester, he was barred from giving lectures. Away from the lectern, he compiled his lectures into a thesis and had it published under the title "Manmong Munhwa" (The Manchu-Mongol Civilization). In it, he claimed that the boundary of Manchu-Mongol civilization was the same as the boundary of the Purham civilization.

The Manchu-Mongol civilization, as asserted by Grandfather, was different from the Manchu-Mongol civilization claimed by China at the time, and also different from the Manchu-Mongol civilization claimed by the Commission on the Northeast Asian History sponsored by the current Chinese government. To the Chinese, the Manchu-Mongol territory existed merely as an outlying region of China, whereas Grandfather's Manchu-Mongol civilization was a distinct cultural entity throughout history, separate from the Chinese civilization. The real purpose of Grandfather's sojourn in Manchuria, I concluded, had been to reveal and to firmly establish this fact.

In his exploration of the Manchu-Mongol civilization, Grandfather brought the Tan'gun myth to the fore. In his thesis "The Manchu-Mongol Civilization," he stipulated that, if Manchukuo were to realize its founding principles, it had to come up with a foundation myth that resonated with all the races in Northeast Asia, and that this myth was the Tan'gun myth. Since the publication of "The Theory of the Purham Civilization," Grandfather had stood by his theory that the Tan'gun myth was the central myth of all of Northeast Asia, and he continued to do so at the National University of Manchuria.

While he was living in the Hŭng'a-dong residence in Manchuria, many Korean students at the university visited him often. On Sundays, or on days that they had no lectures, they came to listen to what Grandfather had to say about the future of their country. According to these students, he always told them not to forget that they were Koreans, and he exhorted them to become the builders of a new Korean future.

While in Manchuria, Grandfather made the prediction that Japan would fall one day. Although he couldn't predict the details of where and when, he let the students know that it was only a matter of time. He felt that Korea needed to be ready for its upcoming independence. In his mind, Grandfather was already making plans for the new country that was about to be born.

The speech Grandfather delivered to Korean students urging them to join the Japanese army could be viewed as an extension of Grandfather's future plans for Korea. Japan, as it was getting hopelessly mired in the Pacific War, had announced the policy of forced mobilization of Koreans. Koreans were, of course, reluctant to comply, and the Government-General of Korea, who viewed Koreans as not sufficiently "Japanized" to serve as Japanese soldiers, opposed it as well. According to Grandfather, the imperialists, in the history of mankind, never allowed the colonized people to acquire any military capability beyond limited, low-level training. But now the Japanese government, with its back to the wall, had offered educated Koreans a chance to gain military skills.

According to Grandfather, the nurturing of higher levels of military manpower equipped with management skills was of paramount importance in establishing the military capability of a country. When Japan's military announced its policy of accepting applications from Korean students for higher military positions, Grandfather suggested that, since it was an opportunity to gain military training and experience, they should take advantage of it. What Grandfather had in mind was the nurturing of nation-building skills and manpower for the independence that was to come. He knew all too well that independence in itself would not ensure the continued existence of a nation. When it was annexed by Japan in 1910, the Yi dynasty was woefully lacking in military capability. Grandfather knew this better than anybody else, and he wanted the elite youths of Korea to acquire management training as military officers by joining the Japanese army. He urged the Korean students at the National University of Manchuria with these words:

> It is very difficult to predict the world's future. However, if the Chosŏn people are to reclaim their just place in the new world order and lay the groundwork for national independence, the cultivation of our capability is a prerequisite. The core of that capability lies in military strength, and we should not let the opportunity to acquire military know-how pass us by. No doubt there will be many sacrifices among the volunteers, but those who survive and return will unquestionably become the leaders of our new destiny.

Many of the students who listened to Grandfather came to understand the need for the cultivation of military capability for their country's future and decided to join the Japanese military. Today, it has become common knowledge that those very students played a vital role in the foundation of the Republic of Korea's military, contributing significantly to the country's development.

In 1941, the year I was born, Grandfather returned to Seoul, and the following year he officially resigned from his professorship at the National University of Manchuria. As I recall, Grandfather's love for his students at the university was exceptional. During his illness, many visitors came to Myo-dong to pay their respects to Grandfather. On a few occasions, the visitors had to be turned away because of his condition, but Grandfather received most of them in a small area adjoining his sickroom. However, for his former students from the university, he made exceptions, welcoming them into his sickroom. Refusing to receive their bows lying down, Grandfather asked me to help him lift his upper body from his bed, and with my arms as his support, he sat up to acknowledge their respectful bows, even if for a brief moment. These visits from his former students, I think, were his happiest moments during his illness.

Around that time, during our meals together, I had a chance to ask him about his stay in Manchuria. He told me he had gone to Xinqing before his official appointment because he found the Government-General's opposition to the appointment increasingly bothersome. Also, the reason he left Manchuria in 1941, before his official resignation from the university, was the deepening of the division within the Kwantung Army. Since the Pacific War started, the Army had a direct hand in managing the university, and its internal division had made his continuation at the university untenable.

After he returned to Seoul, even before he had had the chance to unpack, the Government-General pestered him day and night, finally coercing him to go to Japan to make speeches, urging Korean students there to join the Japanese army. When people asked about these speeches, Grandfather suggested that they speak to the students who had actually heard them. When people made up stories about what he had said, he showed no discernible reaction.

Koreans who were born under Japanese rule grew up receiving a Japanese education, speaking the Japanese language, and learning Japanese history. In short, they had become Japanese citizens, no longer Koreans. Grandfather tried to awaken these young peoples' consciousness as Koreans, and to instill Korean pride in them. Had Grandfather not stoked the embers of "Chosŏn" fire during the dark years, these young Koreans, having been deprived of their own language and history, would have faced the liberation of their country as Japanese citizens.

Chang Jun-ha (1918–1975), the "father" of the present-day Korean activist movement, became the symbol of the struggle against tyranny, as well as the leader of the pro-unification movement of the "386 generation." He belonged to the same generation as my high school teachers, whom I mentioned earlier. Chang grew up reading Grandfather's historical writings, and when he heard Grandfather's speech, he immediately joined the Japanese army. Later, he left the Japanese army to fight with the Liberation Army in China. During Yuggio, he founded the magazine *Sasang'gye* (The World of Ideas), a premier intellectual magazine in Korea. When Grandfather died in 1957, Chang published a special edition dedicated to him, in which he and several other major intellectuals of his generation contributed articles about Ch'oe Nam-sŏn's legacy. In the preface, Chang wrote, "During our country's darkest hours, Yuktang remained our steadfast friend, and we all looked up to him as our mentor.... we knew in our hearts that his sole aim had been to safeguard the destiny of the people of Korea and its culture...."

Chapter 4

The Establishment of the Legitimacy of *Min'guk*

1. *A History of Chosŏn for the Korean People* (國民朝鮮歷史): Writing a "New" History of Korea

It was during the year 1956 that I began to take an interest in the history books that Grandfather had written. What piqued my interest was my firsthand experience of how the Department of Education censored textbooks for middle-school and high-school students. The history textbooks written by Grandfather that had been published by Minjungsŏ'gwan were going through the government censorship procedures. Grandfather had been bedridden for two years, and I was a third-year middle-school student then.

When the editors of the publishing company came with the manuscripts prepared to the specification of the Department of Education (present-day Division of Education and Sciences) and read them to Grandfather, he orally revised them, telling the editors to make certain additions and deletions. When Grandfather wanted to make further changes after the editors had left, he would dictate to me the changed portions to forward to the editors.

One day Grandfather asked me to find and bring down from the attic some newspaper clippings and two history books, *A History of Chosŏn for the Korean People* and *The History of Chosŏn, Revised.* These two history books had been published right after the Liberation.

At the time, as a middle-school student, I wanted to prove to the world that I was a good athlete. I loved rock-climbing, skiing, soccer, and baseball, and I was content to spend all of my free time with friends who shared my love of these sports. Regardless of my wish to be perceived as a budding athlete, I discovered one day that people saw me invariably as "the grandson of Ch'oe Nam-sŏn." On that day, I came to the realization that I had no escape from that perception.

This realization troubled me in that the opinions people had of Grandfather varied greatly and were often contradictory. His contemporaries had many different things to say about him. People in South Korea said that he was a "pro-Japanese betrayer," and people in North Korea said that he was an "anti-socialist reactionary." Some said he was a symbol of resistance against imperialist tyranny, and others said he was an examplar of pro-Japanese collaboration. Some said that he was a pathfinder during a dark era of Korean history, and still others said that he was a stain on the Korean people's name during the difficult times. Grandfather, as he was being talked about by Koreans, was the subject of every opinion under the sun. As a young grandson of Ch'oe Nam-sŏn, I didn't know exactly what to make of these opinions.

As a 16-year-old, I had no one to help me sort through the confusing array of opinions, and I was not entirely comfortable with any one of them. The only certainty I could hold onto was that Grandfather was a historian. I hoped to discover Grandfather in those two history books that he had asked me to bring down from the attic. I felt that "the grandfather I was looking for" could be found in those two history books–not in *Sonyŏn*, not in the poem "From the Sea to Boys," not in the Malmoi Korean dictionary, not in the grand "Declaration of Independence," not in *Sidae Ilbo* and the "Chosŏn People's Policy," and not in one of the sijo from *One-Hundred-and-Eight Agonies*, which I had memorized from my Korean language textbook.

It was also Grandfather's wish that I regard him as a historian–not as a poet, linguist, stylist, or politician. His actions or words that people had labeled as "betrayal" and "reactionary" had little meaning in his apolitical world of a scholar. He had promoted "revolution" as a historian, and he had upheld "integrity" as a historian, not as a politician. Before the age of 20, he had already entered that world, and he would remain there for the rest of his life.

Since I was a member of the post-Liberation han'gŭl generation, the two books, *The History of Chosŏn, Revised* and *A History of Chosŏn for the Korean People,* had too many Chinese characters for me to read with ease. Fortunately, the latter had han'gŭl transcriptions next to the Chinese characters. Also, Grandfather's *A New Dictionary of Chinese Characters*, published by Kwangmunhoe (1915, rev. 1947) and *The Great Dictionary*, published by Ŭlyu Publishing Company (1947–1957), came to my aid.

What led me to finish reading *A History of Chosŏn for the Korean People*, which was quite voluminous, was its preface, which greatly affected me. There I could read Grandfather's dreams, his aspirations, as well as what and why he wanted, at all costs, to teach Koreans about Korean history. In the preface, Grandfather pointed out the tribulations of Korean history brought on by China and Japan:

> Due to an erroneous understanding of the value of its own culture, Korea had long forgotten the sanctity of its own history and its true national character, and just as it was waking up to discover, unearth, and straighten them, the all-out destructive power of an evil foreign power was unleashed to demolish them. On looking back, who among us wouldn't shudder at the nightmare

of not being able to even utter the two words "Korean history"?

With the Liberation on August 15, 1945, Korean history was liberated as well. However, true liberation was not so easily achieved. Grandfather felt that Korean history would truly be liberated at the hand of a great new historian, such as Guizot (1787–1874) of France or Ranke (1795–1886) of Germany.

> Truly, the emergent Korea awaits a great philosopher, a great poet, a great artist, and a great theologian who can speak for the hearts, talents, and aspirations of its people. At the same time, or even more urgently, Korea cries out for a great historian who can enumerate the many facets of its strength. Just as France had Guizot, and Germany, Ranke, and in the manner that the fall of Rome had Gibbon, and the French Revolution, Carlyle, Korean history deserves a historian who can draw out its narrative and discover the value embodied in each fact and event. Within the pages of his book, Korean history will become, for all Koreans, a wellspring of life energy and courage, a whetstone for conscience, and an antidote for cloudy vision and chronic distemper.

In short, Grandfather was yearning for a "backward-looking prophet" who would breathe new life into Korean history, but found that no such historian existed for Korea. He was convinced, however, that, in time, such a historian would emerge and shed light on Korean history "as bright as the midday sun." Until that day, he himself was going to hold up a "small torch" and write "new history." In this endeavor, he said that he had been guided by six points, which he listed as follows:

After three of months of sustained effort, forgoing food, sleep, and company, I have finally completed the first draft. A mere first step toward clarity in response to the urgent demand of our time, it lacks a comprehensive table of contents. As a book of history for a country only recently liberated, it follows these six guidelines:

1. History, traditionally organized by dynastic, politico-military history, has been reorganized by its cultural history.
2. Korea and the world always stand side by side.
3. Within Korean history are embedded creative genius and scientific aspirations, the two indispensable ingredients for mankind's progress.
4. The advancement of Korean history appears slow, but it shows steady progress.
5. Regardless of the circumstances, the Korean spirit has never wavered.
6. More clearly than the history of any other nation, Korean history illustrates that when national life is unified and well regulated, the people enjoy good fortune and glory, and when it is divided and conflicted, the people suffer harm and shame.

It is my hope that readers will find the evidence of my sincere efforts in this book. Forty years ago, unable to simply sit back and watch Korea hanging by a thread, I put an abrupt end to my studies in Japan and, carrying the unfinished manuscripts for *The History of Chosŏn* and *The Geography of Chosŏn*, along with a printing press, I returned to Seoul and hurled myself into the

> storm raging in the country. Since then, I have dabbled in sundry projects, but accomplished little. What remains is the wet and muddy clothing that has weathered a 40-year-long storm. Looking back on those years, I am overcome with emotion.

Grandfather wrote this preface on November 10, 1945, but the book itself did not see its publication until the following year. In *A History of Chosŏn for the Korean People*, Grandfather gave structure to Korean history by dividing it into ancient, medieval, modern, and contemporary periods. Throughout the book, he advanced the proposition that Koreans, as the "*Chosŏn minjok*," have a common entity, sharing cultural heritage and collective memory.

Grandfather believed that the collective memory of a *minjok* is comprised of peace and war, value systems and morality, religion and art, language and territory. Grandfather's idea of *minjok*, as he came to define it, went far beyond the conventional notion of a nation as an entity that relies on military power or imperial tyranny. His idea transcended the recklessness of the Pacific War and the imbecilities of Yuggio. The reason that Grandfather, even during the tumult of war, could not give up his obsession to finish the *Encyclopedia of Korean History* was rooted in his desire to articulate Korea's identity as a nation with a common cultural basis.

Twenty years before, in 1928, Grandfather had submitted an article to the September issue of *Buddhism*, in which he wrote about why he began to study history. At that time, Grandfather had just completed, after six years of sustained work, *The History of Chosŏn,* a book he had started writing during his three-year incarceration for his March First independence activities:

> Angered by how things were going at the time, I kicked away my desk in Japan and returned to Korea to do what little I could to promote its spiritual movement. Our national spirit was in dire need of revitalization. The most urgent task of all was the editing of textbooks, especially in the areas of history and geography, from the Korean point of view....

Grandfather had begun to study history with the objective of writing Korean history from the Korean perspective. When he finished his manuscript, it took three years for it to finally be published in 1931, with the title *The History of Chosŏn*. Soon after, the Government-General stepped in and banned it. After the Liberation, not having had the time to write a brand new book on Korean history, Grandfather added a section on the independence movement to *The History of Chosŏn* and published the book under a new title, *The History of Chosŏn, Revised* (Samchungdang, 1946).

After the publication of *The History of Chosŏn, Revised*, Grandfather spent three months writing *A History of Chosŏn for the Korean People* based on his six guidelines and published it in 1947. The differences between the two books were clearly evident in the description of Imjin Waeran (the Imjin War against Japan). In the former, the character *wae* (倭: derogative term for Japan) in *Imjin Waeran* (壬辰倭亂) had to be deleted and replaced with *Imjinran* (壬辰亂). The character *chŏk* (敵 meaning "enemy") had to be substituted for *chŏk* (賊 meaning "bandit"). Even as he had to make these accommodations, Grandfather continued his writing of Korean history, not an easy task under the rule of *chŏk* (敵). It was only after the Liberation that Grandfather's writing on Korean history and world history could be published as a book with the word *history* in its title.

I wonder whether, at the time of his writing the preface to *A History of Chosŏn for the Korean People*, Grandfather was actually making a prediction about Korea's future. The sixth guideline stated in the preface, "... Korean history illustrates that when national life is unified and well regulated, the people enjoy good fortune and glory, and when it is divided and conflicted, the people suffer harm and shame" reads like much more than a factual statement of his historical viewpoint. *Why did Grandfather, in the preface of a history book, warn Koreans against this possible outcome?* This passage made me pause when I first read the book as a third-year middle-school student, and more than half a century later, it still gives me reason to pause. *Was Grandfather the "backward-looking prophet" whom he himself was waiting for?*

2. *The Encyclopedia of Korean History:* Fifty Years into the Future

In my keeping, I have a little notebook that Grandfather used for miscellaneous purposes. Judging from the content of the items I found between its pages, it appears that Grandfather used the notebook during the period beginning in 1923, the year when he, just released from prison, was involved in the publication of *Tongmyŏng*, to 1936, the year he left for Manchuria. He seems to have had it with him at all times, jotting down reminders to himself, as well as ideas for his writing, whenever they came to him.

The part of the notebook that interested me most was the page that revealed Grandfather's grand plan for what amounted to an encyclopedia of Korea. On the notebook page that I can infer to have been used by Grandfather in 1928, he wrote "The Great Chosŏn Dictionary," followed by the titles of five dictionaries: "The Dictionary of Chosŏn History," "The Dictionary of Notable Persons of Chosŏn," "The Dictionary of Place Names in Chosŏn," "The Dictionary of Chosŏn Arts and Letters," and "The Dictionary of Chosŏn Customs." These titles bring to light that, as early as 1928, Grandfather had conceived the idea of creating a series of dictionaries that together would have represented an encyclopedic coverage of Chosŏn culture.

I believe Grandfather finished the first manuscript of "The Dictionary of Place Names in Chosŏn" around 1931. "The Dictionary of Taedong Place Names," anthologized in volume eight of *The Complete Works of Yuktang Ch'oe Nam-sŏn*, appears to be an alternate title for "The Dictionary of Place Names in Chosŏn" that Grandfather had originally planned. Grandfather had taken the place names from *Tong'gukyŏchisŭng'ram* (a government document that lists geographical features and names) and listed them alphabetically in "The Dictionary

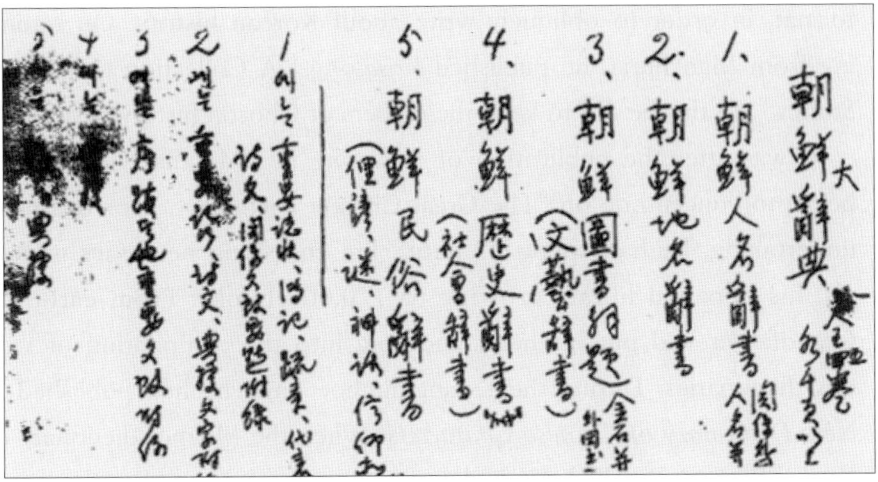

Page from Grandfather's notebook mapping out his long-range plans for an encyclopedia of Korea. As early as the 1920s, Grandfather conceived a multi-volume encyclopedia, a vast compendium of Korea's history, geography, notable figures, art, literature, and customs.

of Taedong Place Names." Based on the fact that one dictionary in the series of five dictionaries listed under "The Great Chosŏn Dictionary" was completed in 1931, I could deduce that, had Grandfather been allowed to remain in his study, he could have completed the remaining titles in the series and had them published one after another, as he had originally planned.

Unfortunately, the time he lived in did not allow him that luxury. Starting from the 1930s, the Government-General mobilized all available techniques to eradicate Chosŏn history. Grandfather, who had come to equate Chosŏn history with the existence of Chosŏn itself, sought to teach its history to its people in whatever way he could devise. Even as the use of the word *history* was barred and history books banned from publication, he used unconventional formats, such as the "daily" format, the "thousand characters" format, and the "common knowledge" format, in order to obliquely write about Korean history. On returning from Manchuria, he published *Kosatong*, "A Collection of Ancient Stories." All this he did to keep the embers of Chosŏn history alive.

It was after the publication of *Kosatong* in 1943 that Grandfather began to concentrate on "The Great Chosŏn Dictionary." For this huge undertaking, he had spent his entire life collecting necessary materials, his personal library growing to 170,000 books. From early on, Grandfather had put his heart and soul into the compilation of various dictionaries. During the Kwangmunhoe days, he had published *A New Dictionary of Chinese Characters*. When the Malmoi dictionary of Korean language stalled, he had sent the manuscript to the Kyemyŏng Club so that its members could continue the compilation. Considering the effort Grandfather dedicated to the completion of the Korean language dictionary, it is more than likely that he had his heart set on the completion of the remaining history dictionary series that he had conceived many years before.

After the Liberation, Grandfather poured all his energy into the compilation of what is now commonly known as "The Dictionary of Chosŏn History." What Grandfather had originally conceived was a combination of all the dictionaries he had listed in his notebook: "The Dictionary of Chosŏn History," "The Dictionary of Notable Persons of Chosŏn," "The Dictionary of Place Names in Chosŏn," "The Dictionary of Chosŏn Arts and Letters," and "The Dictionary of Chosŏn Customs." Grandfather's objective had been the compilation of an expansive, comprehensive dictionary that contained every aspect of Chosŏn culture. All things considered, I feel certain that what he had in mind was something much bigger than a simple history dictionary, and I will go into more detail about this later in this chapter.

Grandfather finished his manuscript up to the midpoint of "ㄱ", the first letter of the han'gŭl alphabet, and was preparing it to go to print when Yuggio broke out. The manuscript, of course, could not be published, and even the printing molds were partially lost. Moreover, Grandfather's library was burned to the ground when Sowŏn was bombed during Yuggio. The collection of 170,000 books housed in the library went up in smoke, along with the tens of thousands of index cards he had prepared over the years.

The year Yuggio broke out was the year of *hwan-ryŏk* (60-year life cycle) for Grandfather. Enduring the inconceivable tragedies of war, he had hardened his resolve to pursue his lifelong goals: to establish Korean identity, to promote Korean spirit, and to secure Korea's place in world history. It was his deep-seated belief that only a correct understanding of history would enable Koreans to prevent the tragic recurrence of fratricide. For this understanding, he set out to reveal everything there was to reveal about Korean history. His obsession to complete "The Great Chosŏn Dictionary" paralleled his zeal to complete the "Chosŏn identity" he helped articulate long ago. Simply put, "The Great Chosŏn Dictionary" was a lifelong goal he had sworn to bring to completion.

According to Grandfather, history was a series of efforts to unearth facts, to present them for the world to see, and to establish them in their rightful place. Without it, a nation or people simply could not exist. In the midst of war, Grandfather returned to Seoul to restart the process of gathering books, which were being sold in the streets at give-away prices. To support his work, he set up a mill business at his house, in the hope of generating some income. During 1953–1954, the entire family stood in awe of the passion with which Grandfather concentrated, day and night, on his work. I, still an elementary-school student, was no exception.

In 1954, I started middle school, and there I had history classes. For the first time, I began to take an interest in Grandfather's work of compiling dictionaries. The center hall at the Myo-dong house was much smaller than the one at the Ui-dong house, where we had lived before Yuggio. In that small space, Grandfather stored 40,000 books. One side of the floor sagged. During my middle-school years, my desk was wedged between his bookcases, and when he asked me to fetch a certain book, I had to make my way around the bookcases to find it.

Grandfather spread the index cards on the floor and filled them with tiny handwriting, and stored them in small boxes labeled with han'gŭl alphabet letters. When guests arrived, he would put the books he had been reading aside in a little pile to make space, and when the guests left, he would spread the books out again and resume work. On some days, he would repeat this several times.

The index cards that had been destroyed at Ui-dong numbered in the vicinity of 300,000, which meant that it had taken Grandfather, working at the pace of 100 cards a day, more than eight years to compile them. The effort he had put in after the publication of *Kosatong* in 1943 had all turned into ash in an instant, and in May of 1952, with the repatriation of Seoul, he started the same process all over again.

By the time Grandfather became bedridden with stroke, he had finished his manuscript from *ka* (가) through *kko* (꼬). This portion of his grand "encyclopedia" has been anthologized in *The Complete Works of Yuktang Ch'oe Nam-sŏn*, under the title "The Dictionary of Korean History."

It is my opinion that the title "The Dictionary of Korean History" doesn't do justice to the scope of Grandfather's work. I had an opportunity to look up some entries, such as *Koguryŏ* (고구려), *Koryŏ* (고

려), *Kojong* (고종), and *kwagŏ* (과거), and I was struck by the extensiveness and thoroughness of each entry. I also had a chance to look up the entries, such as *koch'o* (고초), *kom* (곰), *kat* (갓), and *kyul* (귤), which were ethnological entries written from the viewpoint of exchanges among different cultures. All these entries reminded me of encyclopedia entries, quite different from the entries one would normally find in a history dictionary. I wondered if the title "The Encyclopedia of Korean Culture" or "The Encyclopedia of Korean Studies" would have been more appropriate for a dictionary with these kinds of entries. In terms of sheer volume, the entries from *ka* (가) to *kko* (꼬) would cover approximately 5,000 Korean manuscript pages, so the entire project, had it been completed, would have exceeded 50,000 manuscript pages, or about 20 volumes, according to current publishing practices. Grandfather once told me that he had planned on ten volumes for this project.

Even though only a small portion of his project was completed, the scope of Grandfather's plan can be deduced from the subtopics of an entry. For example, for the topic *military structure* (군제), he listed these subtopics: *army, navy, defense budget, uniform,* and *military organizations of central and local governments*. Some of these subtopics have cross-references to other topics as well. Judging by the detailed nature of these references, it appears that the manuscript for them had already been completed.

There is no doubt that Grandfather conceived this project as something grander in scope than an ordinary history dictionary. He organized it around three levels of topic: main topic (for example: *Koryŏ*), subtopic (for example: *finance, territory, legal system, religion, art*), and sub-subtopic (for example: *land ownership, tribute system,* etc. for the subtopic *finance*). In short, the coverage is so extensive that the content under the main topic *Koryŏ* alone comprised 800 manuscript pages, a size that could easily be turned into a stand-alone book on Koyrŏ history. An ordinary dictionary would have simply listed the topic entries in alphabetical order. The "dictionary," as Grandfather conceived it, was really an encyclopedia, with the expansive and comprehensive treatment of its topics, ranging from legal system, taxation, commerce, religion, customs, language, society, and everyday life, to the arts, among many others.

A Korean dictionary I have gives the definition of *dictionary* as a "book containing words of a language arranged in an alphabetical listing, together with definitions, pronunciations, etymologies, and other information about their uses, forms, and functions." The scope and organization of Grandfather's "dictionary" certainly extends far beyond this definition. Therefore, a more accurate title for Grandfather's "dictionary" as it was originally conceived by him would be, in today's parlance, *The Encyclopedia of Korean Culture* or *The Encyclopedia of Korean Studies*.

In this dictionary, Grandfather faithfully follows the second guideline he had established for *A History of Chosŏn for the Korean People*, namely, "Korea and the world always stand side by side." Grandfather was always wary of ultra-nationalism or exclusivism. He believed that Korean history should be open and interactive with world history. This idea is explored by his choice of topics that show Korean interaction with neighboring countries, as well as with the people and places of other countries.

The topics Grandfather listed in his "dictionary" reveal how neighboring countries have affected the development of Korean culture, as well as how Korea has affected the culture of other countries. For example, among the items related to Korean influence on China, Grandfather listed *koryŏyo* (a Korean cooking technique used in Chinese cuisine), *koryŏgi* (the music and dance of Koguryŏ, popular during the Su and T'ang dynasties of China), and *koryŏji* (Korean paper exported to China). For items related to Korean influence on Japan, he listed *koryŏgŏm* (Koguryŏ sword unearthed in an old Japanese mound), *koryŏja* (a Korean cooking technique used in Japan), and *koryŏjŏk* (a Korean flute played in Japan). He also listed *Koch'ang* (present-day Tibet) and for that entry, included an explanation of how cultural exchange took place between Koch'ang and Korea. With a careful selection of topics, Grandfather adhered to the idea that Korean history always enjoyed an intercultural relationship with world history.

I began to wonder, *If the war hadn't happened, if Grandfather's manuscript hadn't been lost, or if he had lived longer, would Korean Studies have advanced much further than they have now?* A similar regret has been expressed by historian Yi Byŏng-do, who once said, "The fact that Ch'oe Nam-sŏn, after giving his heart and soul to the compilation of the dictionary of Korean history, was not able to complete it due to the war and illness, is a matter of the greatest regret in our history." Chang Jun-ha, the publisher of the magazine *Sasang'gye*, expressed his ardent hope that, "a highly gifted successor would soon be able to step into the shoes of Ch'oe Nam-sŏn and complete the compilation of his dictionary of history, bringing his work to shining fruition."

As far as I know, the encyclopedia that had inherited Grandfather's "The Dictionary of Chosŏn History" materialized in the 1990s. It started as a national project at the beginning of the 1980s, under the auspices of Research Center for Korean Spirit and Culture (the present-day National Research Society for Korean Studies), where it took the work of 4,000 specialists to bring it to publication in 1994. It carried the title *The Great Encyclopedia of National Culture*. More than half a century before, Grandfather had started to tackle a project of such magnitude all by himself.

"The Great Chosŏn Dictionary" represented a synthesis of all the knowledge and energy Grandfather possessed. It also represented the love and sacrifice that he, in his old age, dedicated to his "nim," whom he couldn't forget even in his dreams. Whenever I reflect on the dark times and the personal tragedies that he had to endure as he prepared his manuscript for "The Great Chosŏn Dictionary," I bow before the greatness of the motto An Ch'ang-ho created in the early 1900s for the young people of Korea, *musilyŏkhaeng* (務實力行): "Do your utmost with the task at hand." All his life, Grandfather had himself followed this motto to the letter.

3. *The Maritime History of Korea* (韓國海洋史): The Korean Peninsula, the Junction of Continental and Maritime Cultures

In June of 2004, during my stay in Seoul, a professor of Korean history gave me a set of *Yuktang Ch'oe Nam-sŏn*, published by Yŏknaksa in 2003. The set was a photocopied edition of Grandfather's writings, 14 volumes in all. I shipped home 13 volumes by sea, and I kept the first volume to peruse on my return flight. On the plane, I began to read Grandfather's article "Korean History: A Maritime View," which had originally appeared in 12 installments in *Sonyŏn*. Since the magazine had been confiscated repeatedly during 1908-1909, a portion of the article must have appeared in almost every issue of the magazine.

In the article, which Grandfather had written in a mixture of han'gŭl and Chinese characters, the part that caught my attention was the passage in the preface, titled "On the Beauty of the Sea." It is a short passage, but it captures Grandfather's inimitable style:

> With a gentle *ch'o-ol-ch'ol*, my little waves whisper, and with a thunderous *t'a-ang-t'ang-t'ang*, my big waves explode. When my big waves hit the rocks, they break out in foam, and when they hit the soil, they gouge troughs. Bold at high tide, retreating at low tide, they roll the grains of sand and loosen the soil. Coming and going, they say to the Earth, "How strong can you possibly be, Earth? I will expose your uncleanliness–deceitful, cruel, wicked, and sly people, as well as evil and sinister nations. You, Earth, who hide all manner of misdeeds in plain sight, claiming height with your mountains, hardness with your rocks, and width with your plains, let's see how long you last." Day and night, my waves roar *ch'urŭrŭng, ch'ul-ch'ul, su-u-swa*–as if to bellow, "I will

demolish your soil and cleanse your foul body!"

Once a Korean literary critic suggested that Grandfather's poem "Hae egesŏ Sonyŏn ege," which had appeared in *Sonyŏn* in 1908, was not an original poem by Ch'oe Nam-sŏn, but an adaptation of a translated poem by a foreign poet. I wonder if the critic could have made that preposterous claim, had he read the passage above, which had appeared just a few pages later in the same issue of the magazine.

The literary controversy still hovering in my mind, I turned to the article "Korean History: A Maritime View." As I got deeper into the article, I began to see that the subject of Grandfather's writing was the need for Korea to develop as a maritime nation. Considering Korea's situation at the time, this was an extraordinarily forward-looking vision. Since the Annexation, Japan had claimed that Korea, because of its geographical vulnerability of being a peninsula, had suffered the misfortune of repeated incursions from the continent, resulting in its suzerainty status. Grandfather, as a 19-year-old, had presented a surprising counterargument against this claim.

The purpose of Grandfather's writing about the sea lay not in merely educating Koreans about the geographical value of proximity to the ocean, but also in presenting them with a forward-looking plan for national development. Whenever people asked him about the future of Korea, Grandfather reiterated that Korea's being bordered by the ocean on its three sides provided favorable conditions for its economic development. He said, in addition, that Korea's standing in the world would be determined by the establishment of culture and learning possible only for a people living on a peninsula, as exemplified by the civilizations of the Romans and the Greeks. He advanced the idea that Korea's primary geographical feature would help its civilization become a world-class civilization, an idea that was consistent with his general theory of civilization. Grandfather believed that the characteristics of Korean culture originated from the fact that Korea was a peninsula, a meeting place for both the continental and maritime civilizations.

On January 18, 1952, as Yuggio raged on, President Syngman Rhee of South Korea proclaimed the Rhee Line, a line drawn in the ocean surrounding the Korean Peninsula that indicated Korea's sovereignty. There had been frequent skirmishes between Japanese and Korean fishermen, and the Japanese claimed Tokto as their territory, calling it "Takeshima." Almost all the nations of the world had already laid their claims on the oceans surrounding their territories, so President Rhee decided that it was time for Korea to clarify its maritime borders as well.

At the time, Korea's maritime boundary, called the MacArthur Line, had been tentatively drawn by General MacArthur, but President Rhee extended it by a few miles farther to the east and called it the Rhee Line. This line, drawn up by the Department of Defense, included the Tokto island in Korean waters. During this controversy, Grandfather served as an adviser to the Committee for the Compilation of Korean Naval History in Pusan. He was deeply involved in the Tokto issue and other maritime issues. The project had the full support of Son Wŏn-il, Commander of the Korean Navy. Grandfather invited several history professors who had come down to Pusan as refugees and, with their help, began to compile a history of Korean naval battles. Their work bore fruition when the Committee published the manuscript in 1954, with the title *The Maritime History of Korea*.

Grandfather once told me that Korea was, for all practical purposes, an island. I didn't know then exactly what he meant. At the time, my primary interest during my weekend trips with my friends had been to visit as many mountains and temples as I could, so Grandfather perhaps felt that I needed a reminder that, along with the mountains, the ocean was also an important geographical feature of Korea that I should keep in mind.

During one of our conversations about the oceans surrounding Korea, I remember holding up a map of Korea upside down and asking Grandfather, "When I hold the map this way, the south side of Korea is completely open. Is this the reason Korean kings traditionally sat down facing south?" I couldn't remember the answer that Grandfather had given me that day until several decades later, I read the preface of *The Maritime History of Korea:*

> Proportionally speaking, Korea has the longest coastline among all the maritime nations of the world. Greece and Norway, well known for their lengthy coastlines, have 1 *ri* (1/4 mi.) of coastline per 5 square *ri* of land. Even England, considered the premier maritime nation of the world, has 1 *ri* of coastline per 7 square *ri*. In comparison, Korea has 1 *ri* per 3 square *ri*. With the two rivers, Yalu and Tumen, on the north side, Korea can be considered an island. Actually, a map of Asia published in Europe during the sixteenth century* shows the two rivers as connected, making Korea a big, round island.
>
> (*Source: *the East Indies Waterway Map published in 1596*)

By pointing out that Korea could be considered an island, Grandfather wanted to stress the fact that Korea was a peninsula. Because he had regarded the geographical environment of a nation as "the main source of energy that directs the course of a nation or a civilization," he felt that it was very important for Koreans to have an accurate awareness of Korea's primary geographical feature, and to use that feature for the strengthening of the country. He said, in fact, that one of the most regrettable aspects of Korean history was that Koreans had been oblivious of their proximity to the ocean. Throughout history, nations situated near the ocean enjoyed the glories of a strong nation. The United States, for example, enjoys the status of the strongest nation in the world, thanks to its "ownership" of the two great oceans of the world, the Pacific and Atlantic.

Based on these historical examples, Grandfather advanced the idea that if Korea wanted to become a strong nation, it should focus its efforts on becoming a maritime nation. In the concluding paragraphs of the preface of *The Maritime History of Korea*, Grandfather emphasized that Korea's salvation lay in the ocean, and that the establishment of a strong Korea itself would depend on its nation-building efforts as a maritime nation:

> Who will be Korea's savior? It is someone who can establish Korea as a maritime nation. Exactly how will he accomplish this? He can do this by making Korea into a new nation that stands tall above the ocean. It is my firm belief that the advocacy of this idea and its implementation would provide the basis for fundamental and lasting nation-building. Treasure chest of economy, center of transportation, shortcut for cultural importation, and trade of goods–what better place is there than the ocean? It will be the source of the nation's development, as well as the arena in which the Korean people will hone their skills. The ocean, embedded in our collective memory, can help us retrieve what we have lost and

> then safeguard it. If we accomplish this task with integrity, and since we have amply demonstrated our seaworthy capabilities in the past, we will succeed in realizing our grand dream of saving our nation in the future.

In his late teens, Grandfather had been convinced that "the future of Chosŏn lay in its becoming a maritime nation." Five decades later, in his late sixties, he reaffirmed his conviction that the ocean would play an important role in realizing "our grand dream of saving our nation." Throughout his life, his conviction about the sea was inseparably tied to his lifelong aspiration–the globalization of Korean history.

4. "The Spirit of Truth": Reflecting on Postwar Korean Society

It was the fall of 1954. I was in middle school, and Grandfather, who was then 65 and quite ill, dictated to me his article "The Spirit of Truth." I remember feeling as if he were speaking his last words.

It had been a year since the signing of the Armistice. The division between North and South appeared to be permanent, and Koreans were barely surviving on foreign aid. Thousands of orphaned children roamed the streets in search of food. Amidst the deepening misery, there was rampant political strife. Grandfather again agonized over the fate of the Korean people and the future of their country. He expressed his agony in the article "The Spirit of Truth," along with his reflections on the current state of affairs and his belief about the path Koreans should follow.

Grandfather began his article with these words: "The past half-century has been so full of changes in the country, its society, and its people that it almost feels like a dream. . . ." Born at a time when the country was in imminent danger of losing its sovereignty, Grandfather had lived through the Sino-Japanese War and the Russo-Japanese War, which led to the Annexation, during which he endured the cruelties of colonial rule. Liberation finally arrived, but it was soon followed by Yuggio, which, in turn, split the nation in two, North Korea and South Korea. The national division was the ultimate tragedy for Grandfather, whose sole mission in life had been to bring Korean *minjok* to complete unity.

"The Spirit of Truth" is a long article, but it could be summarized in four words: "*minjok* revolution through truth." "Truth" had been the motto of the Youth Student Association, led by An Ch'ang-ho and Grandfather. First recalling his late-teen days with the Youth Student Association, Grandfather warned that, with the current state of society filled with lies, unification would be impossible. In the following sijo, he expressed his deep consternation about the proliferation of lies in postwar Korean society:

> *I stare at Namsan Mountain and Pugak Mountain.*
> *With so many lies and so much hypocrisy floating around,*
> *I doubt that they are, in truth, standing there on the ground.*

Grandfather's desire for unification was heartfelt. For the country and its people, he believed that unification was essential. For him personally, it was something he yearned for with all his heart. His youngest son, Han-gŏm, was in North Korea, and Grandfather despaired of ever seeing him again.

> Do the people of today's society, filled with lies, dare to hope for peaceful liberty and unification? It is not enough to be fearful of a Russian attack or to be grateful for American assistance. All of us should awaken and strive for the true way of self-reliance and independence. Would Russia bring independence to Korea over its own interests? Would America pursue Korean independence apart from its own Far East policies? The answer to both questions is no.

> The question of the liberty and independence of our land and people will only be resolved by our own self-awakening. It may be hard to put our trust solely in our own strength, but doing so would surely bring about a surer result than relying on others. We have to keep in mind that this self-awakening can only be achieved, above all, by not telling lies.

> With the government and society's leaders telling lies, and the entire society afloat with lies, there is very little left to trust. This is why I have come to question, as I did in my poem, whether Namsan and Pugak Mountains themselves are standing on firm ground. I cannot but feel pessimistic about how deceitful people can possibly extricate themselves from their national crisis. At this juncture, "the spirit of truth" espoused by the youth movement of 50 years ago comes to mind. Sure, the reconstruction of Korea needs anti-communist struggles as well as aid from across the Pacific, but it also calls for something more fundamental. All Koreans must regain their conscience and follow the spirit of truth. Only this spirit will save Korea and pave the way for its everlasting future.

Grandfather warned that telling lies and leaning on other nations would not enable Koreans to achieve unification. Only the Korean people's self-awareness would lead to achieving unification, and that self-awareness called for the "spirit of truth," upheld 50 years ago by Korean youths. Only with the revival of this spirit would Koreans become the pioneers of their new destiny.

In the article, Grandfather continues his warning to the Korean people. He warns, in particular, against refusing to learn from history and repeating the same mistake over and over again. Within 30 years of the Imjin War (1592–1601), Koreans suffered through the Pyŏngja War (1627–1636). Ten years after the Kapsin Coup (1884), Koreans experienced the Kabo Reform (1894). Stagnation in Korean society was all but inevitable. According to Grandfather, a more serious problem for Koreans was that they had fallen into a pernicious habit of putting the blame on others:

> ...we have become accustomed to blaming others for our own falsehood and stagnation. We have fallen into the puzzling habit of thinking that every crisis in our history represents a "transition period" stemming from some circumstances or events in other countries. This was the case during the Russo-Japanese War, the Sino-Japanese War, the Protectorate Period, and the Annexation Period. This habit of self-deception ensures endless misfortunes for our country. Is there any glory in this history of repeated "transition periods," which amounts to nothing more than an acknowledgment of failure and humiliation? In the life of our nation, there is a lack of truthfulness, which undermines a step-by-step progress from period to period.

Pointing out the destructive aspect of viewing every crisis as a "transition period," Grandfather also asserted that simply waiting for changes in geopolitical situations to solve Korean problems was one of the worst evils of Korean society. This evil, he believed, had its origin in *sadae chuŭi* (事大主義), Korea's ingrained stance of subservience to the powerful:

> The notion that all our problems are merely the byproducts of international strife has recurred as the outcome of our misbegotten *sadae chuŭi*. Even today, we rely, unwisely, on the Geneva Convention. The Liberation was handed to us for "free," an incidental situation likely to happen perhaps once in a thousand years. Today's national crisis can only be overcome by the strength

> of our sincere awakening, and we can utilize the international situation, favorable or not, provided we have the independent stance to work with it.

Underlying Grandfather's sharp critical remarks was his belief that true reflection should precede any action. Without reflection, there was no future. Reflecting on his life as a historian, he revisited his ideas of *minjok* and *nation*, the two ideas he kept returning to as a historian. His idea of *minjok* diverged significantly from the way the term had been conventionally used:

> I feel that, fundamentally, *minjok* is not a necessary concept, nor should it exist. In essence, it does not exist, and it comes to the fore only in opposition. Here I am perhaps making an excuse for myself. The concept of race has a short history in human society. Even in the "literary" world of Asia, the term never existed. In the West, also, the term came into existence only after the post-medieval development of city-states, barely 400 years ago. So, in my thinking, the idea of *minjok* originates from a confrontational consciousness. It rises to the surface only when an opposing race is present. It has no place in a world where all peoples live in harmony and equality.

Grandfather had come to the conclusion that *minjok* is a relative concept, devoid of essence. He had also concluded that, for the peace of humanity, the confrontational consciousness that accompanies the idea of *minjok* is a hindrance. However, as long as the world is not ruled by pure socialism, anarchism, or cosmopolitanism, the idea of *minjok* is forced to exist, and the existential mode of a *minjok* is a unified nation.

> Next, what is a nation? It is a group of unified people striving towards a common goal. It is an organization that was formed because, without unification, order cannot be efficiently maintained. Historically speaking, China was a collection of divided states, not a unified entity. In the West, Germany became a nation only in the nineteenth century. Up until then, it had been a collection of 30–40 city-states, but the Germans, in their strong quest for unification, used an opportune moment in history to bring the city-states together to forge one unified nation.

Grandfather yearned for the unification of Korea. The division between the North and South was the worst of national tragedies. He stressed that the only way Korea could overcome this tragedy was "truth" and that what Korea needed was a "truth revolution." The "*minjok* revolution for truth" was a conviction Grandfather held throughout his life, and, with a heartfelt wish for a renewal made possible by such a revolution, he ended his article with these words:

> A revolution for truth is necessary for the revival and unification of our nation. I said once that "A society without revolution is like a human being without blood, or a garden without flowers." These comparisons aptly apply to our history. A nation that "failed to perish" is a nation that cannot rise anew. New shoots cannot grow. What is sorely needed is a *minjok* revolution. Today nobody can predict Korea's future. We are at a critical point in

> history that tests our ability to steer our society away from the prevailing proliferation of lies and perfidy.
>
> At this juncture, I cannot help ruminating on the "people's truth" and the "*minjok's* truth" that I, together with An Ch'ang-ho, cried out for 50 years ago in order to bring about the "*minjok* revolution for truth." Whether or not we can be truthful will determine the future of our nation. For this reason, we have to wage a moral war against lies and wickedness, in order to effect a spiritual revolution. Good cannot come out of evil. To expect that it will is the road to self-destruction. Only when the might of good defeats evil, will the light of good shine.

Now, as I reread Grandfather' piercing final words, "A society without revolution is like a human being without blood, or a garden without flowers," I am profoundly affected by them. I hear his loud cry at the possibility that Korea could neither grow its new shoots nor enjoy the return of goodness. He shouts at the top of his lungs that the only thing Korea, his beloved *nim*, needs is truth. The last words of my grandfather, who understood history as nobody else probably could, carry their full weight into the present day, more than half a century later.

PART THREE

The Future of Yuktang Study

Chapter 1

After Yuktang's Death

1. "Pro-Japanese" Criticism and the Sowŏn Monument

Two years had already passed since the Liberation, but during the winter of 1947, the Korean peninsula was in the throes of a struggle between two political ideologies: "capitalist liberty" and "socialist equality." The struggle seemed to hurtle Korea toward an inevitable bifurcation. Neither of the two opposing ideologies, both products of Western philosophy, was a good fit for Korea, which had just been liberated from colonial rule.

Away from the clamor of this struggle, Grandfather concentrated on compiling the *Encyclopedia of Korean History* in his study at Sowŏn. Still, many visitors came to see him. In fact, there were so many that sometimes I found the chore of showing them to Grandfather's study a bit burdensome.

In December of that year, Grandfather reminded Koreans, through a brief thesis titled "The Essence of Korean Culture," of the three points they should keep in mind and reflect on: first, Korea should stand tall vis-à-vis the West; second, it should free itself from Chinese influence; and, last, it should rid itself of Japanese influence. He wanted the Koreans of the "new Chosŏn" to reflect on these three points so that they could hold their own in the world as an independent country. In all likelihood, the geopolitical situation would not have let Koreans stand alone, but regardless, neither Seoul nor Pyongyang heeded Grandfather's urgent call for cultural reflection, which he felt was essential for

Korea's future.

In looking back on what transpired in Korea over the last half century, it appears that Grandfather fulfilled the role of "prophet-historian." Unfortunately, the politicians of both North Korea and South Korea, with Western powers at their backs, did not heed his words.

Grandfather concluded his short thesis with these cryptic words: "*Minjok* is small and culture is large. History is short and culture is long." The "national independence" that Grandfather pursued all his life was "Chosŏn as common cultural entity," and his idea of *minjok* and his historiography were instruments he employed to reach this goal. He consistently put forth the idea that Korea should be founded on the framework of its own unique culture, not on ideas borrowed from the West, such as capitalism or communism.

After finishing my military duties, I arrived in Boston as a 27-year-old foreign student in 1967, ten years after Grandfather's death. Since then, I have made yearly trips back to Korea. The number of years I have lived in the United States notwithstanding, my feelings toward Korea remain unchanged. I am very proud of Korea's recent political and economic progress, and I am particularly proud of the Koreans of my generation for the success they have achieved through their sheer stamina and perseverance. I feel that, to a certain extent, Grandfather's dream of modernization and globalization for Korea has been achieved. It goes without saying that the interest I have in Korea is closely tied to the interest I have in Grandfather and what he stood for.

Listening to public opinions about Grandfather shift with the changes in the political trends and regimes in Korea, I sometimes get an odd sensation that my grandfather, Yuktang Ch'oe Nam-sŏn, is a living person who is still among us today, not someone who is dead and gone. Were he merely someone who once existed, it does not seem possible that public perception of him could go through such highs and lows with every wind of political change. It is not an exaggeration to say that, in Korea, Yuktang Ch'oe Nam-sŏn and his work live on in almost all areas, including politics, culture, and other humanistic endeavors.

One point that is even clearer is that there is a significant difference between my generation's view of him and that of the new generation, which has not experienced colonial rule. In his "Open Letter," Grandfather wrote, "the popular anger toward me comes from the love they feel toward me." He understood that people were angry with him because they loved him. Indeed, many Koreans did not turn their backs on him, as shown by the words of Chang Jun-ha, one of the leading intellectuals of the "386 generation," who dismissed the remarks critical of Yuktang as "the mere babbling of the immature and uneducated."

In 2006, there was a small gathering at the Korea Society in New York, celebrating the publication of the English translation of Yi Kwang-su's novel *Mujŏng* (The Heartless), the first "modern" novel of Korea, published in 1917. A number of professors of Korean Studies from various American universities engaged in a discussion on "the Literary Period of Yuktang and Ch'unwŏn (pen name for Yi Kwang-su)." The discussion was followed by the introduction of Yi's granddaughter, Ann S. Lee, who talked about the challenges and rewards of translating her grandfather's novel. Afterwards, I had the opportunity to talk to her father, Yi Yŏng-kŭn, who had come to New York to attend the celebration.

During our talk, Yi told me about what he had learned during his trip to North Korea in 1991. As Yi Kwang-su, his father, was being abducted to the North, he suffered from extreme frostbite. On reaching the city of Kang'gye, he asked Hong Myŏng-hi, his long-time friend, for help. Hong, with Kim Il Sung's permission, took Yi to his quarters to take care of him. Yi, already quite ill with tuberculosis, subsequently died in a People's Army hospital on October 25, 1950.

After the Armistice, the North Korean authorities set up a burial site for all the notable figures from South Korea who had died during or since the war. These included many well-known figures such as Chŏng In-bo, An Chae-hong, Hyŏn Sang-yun, Kim Yak-su, and Won Se-hun. Their graves, then scattered all over North Korea, were being excavated and moved to this burial site. Many North Koreans expressed strong opposition to moving Yi's grave to this site, but Kim Il Sung stepped in and ordered it moved. It was said that Kim had made the decision that Yi, with his pioneering literary work, had represented the "conscience of the Korean *minjok*," and that, even if he had engaged in pro-Japanese activities, the time Yi lived in merited consideration. As I listened, my first thought was that Kim Il Sung's decision was only possible because he had himself lived through the same era that Yi had.

It was the spring of 1957, and I was a first-year student in high school. I don't quite remember whether it was March 1 (Day to Commemorate March First Movement) or April 26 (Grandfather's birthday), but when I got back from school, I saw a pot containing a small plum tree on my desk in Grandfather's room, As I put down my book bag, Grandfather asked me to water the plant, which I did, and nothing more was said about it. My mother later told me that the plant had been delivered by a secretary from Kyŏngmudae (the official residence of the President) that morning, adding that Grandfather was being considered for "the Merit Award for the Foundation of the Country" the following year.

Grandfather died in October of that year.

Two years later, in 1959, there was a commemorative ceremony at Sowŏn, at which a monument erected in Grandfather's memory was unveiled. On the monument were inscriptions of the epitaph written by the historian Yi Byŏng-do and the entire text of the Declaration of Independence. My family received word that President Rhee would attend the ceremony, but at the last minute, he sent word that he could not, due to some pressing matters of state. A few days later, President Rhee visited Sowŏn unannounced and, after a few minutes of silent meditation in front of the monument, returned to Kyŏngmudae. This was six months before Rhee was forced to leave office as a result of the April 19 Student Uprising.

It is my opinion that President Rhee's actions regarding Grandfather stemmed from his having experienced the era of colonial rule himself. The colonial era was cruel to all Koreans, whether they sided with the political left or right, and they knew this fact through personal experience. In contrast, Koreans of later generations, who never experienced colonial rule tend to be critical of Grandfather, to the point of making criticism for criticism's sake. I think that this blind posture comes partly from their inability or unwillingness to accept the facts of the past.

History is not merely a superficial record of historical events, but a record of how and why those events occurred, and how they stand in a continuum with those that follow. The study of history strives to reveal the motives, context, progress, outcome, and effect of the actions of historical figures or events. In the absence of a full analysis of the progression of historical events, they cannot be fully understood as facts. In addition, a person who is unable or unwilling to understand the past as fact is just as unable to make sensible plans for the future.

Unveiling of the Sowŏn monument commemorating Grandfather in Ui-dong on October 10, 1959. The ceremony was attended by Chin Hak-mun, Kim Yŏng-sang, Hong Il-sik, Pak Chong-hwa, Cho Yong-man, and Sim Chŏng-sŏp, among other notable intellectuals of the day. Grandmother, in white, stands in the front center.

During Yuggio, Sowŏn, Grandfather's home at Ui-dong, was all but reduced to rubbles, except for the main house, which, in its half-burned state, looked as if it would collapse at any moment. In preparation for the commemorative ceremony, however, Second Uncle, Han-ung, had some renovations done on the house and also planted several small trees in the front yard. Finally the place was presentable enough for the occasion. With the erection of the monument, Sowŏn became the place where a commemorative ceremony for Grandfather was held every year, and where people came to pay their respects throughout the year.

However, with time, Sowŏn deteriorated. To obtain funds for a major renovation of Sowŏn to its original state, the Committee for the

Memorialization of Yuktang, along with the Kangbuk District Office, repeatedly requested that the Seoul City Administration designate Sowŏn as one of the city's "cultural treasures." But this request was voted down at the meeting of the Committee for Cultural Treasures of the City of Seoul in January of 2003. The reason given was that Sowŏn was a "place where Ch'oe Nam-sŏn, in addition to other pro-Japanese activities, urged Korean youths to participate in the Japanese war through his newspaper articles and columns. Moreover, the condition of the structure, being more than 65 years old, does not warrant the cost of renovation."

There was much controversy surrounding the city's decision. To ameliorate the situation, the city government promised that it would consider placing a plaque at the original site of Kwangmunhoe in Samgak-dong to memorialize Yuktang's service as "the poet who first wrote free-style poetry, thus making a contribution to the modern literature of Korea." However, I have yet to hear that this plaque has been installed.

When I was living at Sowŏn, a few big rocks dotted the front yard. I remember the touch-me-nots that were growing in their shades, whose red flowers I crushed to dye my little sister's nails. Years later, one of those rocks was moved to a spot beside a nearby stream. In 2007, the Kangbuk District Office had the characters "So-wŏn" inscribed on the rock and moved it back to its original site at Sowŏn. Presently, the rock with this two-character inscription stands next to a guidepost on which these words appear: "This is the site where Yuktang Ch'oe Nam-sŏn, the author of the Declaration of Independence, pioneered modern Korean literature by composing free-style poetry."

When I learned in New York that Sowŏn had been demolished by apartment developers, I was devastated. Apart from my personal memories of the place, I thought: *Why did the Korean people fail to under-*

stand that it was a historical building? Why would Korea tear down a building with genuine historical significance, while other countries have been known to build structures that have questionable historical authenticity? When I consider all the things to which Grandfather dedicated his life–how he stressed, through his scholarly works, travel writings, radio lectures, and all the other media he could employ, the importance of historical remains and artifacts as manifestations of the Chosŏn spirit and, therefore, the importance of their preservation–the one brief sentence on the guidepost breaks my heart. I am again reminded of Grandfather's cry when, in 1923, he had to discontinue his magazine, *Tongmyŏng*:

> People of Chosŏn! If you have the courage, say "Yes!" It is not the people of Chosŏn that deserve pity, but Chosŏn itself–its mountains and rivers. It is the spirit of Chosŏn that resides in its mountains and rivers.

But that was then, when Korea was under Japanese rule. Shouldn't things be different now, even a little?

2. Biographies, Collections, and the Yuktang Archive

I have wanted to write a book about Grandfather for quite a while, but it was only after I retired in 2005 that I had the time to actually embark on this project. My first task was to compile a bibliography of Grandfather's works, along with a chronology of his life and works. During the process, I was quite dismayed at how much misinformation exists about Grandfather, and also at how often this misinformation has been repeated and therefore perpetuated. I also discovered that a significant portion of Grandfather's works had been lost, probably never to be found again.

It took me a whole year just to get the chronology and bibliography into their current shape. Concurrently with this task, I collected information concerning the history of the intellectuals of modern Northeast Asia that was relevant to Grandfather's life and work. In so doing, I wanted to reach an understanding of Grandfather's work, not only within the framework of Korean Studies, but also within the larger framework of the modern intellectual history of Northeast Asia.

Soon after I embarked on this book, I also began to plan for an English translation of it. I wanted to pass on what I know and have discovered about Grandfather to my children, who were born and raised in the English-speaking world. The most salient feature of my book, of course, is my memory of Grandfather as I was growing up, but I did not want the book to recount solely the memories of a young grandson. I also wanted to convey how I have come to understand the works of Yuktang Ch'oe Nam-sŏn as a historian and a public figure during the tumultuous period of Korean history in which he lived.

To my recollection, Grandfather rarely talked about himself. He responded to my childish questions with simple answers that a young grandson would easily understand, and there were many questions I wasn't mature enough even to ask. Grandfather never responded to the unfounded rumors that were spread about him nor to the malicious remarks some people made about his actions. He didn't have the time. I don't think he would have written a memoir even if he had lived longer. He would have used the time compiling the *Encyclopedia of Korean History*.

There was, however, a graduate student named Hong Il-sik who did write about Grandfather. Hong was introduced to Grandfather by Ku Cha-gyun, a professor of Korean literature at Korea University. For a year and three months, Hong visited Grandfather at his sickbed twice a week to talk to him, and recorded their conversations. When he didn't show up on a Sunday, one of his regular visiting days, Grandfather, as well as I, wondered if anything had happened to him. As far as I know, Hong was the only person who heard directly from Grandfather about his life story and also about his work as a scholar and poet. Based on these conversations, Hong wrote his doctoral thesis, which was published two years after Grandfather's death. Hong's *The Study of Yuktang*, at once a biography and scholarly study, is the first book ever written about Yuktang. In the sense that the book contains Grandfather's own words, even though it lacks some important details about his life, it is quite valuable.

With the erection of the commemorative monument at Sowŏn two years after his death, a serious discussion began in the academic community about the writing of an exhaustive biography of Yuktang. Among several candidates, Cho Yong-man and Kim Chong-mu were chosen as authors. Kim Chong-mu had once studied under Grandfather, who thought highly of him. Cho Yong-man, a professor of English

Literature, a novelist, and a founding member of Kuinhoe (Group of Nine Novelists), as well as a distant relative of Grandmother's, had a long teacher-student relationship with Grandfather. It was decided that Kim would be responsible for the section on Grandfather's writings on historical and other scholarly subjects, while Cho would write the section about Grandfather's writings on literary and cultural subjects. Sŏ Chae-su, president of Samchungdang Publishing Company, offered to publish the biography as soon as the manuscripts became available. Sŏ had published, under severe censorship, Grandfather's *Kosatong* during Japanese colonial rule.

While Kim's manuscript was being delayed for one reason or another, Cho's manuscript was completed on schedule. For his manuscript, Cho obtained verbal testimony from Grandmother, Ch'oe Tu-sŏn (Ch'oe Nam-sŏn's younger brother), Chin Hak-mun (Grandfather's lifelong friend), and Kim Yŏ-che (a Sinmun'gwan colleague), some of whom also gave him access to valuable materials they had in their possession. When Kim couldn't finish his manuscript and resigned from authorship, Cho took over the section on history as well. The biography was finally published in 1964, with the title *Yuktang Ch'oe Nam-sŏn*. This book has remained the definitive biography of Yuktang to the present day, but it should be noted here that the section on Grandfather's historical works is far from being exhaustive, and needs major expansion.

Over the years I wondered why there had been, for several decades, a near-total absence of books on Grandfather since the publications of Hong Il-sik's *The Study of Yuktang* and Cho Yong-man's *Yuktang Ch'oe Nam-sŏn*. The minor publications that did come out were mostly about Grandfather's life, but most of the information in them had already been covered by the two previous books. The two books represented serious attempts at thorough coverage, but there were still areas that even I knew had not been touched. There were some items that the authors simply did not have access to and other items that could not be revealed at the time the books were written. The omission of these items, unfortunately, played a role in generating misunderstandings and prejudicial opinions over the years. Rectifying this situation is one of the reasons I am writing this book.

After the publication of Cho's biography, our family announced in 1967 that it would donate Grandfather's collection of books and documents to Korea University. This was the collection that Grandfather had restarted after the destruction of the Sowŏn library. To house the collection, Korea University built a section called the "Yuktang Archive" in its main library, and soon published a list of its contents. Korea University and Grandfather had enjoyed a special bond over the years. When Kim Sŏng-su, the future founder of Korea University, took over Posŏng Institute, he sought Grandfather's advice. When Posŏng Institute did not have enough land to build an extension, Grandfather persuaded his good friend Pak Han-yŏng, then principal of the Chung'ang Buddhist School and director of the Chosŏn Buddhist Organization, to donate part of the land the school owned. In addition, Grandfather's younger brother, Tu-sŏn, once served as the executive director of Posŏng Institute.

On the tenth anniversary of Grandfather's death, on October 10, 1967, the entire contents of Grandfather's library were physically moved to Korea University: 22,189 books and approximately 900 other documents that included Grandfather's handwritten manuscripts, sijo, photo albums, maps, and other miscellaneous items. Among these were rare copies of *Yong'gamsugyŏng* (龍龕水鏡), *Hunminchŏng'ŭm Ŏnhae* (訓民

正音諺解), and *Wŏlinsŏkbo* (月印釋譜).

Yong'gamsugyŏng, designated as "National Treasure, Number 130," is a Chinese dictionary, originally published during the Liao dynasty of China, used to read Buddhist sutra. Here I would like to recount the story behind how this book survived the Sowŏn library's fiery destruction. Just before Yuggio broke out, the National Museum of Korea had borrowed the book so that it could be displayed in its exhibition of national treasures. When the war broke out, the book was moved to a safe place, along with other national treasures, and was returned to Grandfather when the war ended.

Hunminchŏng'ŭm Ŏnhae, the annotated edition of the Korean alphabet in its original form, also has its own serendipitous backstory. While Grandfather was living in Taegu as a refugee, he had a chance encounter with Pak Chŏng-sŏ, son of Pak Sŭng-bin, who subsequently presented Grandfather with *Hunminchŏng'ŭm Ŏnhae,* a book his family had treasured for generations. It was one of two copies of the book extant in Korea. Pak probably did this in honor of his own father's close friendship with Grandfather.

It took almost two years for the Research Committee for Asian Issues at Korea University to catalogue Grandfather's collection. In 1969, the Committee held an event to commemorate the publication of the *Bibliography of the Yuktang Collection*. Along with an exhibition of the collection, Kim Tu-chong, the premier bibliographer, gave a lecture on the significance of the Yuktang collection. I think it is very fortunate that Grandfather's collection is preserved and managed to this day by Korea University. My greatest regret, of course, is the irrevocable loss of the Sowŏn library collection during Yuggio. Prior to moving to Ui-dong,

Grandfather had a library at his house in Yangsakkol, which he named *Illamgak*, "a place where the world can be seen at a glance." Viewed as a library comparable to that of Kyŏngsŏng Imperial University, it had been a place where prominent literary and scholarly figures of the time gathered for readings and discussions.

After the publication of the *Bibliography of the Yuktang Collection*, Korea University organized a committee to compile a collection of Yuktang's works. As its director, Kim Chun-yŏp was chosen, and several advisors were invited, such as Kim Tu-chong, Pak Chong-hwa, Pak Nak-chun, Yi Byŏng-do, Yi Chong-u, and Ch'oe Tu-sŏn. Among its members, well-respected experts from various fields, such as Kim Sam-su, Kim Yong-dŏk, Kim Chong-mu, Pak Sŏng-ŭi, Yi Sang-ŭn, Chŏng Chae-kak, Cho Ki-chun, Cho Yong-man, Ch'ŏn Kwan-u, Ch'oe Yŏng-hi, Ch'oe Han-ung, Han U-kŭn, and Hong I-sŏp, were represented.

The compilation effort faced many challenges, however. Yuktang's writings, which had appeared over a long span of years in a variety of media, including books, magazines, and newspapers, were not easy to collect. Depending on the time of publication, there were variations in orthography as well. After two years of intense debate, editorial guidelines were finally established, and the process of compilation began, which was to last four years. The finished manuscript was sent to Hyŏnamsa Publishing Company, but the printing of the collection itself faced many challenges, because Grandfather's writings, apart from their sheer volume, were full of rarely used Chinese characters. The cost of the printing turned out to be astronomical, and the proofreading expense alone exceeded the entire cost of other collections the company had previously published.

On more than one occasion, Hyŏnamsa Publishing Company teetered on the brink of bankruptcy while publishing *The Complete Works of Yuktang Ch'oe Nam-sŏn*. I remember reading a newspaper interview with the company president, Cho Sang-wŏn, in which he said that the publication "posed the greatest threat to the company since its foundation." He added that "only with the conviction that if we were to give up, we would lose our identity," was he able to see the project to its completion. The original plan had been to publish the collection in 17 volumes, but the final number of volumes came to 15. The first 14 were published during 1973–1974, and the final volume in 1975. It had taken nine years since Grandfather's collection was moved to Korea University.

Kim Chun-yŏp, director of the Research Committee for Asian Issues at Korea University, pointed out in his remarks on the publication of *The Complete Works of Yuktang Ch'oe Nam-sŏn* that the purpose of its publication was the objective study and evaluation of a "new cultural movement in modern Korean history." Kim saw the significance of *The Complete Works* as extending over the entire period that Yuktang represented, not limited to just Yuktang. Kim, who later became the president of Korea University, had joined the Japanese army toward the end of colonial rule and then left it to join the Liberation Army in China, where he fought side by side with Chang Jun-ha.

The Complete Works of Yuktang Ch'oe Nam-sŏn is a comprehensive anthology that represents 50 years of Grandfather's writings. Were it not for the publication of this collection, many more of Grandfather's writings would have been lost. Twenty years before its publication, Hong Il-sik, who had attempted to personally locate individual works written by Grandfather, lamented in the preface of his book *The Study of Yuktang*, "...now it is difficult to find the writings of Yuktang." Without this collection, I myself would have found it next to impossible to write this book, sitting in my study in New York. The collection includes about 85 percent of Grandfather's *oeuvre*, representing about 100,000 Korean manuscript pages and 20 million characters in all. It appears that Grandfather wrote at a greater speed than I could read his writings, a fact that still causes me to marvel. I remember Grandfather once telling me, "Even in the dead of winter, if you dip your pen often and fast enough, the ink won't freeze." Even in prison, Grandfather had written furiously and incessantly.

In 2003, Yŏknaksa Publishing Company came out with another version of *The Complete Works of Yuktang Ch'oe Nam-sŏn*, in 14 volumes. Unlike Hyŏnamsa's *The Complete Works*, which was a printed version, Yŏknaksa had published a photocopied version of Grandfather's writings as they originally appeared in various contemporary media. The collection is useful in that it provides scholars with access to Grandfather's works in their original form, and also includes material that had not been included in Hyŏnamsa's *The Complete Works*. I surmise that the Yŏknaksa's photocopied version was made possible by the surge of interest in Yuktang among younger scholars. These two publications of Yuktang's complete works undoubtedly provide the foundation for the study of Yuktang, and it is my sincere hope that this study will continue, leading to the full establishment of "Yuktang Study."

3. The Reconstruction of Kwangmunhoe, the Cradle of Korean Modernity

In 1967, when I left Korea to study in the United States, Ch'ŏng'gech'ŏn, a river that flowed through the heart of Seoul, had been filled in and a three-lane highway built over it. Forty years elapsed before the river was uncovered and allowed to flow again. On hearing the news of Ch'ŏng'gech'ŏn's restoration, my thoughts turned to the Kwangmunhoe building that had once stood near the river.

The site where Grandfather began his cultural movement had been a two-story building that housed Sinmun'gwan on its first floor and Kwangmunhoe on its second floor. The building was torn down in the late 1960s, when the streets around Ŭlchiro were widened to accommodate increased traffic. Many people had voiced opposition to its demolition, but in the end, the voice of expansion won over that of preservation.

In my mind, the fate of Ch'ŏng'gech'ŏn intersects with that of the Kwangmunhoe building. The restoration of Ch'ŏng'gech'ŏn represents Korea's return to its appreciation of nature and culture, as opposed to blind pursuit of economic development. Just as Ch'ŏng'gech'ŏn, once sacrificed to modern urban expansion, was rescued from its tomb, it is time for Kwangmunhoe to be reconstructed and rescued from oblivion. The reconstruction of the building, which was once the cradle of Korean modernity, will surely signal Korea's maturity as it shows appreciation for its history and culture in the center of its capital.

Whenever I visit Seoul, my steps lead me to the site of Kwangmunhoe, the site I passed by whenever I ran Grandfather's errands to the offices of *Dong-a Ilbo* and *Chosŏn Ilbo*, as he lay sick in bed in his final years. In 1985, I spotted a small plaque with the words "The former site of Kwangmunhoe" in one inconspicuous corner of this site, appearing incongruously meager in proportion to Kwangmunhoe's historic role as the birthplace of Korea's modernity.

Over the last few years, a few prominent figures of Korean society have advocated the reconstruction of Kwangmunhoe. In 1995, the Research Committee for Kwangmunhoe Spirit was organized, with ex-Prime Minister Kang Yŏng-hun serving as adviser, and former president of Korea University Hong Il-sik serving as president. The Committee repeatedly submitted its reconstruction requests to various city organizations, but to no avail. However, in 2005, with the restoration of Ch'ŏng'gech'ŏn, the area where Kwangmunhoe once stood opened up and was designated as a public park. When the city government announced that it would name the triangular-shaped area "Berlin Park," many citizens objected to the idea of constructing a park totally devoid of any historical connection. Instead, they supported the idea of using the site for the reconstruction of the Kwangmunhoe building, which, they felt, once housed the "soul of Korean *minjok*."

The year 2005 also saw the creation of the Commission for the Inquiry into Japanese Collaborators by the Korean government, which ignited a fierce controversy in Korean society. One group raised a shrill voice, saying that under no circumstances should Kwangmunhoe be reconstructed because it was founded by "pro-Japanese Ch'oe Nam-sŏn." Another group strongly supported the reconstruction of the building for its historical significance, regardless of the debate over Ch'oe Nam-sŏn. Public opinion, in the end, seemed to be leaning toward the reconstruction.

By 2010, a hundred years after the Japanese annexation of Korea, public sentiment had grown in strong favor of the reconstruction of Kwangmunhoe, and the Seoul City Government announced that it could allocate 20 percent of the triangular park for the new Kwangmunhoe building. In response, the Research Committee for Kwangmunhoe Spirit announced that, if given the land, it would collect public funds to cover the cost of reconstructing the building to its original two-story structure, and on its completion, it would donate it to the city government. The Committee also promised that, in addition to the structure, it would erect a large monument memorializing Kwangmunhoe's significance, as well a kiosk of modern digital displays of its various achievements. When the reconstruction is completed, I look forward to donating the Yuktang memorabilia I have in my possession to be displayed there.

Witnessing the debate over the Kwangmunhoe reconstruction, I was reminded of the controversy that arose about ten years ago over the National Treasure status of "The Declaration of Independence." It has become common knowledge now that Kwangmunhoe was the place where the Declaration was conceived and where the March First Movement was born. If the demolition of the Kwangmunhoe building was the result of a thoughtless dictatorial government intent on modernization, the refusal to confer National Treasure status to the Declaration was the result of narrow-mindedness or a lack of historical consciousness on the part of the younger generation of scholars, those with no experience of colonial rule.

On March 1, 1997, the anniversary of the March First Movement, the Committee for National Treasures made a preliminary announcement that "The Declaration of Independence" would be included in the list for consideration for National Treasure status. However, the Research Society for Minjok Issues rose in opposition, citing Grandfather's "pro-Japanese" activities. The end result was its elimination from the list, and Kim Ku's diary, *Paekpŏm Ilchi,* being conferred the status of National Treasure Number 1235. I record this incident in my book because I would very much like to know who was behind the decision and exactly why and how this decision was reached.

Regardless of who wrote "The Declaration of Independence," the document speaks for the Korean people in their will to independence. At a time when the word *independence* itself was banned from people's lips, the public declaration of Korea's independence was an act of extraordinary courage. To deny this fact is to deny the historical fact of the March First Movement. To deny the March First Movement is to deny the legitimacy of the Korean nation. I say this, of course, not to minimize the importance of the diary of Kim Ku, a great Korean patriot, but to point out that the Declaration of Independence has a deeper, more far-reaching influence in Korean history. The Declaration has long been anthologized in Korean textbooks in order to transmit the spirit of the March First Movement to Korea's young citizens. A serious question, I believe, needs to be raised as to why this document of major significance has been eliminated from the list of national treasures, and whether this decision is still justified.

Chapter 2

Establishing Yuktang Study

1. The Concepts of *Minjok* and *Nation*

The word *minjok chuŭi* (民族主義), as it is used today, is translated into English as *nationalism* without any problem. However, translating the word *nation*, as it is used in modern history, as *minjok*, causes hesitation or confusion. I think this is because we use the word *minjok* as an abstract noun to refer to a cultural entity that embodies a common cultural life or system of values, but its existential reality is the unit called *nation*.

Until the 1900s, the word *minjok*, in its modern sense, did not exist in Korea. *Is it possible for people to have been conscious of* minjok *when there was no word for it?* At the end of the Korean Empire, the word *minjok*, as it was commonly used by the *yangban* class, was synonymous with the English word *race*. For example, when they warned about the "encroachment of the white *race*," they felt that "the yellow race, firmly standing on *minjok chuŭi*, should advance "*Tong'yang chuŭi* (Easternism)."

In March of 1907, Grandfather declared, in the newsletter *Korean Students Abroad*, that "20 million people living under the Paektu Mountain are our *minjok*" and called for an "awakening of unique national characteristics." It was this declaration, in my opinion, that helped awaken the Korean people's consciousness of "their responsibility to work together for the common good of the *minjok*."

A few years later, when Korea lost its sovereignty, Grandfather felt the need to promote the idea of *minjok* in order to, in his own words,

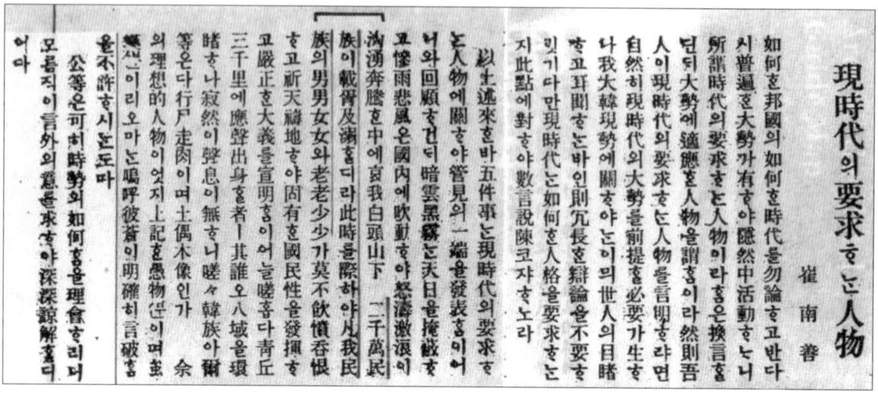
現時代의要求ᄒᆞᄂᆞᆫ人物

崔南善

如何ᄒᆞᆫ邦國의如何ᄒᆞᆫ時代를勿論ᄒᆞ고반다
시普遍ᄒᆞᆫ大勢가有ᄒᆞ야隱然中活動ᄒᆞᄂᆞ니
所謂時代의要求ᄒᆞᄂᆞᆫ人物이라ᄒᆞᆷ은換言ᄒᆞᆯ
딘ᄃᆡ大勢에適應ᄒᆞᆫ人物을謂ᄒᆞᆷ이라然則吾
人이現時代의要求ᄒᆞᄂᆞᆫ人物을言明ᄒᆞ랴면
自然히現時代의大勢를前提ᄒᆞᆯ必要가生ᄒᆞ
나我大韓現勢에關ᄒᆞ야ᄂᆞᆫ이믜世人의目睹
ᄒᆞ고耳聞ᄒᆞᄂᆞᆫ바인則冗長ᄒᆞᆫ辯論을不要ᄒᆞ
깃기다만現時代ᄂᆞᆫ如何ᄒᆞᆫ人格을要求ᄒᆞᄂᆞᆫ
지此點에對ᄒᆞ야數言說陳코자ᄒᆞ노라

以上述來ᄒᆞᆫ바五件事ᄂᆞᆫ現時代의要求ᄒᆞ
ᄂᆞᆫ人物에關ᄒᆞ야管見의一端을發表ᄒᆞᆷ이어
니와回顧ᄒᆞ건ᄃᆡ暗雲黑霧ᄂᆞᆫ天日을掩蔽ᄒᆞ
고慘雨悲風은國內에吹動ᄒᆞ야怒濤激浪이
洶湧奔騰ᄒᆞᆫ中에哀我白頭山下　二千萬民
族이載胥及溺ᄒᆞᆫ디라此時를際하야凡我民
族의男男女女와老老少少가莫不飮憤呑恨
ᄒᆞ고祈天禱地ᄒᆞ야固有ᄒᆞᆫ國民性을發揮ᄒᆞ
고嚴正ᄒᆞᆫ大義를宣明ᄒᆞᆷ이어ᄂᆞᆯ嗟홉다靑丘
三千里에應聲出身ᄒᆞᆯ者ㅣ其誰오八域을環
睹ᄒᆞ나寂然이聲息이無ᄒᆞ니嗟々韓族아爾
等은다行尸走肉이며土偶木像인가　余
의理想的人物이엇지上記ᄒᆞᆫ愚物뿐이며至
[illegible]ᄒᆞ니이리오마ᄂᆞᆫ嗚呼彼蒼이明確히言破ᄒᆞᆷ
을不許ᄒᆞ시ᄂᆞᆫ도다

公等은可히時勢와如何ᄒᆞᆷ을理會ᄒᆞ리며
모름직이言外의意를求ᄒᆞ야深深諒解ᄒᆞᆯ디
어다

In his article published in the first issue (March 3, 1907) of *Korean Students Abroad*, Grandfather used the term *minjok* for the first time. Starting in his late teens, his scholarly efforts revolved around developing and establishing the concept of *minjok*.

"extricate Chosŏn from Chinese value systems and, at the same time, regain the identity stolen by the Japanese." Under the given circumstances, Grandfather had no choice other than the rationale of *minjok chuŭi*, which he used as an instrument to pursue nationalism, with the ultimate goal of regaining sovereignty. Grandfather's *minjok chuŭi* was, in essence, nationalism, and thus was closely tied to his study of Tan'gun as the father of the nation.

In contrast to the conventional concept of a *nation* as defined by the territory it occupies, Grandfather's concept of *minjok* was defined by a common system of values upheld by the people, such as the ideals of "hong-ik" (benefit to all) in Korea. Grandfather's concept of *minjok*, however, was not written in stone from the time he first used the word in 1907 to when he died in 1957. On the contrary, Grandfather continually revisited the concept, modifying its definition.

After the establishment of the Democratic Republic of Korea in 1948, when the word *nation* referred to Korea, not Japan, Grandfather re-examined the meaning of *minjok*. In his article titled "The Spirit of Truth," published in 1954, he wrote, "As a historian and a member of our *minjok*, I have long wrestled with the concept of *minjok*." He then stressed the intrinsically relative nature of the concept and its short history in the evolution of human society.

When the Republic of Korea was established in 1948, Grandfather declared that the unit necessary to become a member state of the world was not *minjok*, but a nation. At the same time, he declared that the *minjok* should be unified in order to become a nation, and in order for the nation to become a developed one. In the face of national division, Grandfather struggled with the twin issues of *minjok* unification and national development. He had "discovered" *minjok* through the March First Movement, and had sought since then to "complete" *minjok* through the establishment of Chosŏn Studies. Now, the unification of the divided *minjok* had become the indispensable ingredient for the development of an independent nation.

Grandfather subscribed to neither the doctrine of the left nor that of the right. I really wish that he had lived a little longer and clarified for me the concepts of *minjok* and *nation*, these ideas that remain somewhat conflated in my mind. Although the March First Movement succeeded in solidifying the concept of *minjok*, the left-right division, which dates back to the dissolution of Sin'ganhoe in 1931, still persists on the Korean Peninsula.

2. "Open" Nationalism

I have heard that in today's Korean academic community there is strong criticism of the concepts of *minjok chuŭi* and nationalism. I regard this critical stance as originating from an earnest attempt to reflect on the past in preparation for a better future. All ideas and trends inevitably fade once their timely relevance recedes. Korea had embraced exaggerated *minjok chuŭi* during its modernization period, and extreme nationalism to justify its rapid development. It is shortsighted, however, to render criticism on the ideas and trends of the past from today's vantage point. Those ideas and trends provided solutions to the problems people faced in those particular times, and they represented the most logical and effective tools available to the people. I believe Grandfather's *minjok chuŭi* was one of them.

Grandfather's *minjok chuŭi* had a few characteristics that diverged significantly from the conventional conception of *minjok chuŭi* at the time. The *minjok chuŭi* he upheld transcended his time and looked forward to the future. It was an "open" *minjok chuŭi*. Not taking this aspect of his *minjok chuŭi* into consideration, and criticizing it for its exclusivism or romanticism is, in my opinion, a form of prejudice, if not ignorance. My own interpretation of Grandfather's *minjok chuŭi* is as follows:

Sinocentrism and *Minjok chuŭi*

One thing the critics should bear in mind is that Grandfather's concept of *minjok* originated from Korea's need to extricate itself from its sinocentric past. Grandfather felt that Korea's history, for a thousand years, had been mired in its subservience to China. He equated a break from this mentality of subservience with the idea of *minjok*, a modern *minjok*.

Grandfather never once referred to China as "the Middle Kingdom." He always referred to it as "Chi-na," because the name "The Middle Kingdom" presumed a sinocentric worldview. To him, China, instead of being the center of the world to which Korea should kowtow, represented a "medievalism" that Korea would do well to divest itself from. Domestically, Korea needed to rid itself of the Confucian ideology and class system, and internationally, it needed to show to the world that it had made a clean break from China's influence. Only then could Korea free itself from its deeply entrenched sinocentric past.

In the very first sentence of the Declaration of Independence, Grandfather declared "the independence of Korea." Later, he explained why he called out this point at the very beginning of his Declaration:

> Among the leaders in the independence movement, some made excuses for Korea's long history of suzerainty to China, and I was determined to counter this attitude. I wrote the first sentence of the Declaration of Independence with this attitude specifically in mind.

In 1919, many Koreans considered their country a suzerainty of China. In order to bring about a fundamental change in this attitude, Grandfather sought to create a sense of *minjok* among Koreans. He sought to establish Chosŏn Studies, in an effort to do away with sinocentrism and bring *Chosŏn chuŭi* to the fore. In this context, it can be said that the aim of Grandfather's first sentence in the Declaration was to eradicate sinocentrism, not Japanese imperialism. Once divested of sinocentrism, *Chosŏn chuŭi,* he believed, was an effective tool for Korea in its fight against the Japanese imperialism that pillaged its language and history.

Globalism and *Minjok chuŭi*

Grandfather's *minjok chuŭi*, as I discussed earlier, always stood side by side with the world at large. He advocated a *minjok chuŭi* that was open to the world. Starting in his late teens, he urged Koreans to march in step with the rest of the world, and, throughout his life, he continued to advocate the need to be connected to the world. He stressed this connection in his study of Tan'gun, in his study of Korean history, and in his study of Asian cultural history. In all his scholarly endeavors, including his compilation of the *Encyclopedia of Korean History*, his *minjok chuŭi* was closely connected to globalism.

For Grandfather, Korean independence was inextricably tied to the current of world history. In his article "The Declaration of Independence as I Wrote It," Grandfather pointed out that "the independence movement of Korea did not originate from selfish reasons, but from the desire to bring peace to the world and to prove its inevitability in the trend of world history." Among the many factions of the nationalist movement, one suggested that armed resistance was the only way to gain independence. Grandfather thought otherwise, and the geopolitical situation at the time proved him right. *In a world where a few powerful nations set up colonies in different parts of the world, what people could rise up in arms to claim independence?* The demise of imperialism and the end of colonies were possible only with the advent of a new world order.

Grandfather had the entire world in mind as he explored his idea of *minjok*. In this sense, he was a globalist. Fully aware that a false sense of self-importance would get Koreans nowhere, he pursued his study of Tan'gun and his study of Chosŏn history in connection with the world. He compiled the *Encyclopedia of Korean History* from this viewpoint as well. He viewed Korea as a country involved in a continuous exchange with the rest of the world. Ironically, this global aspect of Grandfather's thinking led to his wholesale condemnation as a "pro-Japanese collaborator." In Grandfather's worldview, Japan represented just another part of the world with which Korea had exchanges. Viewed from the vast perspective of the world's cultural history, Korea and Japan were, in fact, closely connected.

Civilization and Culture, and the Postmodern Narrative

Without a doubt, Grandfather was a modernist. His exploration of *minjok chuŭi* was his effort to establish the identity of Chosŏn as he sought to modernize it. For this reason, he is not just a "modernizer of civilization," nor solely a "Chosŏn culturalist." He was forward-looking towards modernization even as he explored the identity of Chosŏn culture. He founded both Kwangmunhoe and Sinmun'gwan. He experimented with new forms of poetry even as he revitalized traditional sijo. His study of Chosŏn history proceeded in tandem with his study of world history. The seemingly contradictory trajectories of his endeavors were always complementary at their core.

With the start of the new millennium, academics in various disciplines began to show renewed interest in the study of Yuktang, and this trend seems to be continuing to the present day. In the early 2000s, a postmodern narrative of Korean history swept the Korean academic community. Within the context of modernism's demise, Grandfather's ideas seem to have caught the attention of scholars. *Why would Grandfather, traditionally viewed as a pioneer of Korean modernity, be undergoing re-evaluation within the postmodern narrative?* I think this phenomenon arose as a result of the re-evaluation of the existing notions of modernity, which gave birth to the postmodern narrative.

If the modern narrative of Korea has been dominated by anti-imperialism and anti-sinocentrism, the postmodern narrative of Korea is characterized by globalism. The relationship between Korea and the rest of the world is the central issue in this narrative. Grandfather's vision for Korea's modernization proceeded hand in hand with globalization. As he worked toward the casting off of sinocentrism, he sought modernization through close interactions with the world. The postmodern discourse in Korea posits that the most Korean things are global, and *vice versa*. In this proposition, I hear clear and interesting echoes from Grandfather's writings.

Postmodernist history aims to dissolve the notion of nations as separate *minjok* units. Where the narrative of *minjok chuŭi* ends, postmodern narrative begins. As I mentioned previously, Grandfather asserted that "*Minjok* is small and culture is big. History is short and culture is long." Grandfather caught the attention of the postmodernists because he had long ago put the spotlight on *minjok* and history from the broader, more universal vantage point of culture.

Grandfather's concept of globalization through culture resonates with the trend of globalization in contemporary Korean society, which proves that his ideas retain relevance beyond Korea's modern era. This, I believe, is just one of the reasons a systematic study of Grandfather's works should be established.

3. An Interdisciplinary Approach

For some time now, the word *consilience* has become fashionable in academic communities all over the world. According to my dictionary, the word means "the putting together of knowledge" or "the unity of knowledge." The concept of consilience suggests that only with the combination of knowledge gained from both scientific and humanistic disciplines can the true nature of ideas or events be discerned or understood. For example, to understand philosophy, one needs to understand physics, and *vice versa*. That said, I get the distinct impression that in the Korean academic community, the putting together of knowledge seems hard to come by, even within the same discipline. This impression is reinforced when I encounter discussions of Grandfather's works in various academic circles.

Grandfather approached the study of Tan'gun through many different disciplines, such as history, ethnology, anthropology, paleontology, linguistics, mythology, religion, and other disciplines that had not even been introduced in Korea at the time. Using knowledge gained through these disciplines, he reached and advanced his theory of Tan'gun, as well as the theory of the Purham Civilization.

Realizing the inadequacy of a single discipline to reach a full understanding of Tan'gun, Grandfather explored and utilized the methodologies of various disciplines and beyond. He felt that the meaning of Tan'gun lay in the Chosŏn spirit and the Chosŏn soul, which he knew would not to be discoverable in the usual domain of scholarship. He therefore went on pilgrimages around the Chosŏn land, and he also engaged in the revitalization of Chosŏn's unique literary form, sijo.

Grandfather laid the foundation for almost all branches of Korean Studies. During his time, Korean Studies had yet to undergo specialization, so the subject of his Chosŏn Studies was all of Chosŏn. The field of his study was not yet compartmentalized, which is why Grandfather pursued Chosŏn Studies through an interdisciplinary approach.

At present in Korea, the study of Yuktang seems to proceed in parallel universes in different disciplines. Departments of history, literature, ethnology, anthropology, and mythology each pursue their own studies. *Is it because today's academic world has undergone extreme specialization?* I realize that specialization often spurs the advancement of specific knowledge, but when it comes to the unique nature of Grandfather's work, the specialized approach seems to present a major stumbling block. Depending on the specialty, the same subject of study often results in inconsistent evaluations and contradictory conclusions.

A few years ago, I heard that Lee Young-hwa, a noted scholar of modern Korean history, and Kang Hae-su, a specialist in the comparative study of Japan and Korea, were engaged, along with several other younger scholars, in the study of Yuktang for a little over a year. Aiming for an interdisciplinary approach, the group included specialists in history, literature, ethnology, anthropology, mythology, and comparative ideologies. Once every month they met to present and discuss their findings.

I learned later that these scholars from different disciplines faced many challenges in combining or synthesizing their ideas. The terms and concepts employed by each discipline varied, and their points of interest and emphasis also diverged. As a result, they could not arrive at a consistent overarching idea in their evaluation of Grandfather's works. Though all the scholars agreed that Yuktang study was important, and all made a serious attempt to go beyond the limitations posed by existing paradigms, they still found it hard to overcome the challenges of digesting the methodologies of disciplines not their own.

I would also like to point out here the tendency among the Korean academic community to steer clear of the study of Yuktang. Given that Grandfather himself wanted to be known primarily as a historian, I find this profoundly ironic. Even as it acknowledges that Grandfather's historical studies are modern in their approach and that Grandfather laid the foundation for the study of Korean history, the academic world seems deeply conflicted about conferring the rightful level of recognition upon Yuktang in Korean historiography. This trend may have intensified after the 1987 Democracy Movement, as the students who were involved in the movement entered the academic world and began to wield influence.

Another point I would like to make here has to do with instances of plagiarism I have witnessed over the years. Whether or not Grandfather was "pro-Japanese" could perhaps be a legitimate subject for academic inquiry, so I will not take exception to it, but I have been shocked, on numerous occasions, to see Grandfather's words or ideas taken without credit. Any form of plagiarism, I believe, should be considered unacceptable in the academic domain.

As early as the 1910s, Grandfather had laid the foundation for Chosŏn Studies with his work at Kwangmunhoe. In 1922, he proclaimed the establishment of Chosŏn Studies in his magazine *Tongmyŏng*. Nonetheless, some of today's academics have theorized that the "Chosŏn Studies Movement" was initiated in the mid-1930s by others. Additionally, in spite of the fact that Grandfather, in his book *A Series of Lectures on Chosŏn History*, codified the ideas and terminology of Sirhak, along with its chronology, in 1928, the Korean academic community has suggested that the first study of Sirhak was begun as late as the 1960s. This is a major misrepresentation in search of overhaul for future scholars of Korean history.

In September of 2008, the Yuktang Research Society was formed. Kim Yong-jik, a prominent member of the Korean Academy of Sciences, was appointed as its president. To my knowledge, this is the first official organization created for the study of Yuktang. After two years of research, the Society collected its research findings and published them in 2009 in a book titled *Rereading Ch'oe Nam-sŏn: The Birth of Chosŏn Studies Through the Eyes of Ch'oe Nam-sŏn*. At the risk of sounding presumptuous, I would like to see Yuktang research develop into a full-fledged field of "Yuktang Study." I am convinced that, beyond the narrow focus on Ch'oe Nam-sŏn the individual, a comprehensive study of the structure of his ideas and scholarly discoveries would confer immeasurable, eye-opening benefits upon future scholars of Korean history.

It is of paramount importance that contemporary scholars across diverse academic disciplines fully embrace an interdisciplinary approach in their evaluation of Yuktang's work and its role within history. Only through such a change in approach will an objective re-evaluation of Yuktang's legacy emerge. My greatest wish is for an in-depth re-examination of my grandfather's lifelong quest to arrive at an inclusive form of nationalism, which laid the foundation for Korea's modern identity and relationship with the world at large.

Afterword

Last year, the year 2010, was the centennial of Korea's falling into foreign hands. It was also the second *hwan-ryŏk* (還曆: 60-years, a full life cycle) of Grandfather's birth. He lost his country at age 21, and got it back after nearly four decades of tribulations, only to see it split in half.

Grandfather lived for seven more years after his first *hwan-ryŏk*, the year that Yuggio began, but not counting the three years of the war and three years of his illness, it amounted to merely a year that I, as a young grandson, could claim my place next to him and be a carefree, playful companion to him. During those seven years, however, I ate with him every day and slept beside him every night, so becoming closer to him than anybody else could. As I approached maturity, Grandfather towered like a tall mountain to me, and as my intellectual curiosity broadened, the mountain grew taller and taller.

Before he became my grandfather, Ch'oe Nam-sŏn was already a public figure of great renown. Apart from a grandson's recollections presented here, I would surmise that my generation and the previous generation, which survived the colonial rule and Yuggio, would have little problem understanding and appreciating Yuktang Ch'oe Nam-sŏn and his work. However, the worldview of the younger generations, whose experiential realm does not include the indignities of colonial rule and the savagery of war, inevitably differs from our own, and thus the prism through which they view the work of their predecessors also differs. This is probably even truer of my own children, who grew up and now have settled into their lives in the English-speaking world.

Along with an unvarnished narrative of my own family, I have attempted to present the history of modern Korea as I have come to understand it. I took it upon myself to be as objective as possible, but discovered that there were still many areas in which I was hard pressed for an explanation without resorting to subjectivity. Many times, I have asked myself: *Is my ignorance or laziness culpable?* Often, my self-questioning was coupled with another question: *If certain aspects of Yuktang's work still call for subjective interpretations on my part, could objectivity somehow be lacking in the existing study of Yuktang?* The study of Yuktang, I felt, still needed to extricate itself from the deflections and inclinations of our time.

As I have already indicated, this book is, first and foremost, a record of the life of Yuktang who, at great personal pain and sacrifice, steadfastly pursued his goal, with his feet firmly planted on the Korean Peninsula, in the northern tip of Northeast Asia. The aim of this record is quite clear: that future generations of Koreans, through an accurate understanding of Yuktang and his historical milieu, can better understand themselves and, equipped with this understanding, draw the best possible roadmap for their country's future. To further this accuracy, I would hope that the study of Yuktang will mature into a more comprehensive interdisciplinary undertaking, unfettered by the exigencies of the day.

A few months ago, I was presented with a scroll by a professor of Korean history, who visited me while attending a conference at an American university. On it was a line by Ssu-ma-Ch'ien (司馬遷 135 BC–86 BC, the father of Chinese historiography) from his *Shih-chi* (史記). The brushwork was quite extraordinary, both in its technique and elegance.

桃李無言 下自成蹊

Under the silent peach tree and plum tree, a path is made.

The professor had presented the scroll to me, but he obviously had my grandfather in mind. Yes, my grandfather, Yuktang, was that peach or plum tree. He didn't say much about himself, but his very existence opened up a path, a path we have all walked on. With the passage of time, when the tree falls and the ground it stood on shifts, the path will remain, and others will continue to walk the path on which we once walked.

Hak Joo Choi

On March 1, 2011,
the 92nd anniversary of the March First Movement,
standing on the former site of Kwangmunhoe,
Seoul, Korea

Chronology

1890 Born on April 26 as second son to Ch'oe Hŏn-gyu (崔獻圭), who amassed wealth by trading in medicinal herbs with China.

1894 Masters the Korean phonetic alphabet.

1895 Starts attending *kŭlbang*(書堂) where he studies Chinese characters.

1899 Reads novels written in Chinese and "Western" books, such as the Bible and *Pilgrim's Progress*, in Korean translation.

1901 Submits an article, titled "28 Points for the Development of Chosŏn," to the *Hwangsŏng newspaper*. In April, marries Hyŏn Yŏng-ch'ae.

1902 Enters Kyŏngsŏng School and studies Japanese. After three months of study, is able to read Japanese newspapers.

1904 In October, goes to Japan as head of the Royal scholarship students. Ch'oe Rin is one of his fellow students.

1905 In January, leaves school and returns to Korea. Is incarcerated for a month by the Japanese police for his article in the *Hwangsŏng* newspaper, in which he urges Koreans to boycott Japanese currency.

1906 In March, goes to Japan for the second time to attend Waseda University, enrolling in the department of geography and history. Edits the newsletter *Korean Students Abroad*. In June, leads his fellow students to protest the university's mock Diet denigrating the Korean king. Develops friendship with Yi Kwang-su and Hong Myŏng-hi.

1907 Chosen as editor-in-chief of *Korean Students Abroad*. In its first issue, publishes an article titled "The Kind of People the Modern Age Needs," in which he first uses the term *minjok* (民族). In August, renovates one of his father's houses to set up Sinmun'gwan (新文館: The Institute for New Learning).

1908 In November, launches *Sonyŏn* (少年: Boys), where his "free verse" poem "Hae egesŏ Sonyŏn ege" appears. Also begins to serialize "Korean History: A Maritime View" in the magazine.

1909 In *Sonyŏn*, publishes "Tolstoy's Teachings," "Our Nim"(님), and "Chosŏn with Sea on Three Sides." Becomes a founding member of the Youth Student Association and embarks on speaking tours all over Korea. In April, his daughter, Han-ok, is born.

1910 Founds *Chosŏn Kwangmunhoe* (朝鮮光文會: The Institute for the Illumination of Chosŏn Culture). Begins the compilation of a Korean dictionary. Publishes, in *Sonyŏn*, the mission statement of the Youth Student Association.

1911 In January, *Sonyŏn* is confiscated and banned. In May, after 4 years and 23 issues, it is discontinued. In December, publishes *Yŏlha Ilgi* (熱河日記).

1912 In July, launches the magazine *Pulkŭn Chŏgori* (Red Jacket).

1913 In September, launches the magazine *Aidŭl Boi* (A Reader for Children), in which he first uses the name *han'gŭl* for the Korean alphabet. In December, rewrites and publishes *The Story of Ch'unhyang*.

1914 In July, *The History of the Three Kingdoms* (三國史記) is published by Kwangmunhoe. In October, launches *Ch'ŏngch'un* (靑春: Youth), a monthly magazine, in which he publishes his poem, "Nim" (님: Beloved). In November, gives a lecture at Hwimun High School titled "The Activities of the Ancient Koreans Abroad."

1915 In March, *Ch'ŏngch'un* is suspended. In August, his first son, Han-in, is born. In December, *Sinjajŏn* (The New Dictionary of Chinese Characters) is published by Sinmun'gwan.

1916 In January, *Simundokpon* (A Reader of Modern Writing) is published by Sinmun'gwan. In May, resumes the publication of *Ch'ŏngch'un*.

1917 In July, publishes the essay, "Perseverance." In August, edits and publishes *A Short History of Buddhism in Chosŏn* by Kwŏn Sang-no. In September, celebrates his father's *hwan'gap*, 60th birthday. In December, his second son, Han-ung, is born.

1918 In June, publishes a thesis "Kyegoch'ajon" (稽古箚存) in *Ch'ŏngch'un*. In June, publishes an essay, "The Reform of Public Morals." Starting in the fall, initiates a debate on the *minjok* movement at Kwangmunhoe.

1919 In January, meets with Ch'oe Rin, Song Chin-u, Hyŏn Sang-yun, and others to plan the Korean independence movement. In February, composes "Declaration" (宣言書), "Announcement to the Japanese Government," "A Letter of Appeal to President Wilson of the United States," and "A Message to the Versailles Peace Conference." On March 1, independence is declared and the movement ignited. On March 3, arrested with 47 other nationalists and incarcerated at Sŏdaemun prison.

1920 In September, sentenced to 2 years and 6 months in prison.

1921 In October, released on parole.

1922 Moves his family to Yangsakkol and names his study "Illamgak." His brother, Tu-sŏn, departs for Germany to study philosophy. In July, disbands Sinmun'gwan. In September, launches Tongmyŏng Publishing Company and starts the weekly, *Tongmyŏng*. Serializes "Chosŏn Minsiron" in 11 installments. Serializes "A Series of Lectures on Chosŏn History" (朝鮮曆史講話). In December, his third son, Han-gŏm, is born.

1923 In June, gives a lecture, "A Regional History of Chosŏn." Discontiues *Tongmyŏng* with issue no. 23.

1924 In March, starts publication of *Sidae Ilbo* (時代日報: Times Daily), with Chin Hak-mun as editor-in-chief. In September, resigns from the newspaper due to funding issues. In October, takes a trip to Kŭmgang Mountain and on his return publishes his travelogues titled "Pung'ak Kiyu" (楓嶽記遊) in *Sidae Ilbo*, in 52 installments. Holds monthly poetry readings in his study, "Illamgak."

1925 In March, takes a trip to Chiri Mountain and publishes his travelogues titled "Simch'un Sullye" (尋春巡禮) in *Sidae Ilbo*, in 77 installments. In August, starts writing columns as writer-at-large for *Dong-a Ilbo*. In October, his brother, Tu-sŏn, returns from Germany on completion of his study. In December, begins writing "The Theory of the Purham Civilization" (不咸文化論). With Pak Sŭng-bin, starts the Kyemyŏng Club, where work resumes on the dictionary of Korean language.

1926 In March, begins to publish "The Theory of Tan'gun" (檀君論) in *Dong-a Ilbo*, in 77 installments. In May, *Simch'un Sullye* is published. In July, begins to serialize "The Travels to Paektu Mountain" (白頭山覲參記). In October, finishes compiling *A Sijo Selection* (時調類聚). In December, publishes *One-Hundred-and-Eight Agonies* (百八煩惱).

1927 In January, publishes "A Survey of Korean Folk Songs" (in Japanese). In *Tongkwang* (東光: Eastern Light), publishes "Yuktang's Reminders" (自警). Discusses the founding of Sin'ganhoe (新幹會: New Korea Society) with Hong Myŏng-hi and Sin Sŏk-u. In February, publishes "The Beginnings of Chosŏn History" (兒時朝鮮). In *Kyemyŏng*, publishes "An Analysis of the *History of the Three Kingdoms*" (三國遺事 解題). In May, publishes "An Interpretation of Shamanism" (薩滿教箚記). In August, publishes "The Theory of the Purham Civilization." In *Buddhism*, publishes articles on Chosŏn Zen Buddhism and Silla Buddhist monks.

1928 In January, begins to serialize "A Series of Lectures on Chosŏn History" in *Hanbit*. In April, *A Sijo Selection* published. In *Pyŏlgŏn'gon*, publishes "A Study of Tangun" (壇君及其研究). In June, starts serializing "Songs About Travels Across Chosŏn" (朝鮮遊覽歌) in *Dong-a Ilbo*. In July, publishes *A Paean to Kŭmgang* (金剛禮讃). In August, publishes "Tan'gun and the Three Emperors and Five Kings" in *Dong-a Ilbo*. Publishes a novella titled "Morning" in *Pyŏlgŏn'gon*. In October, completes *The History of Chosŏn* (朝鮮歷史). Enters the Commission for the Compilation of Chosŏn History.

1929 In January, publishes "Kim Tae-mun, an Advocate of the Chosŏn Heart." In May, launches *Kwegi* (Mystery) and publishes in it "Chang Pogo, the Maritime King of 1,100 Years Ago," "A Western-Style Structure by a Koguryŏ Builder," "Silla Prince Chŏn Ilch'ang, a Great Colonizer," and "The Source of Religious Culture." In September, discovers King Chinhŭng's Maunryŏng Monuments at Unmubong. In December, publishes "Kija in Chosŏn History Is Not the Kija in Chinese History" in *Kwegi*.

1930 In January, begins the 51-installment serialization of "A Series of Lectures on Chosŏn History" in *Dong-a Ilbo*. In August, publishes "The Political Structure in Ancient Chosŏn" in *Chosŏn Hakbo* (a Japanese magazine), later delivered before the Kyŏngsŏng Imperial University faculty. Publishes in *Buddhism*, "Buddhism in Chosŏn," later submitted to the Pan-Asian Buddhism Conference held in Hawaii. In November, publishes "King Chinhŭng's Three Monuments and the Newly Discovered Maunryŏng Monument" in *Ch'ong'guhakch'ong*.

1931 In March, publishes in *Tongmyŏng*, "The Chronology of the Literature of the Three Kingdoms Period," "The Notable Writers of the Three Kingdoms Period," and "Essential References for the Three Kingdoms Period." In June, publishes *The History of Chosŏn*. It is immediately banned. In July, *Imjinran* (壬辰亂) is published by Tongmyŏng Publishing Company.

1932 In September, appointed lecturer at Chung'ang School of Buddhism. Plans for study in France, but gives up the plan due to his father's illness.

1933 In April, his father dies at age 77. In November, gives a lecture on "The Historical Remains of Chosŏn."

1934 In April, begins to write a column for *Maeil Shinbo*. Also serializes in 8 installments, "Yi Sun-sin and Nelson." Moves his family from Yangsakkol to Hyoje-dong. Gives radio lectures on the culture, geography, and historical remains of Chosŏn.

1935 In February, visits An Ch'ang-ho, who has just been released from prison. In June, begins a 365-installment serialization of "Kosa Chŏnja" (故事千字) in *Maeil Shinbo*. In July, publishes "Life and Religion."

1936 In January, gives a lecture on "The Myths of Chosŏn." In February, gives a lecture, "The Indigenous Religion of Chosŏn" at Kyŏngsŏng Imperial University. In November, his first son, Han-in, marries Sŏn-yŏng, first daughter of Yi Ik-sang.

1937 In January, begins to serialize in *Maeil Shinbo*, "Common Knowledge About Chosŏn," in 160 installments. In February, publishes "Issues Facing Chosŏn Culture." In October, publishes "The Particularities of Northern China," in 7 installments. Publishes "Songmak'yŏnunrok" (松漠燕雲錄) in 84 installments.

1938 In April, travels to Xinqing and works as an advisor at *Manmong Ilbo* (滿蒙日報). Publishes, in 15 installments, "The Folktales of Chosŏn." In September, publishes "Pilgrimages to the Three Cities." Begins a 14-installment serialization of "The Cultural History of Cheju Island." In October, publishes "Scenes from Manchuria" and "Russia's Incursions in the East."

1939 In January, publishes "The Myths of Chosŏn" in 20 installments. In February, begins a 224-installment serialization of "Past Events of Today" (昔年今日). In March, publishes "The Appellation of Manchuria" in *Mansŏn Ilbo*. In April, appointed professor at the National University of Manchuria, where he lectures on "The Cultural History of Manchuria." Writes an article titled, "The Concept of the Sacred Among the Ancient Peoples of the East." Travels frequently to Beijing to purchase books and to confer with Chinese scholars.

1940 In May, obtains permit to publish the revised edition of *Samguk'yusa* (三國遺事).

1941 In April, publishes "The Study of Books and Stone Monuments" in *Ch'unch'u*. In November, grandson, Hak-joo, is born to his first son, Han-in. In December, with the outbreak of the Pacific War, predicts Japan's fall and Korean independence. Returns from Manchuria to his home in Hyoje-dong, Seoul.

1942 In July, gives a lecture, "The Three Seas of Chosŏn." In November, resigns from his teaching position in Manchuria due to poor health.

1943 In October, Samchungdang publishes *A Collection of Ancient Stories* (故事通), which sells 30,000 copies. Learns of the Cairo Declaration. In December, under the coercion of the Government-General, goes on a speaking tour with Yi Kwang-su to Japan and urges Korean students to join the Japanese army to learn military skills. Writes articles, "Kando and the Chosŏn People," "The Appellation of Mongolia," and "A Short History of Manchuria." Meets frequently with Hong Myŏng-hi and Chŏng In-bo.

1944 Moves his family to Ui-dong. Concentrates on the compilation of the *Encyclopedia of Korean History* (朝鮮歷史辭典).

1945 In August, declines Yŏ Un-hyŏng's invitation to participate in the Committee for the Preparation of Korean Independence and instead recommends his brother-in-law, Pak Sŏk-yun, in his place. On August 15, Korea is liberated. In October, resumes the work of Tongmyŏng Publishing Company.

1946 In February, publishes *A History of the Korean Independence Movement* and *A History of Chosŏn, Revised*. In June, publishes *Questions and Answers on Common Knowledge About Korea, Volume 1*. In November, publishes *A Quick and Easy History of Korea*. Engages in frequent discussions about the Korean situation with Yu Tong-yŏl, Yi Si-yŏng, An Chae-hong, Chŏng In-bo, and Kim Sŏng-su.

1947 In January, publishes *A History of Chosŏn for the Korean People* (國民朝鮮歷史). In April, publishes *Daily History, Volume 1*. In October, publishes *The Landscape of Korea*. In December, publishes *Questions and Answers on Common Knowledge About Korea, Volume 2* and *A Historical Map of Korea*.

1948 In February, publishes *The Historical Remains of Chosŏn*, *Common Knowledge About Chosŏn: Geography*, and *The Culture of Chosŏn*. In July, publishes *Daily History, Volume 2* and *Common Knowledge About Chosŏn: Institutions*. In August, publishes *National History for High School Students, Revised Edition*, *The History of Asia for High School Students*, and *The History of the West for High School Students*. In October, publishes *Common Knowledge About Chosŏn: Customs*.

1949 In February, incarcerated at Sŏdaemun prison for allegedly violating the Anti-National Law. In March, submits his "Open Letter" (自列書) to the court. Paroled in one month. Case suspended in September.

1950 On April 26, celebrates his *hwan'gap*. His third son, Han-gŏm, is married. On June 25, the Korean War breaks out. In September, his daughter, Han-ok, is murdered by the North Korean People's Army. In December, takes refuge at the home of his second daughter-in-law in Taegu.

1951 In January, stays with his eldest son, Han-in, in Pusan. In April, works as editor of *The History of Naval Battles*. In May, sends Han-in to Ui-dong to gather materials for the book. Learns of the burning of his book collection.

1952 In May, returns to his house in Myo-dong, where his wife stayed during the war. In July, his eldest son, Han-in, dies. In August, publishes in *Chayu Segye* (Free World), "Overcoming National Crises." In October, goes on a lecture tour at the invitation of the Korean Army. Continues work on the *Encyclopedia of Korean History*.

1953 In April, publishes in *Sinchŏnji* (New World), "A Historical Study of the Korea-Japan Relationship." In May, publishes in *Chibang Haengjŏng* (Local Administration Newsletter), "The Spirit of the March First Movement." In July, publishes in *Seoul Sinmun* (Seoul Newspaper), "Korea's Future, Eight Years After Liberation." In October, serializes in *Hŭimang* (Hope), "The History of How Korea Overcame National Crises." Publishes in *Seoul Sinmun*, "Ullŭngdo and Tokto."

1954 In February, publishes in *Sasang'gye* (The World of Ideas), "The Interpretation of Old Tan'gun Records." In March, publishes in *Hyŏndae Kongron* (Modern Discourse), "A Historical Study of the March First Movement." In April, publishes in *Ungbyŏn Digest* (Oratory Digest), "Korea and the World." In May, writes the foreword to *The Maritime History of Korea*. Suffers a stroke on returning from a lecture tour. In September, publishes in *Saebyŏk* (Daybreak), "The Spirit of Truth."

1955 In March, publishes in *Saebyŏk*, "The Declaration of Independence as I Wrote It." In April, invited as advisor to the Committee for the History of Seoul. In July, publishes in *Saebyŏk*, "Underdevelopment Due to the Neglect of Sirhak." Publishes "The Fundamental Spirit of Learning" in the University Bulletin of Sookmyung University. In November, baptized a Catholic with the name Peter. In December, publishes in *Han'guk Ilbo*, "Life and Religion."

1956 In March, publishes in *Sinsegye*, "A Modern Interpretation of the March First Movement." Publishes in *Saebyŏk*, "The Uselessness of Political Parties."

1957 In January, publishes in *Saebyŏk*, "Heaven, My Home." In February, publishes in *Dong-a Ilbo*, "In Memory of Inch'on." On October 10, after a bout of flu, dies at 5:00 p.m. at his residence in Myo-dong, Seoul.

Appendix A

The Declaration of Independence

by Ch'oe Nam-sŏn (1919)

translated by Yer-ae K. Choi (2010)

We herewith proclaim the independence of Korea and the liberty of the Korean people. This we proclaim to all the nations of the world in witness of human equality. This we proclaim to our descendents so that they may enjoy in perpetuity their inherent right to nationhood.

Inasmuch as this proclamation originates from our five-thousand-year history, inasmuch as it springs from the loyalty of twenty million people, inasmuch as it affirms our yearning for the advancement of everlasting liberty, inasmuch as it expresses our desire to take part in the global reform rooted in the human conscience, it is the solemn will of heaven, the great tide of our age, and a just act necessary for the co-existence of all humankind. Therefore, no power in this world can obstruct or suppress it!

Victims of the outdated notions of aggression and brute force, we have now suffered for a decade, for the first time in our long history, under foreign tyranny; our right to existence deprived, our spiritual growth stunted, our national pride and honor damaged, and our opportunity to make our own creative contribution to the progress of world civilization lost.

Surely, if we are to eradicate our longstanding sense of injustice, if we are to extricate ourselves from today's pain, if we are to forestall tomorrow's threat, if we are to resuscitate our trampled national pride, if we as individuals are to reach our full potential, if we are to deliver our children from the legacy of shame, if we are to bequeath to our future generations blessing and prosperity, our first and foremost duty is to secure the independence of our people. If each and every twenty million of us carry a sword in our hearts and if we are supported by today's shared human conscience, ready to stand by us equipped with arms of justice and morality, what can stop us from pressing forward to defeat the strongest? If we regroup and build up our strength, what aim can we not accomplish?

Though Japan has repeatedly violated its promises since the Treaty of 1876, we do not here condemn its perfidy. Though its scholars and government officials dismiss our great dynastic achievements in order to prop up its claim that our history began as a foreign colony with a primitive civilization, though it merely seeks a conqueror's gratification willfully ignoring the ancient foundation and the outstanding characteristics of our people, we do not here take it to task. We are pressed to reprimand ourselves, and thus have little time to reproach others. Busy with today's work, we have little time to chastise yesterday's actions.

Today, our only duty is to rebuild ourselves, not to demolish others. It is to explore our new destiny according to the solemn dictates of our conscience, not to squabble with others over fleeting grudges and old animosities. It is to restore our natural, rational foundation by rectifying the unnatural, irrational ambition of the Japanese politicians in the grip of obsolete ideas. The annexation made without national consensus has inevitably led to intimidation used as a temporary measure, inequality caused by discrimination, and statistics falsified to justify it. Just look at the result today! The chasm of rancor has grown so wide that bridging the two peoples with diverging interests seems all but impossible.

To boldly right old wrongs, opening a new relationship based on true mutual understating, is certainly the best way for both countries to avert disaster and foster amity. To forcibly bind twenty million people filled with bitterness and enmity will not secure lasting peace. Moreover, it will exacerbate the apprehension and distrust of four hundred million Chinese people who hold the key to East Asian stability, which will undoubtedly lead to the unrest and eventual downfall of the entire region. Therefore, establishing Korean independence today will permit Koreans to return to their rightful lives, will enable the Japanese to break away from their wrongful path and concentrate on their responsibility as a major player in East Asia, and will free the Chinese from their nightmare of uncertainty and anxiety about Japan. Korean independence will indeed be an indispensable step toward the stability of East Asia, which will, in turn, contribute to the attainment of world peace. With the well-being of all humanity at stake, the establishment of Korean independence is a grave issue that transcends mere animosity between two nations.

Behold! A new world is approaching before our very eyes! The age of might has receded, and the age of morality has arrived. The spirit of humanism cultivated throughout the past century now begins to throw its light on a new chapter in world history. Just as a new spring has come, hastening the rebirth of every living thing, our pulse, once frozen in the bitter cold and snow, now quickens in the warm breeze and sunshine. The good fortune of heaven and earth has returned to us, and we ride the changing tide of the world. Do not hesitate or flinch! By protecting our inalienable individual right to freedom, we will enjoy our lives to the fullest. By realizing our bountiful creativity, our national civilization will flower in the warmth of spring that pervades the world.

We hereby rise up! Conscience is on our side, and truth marches with us. Men and women, young and old, leave your darkened corners and partake in the joyful resurrection along with all creation! The spirit of our many ancestors protects us from within, and the tide of the new world from without. To begin is to succeed! Let us march straight into the light!

We hereby pledge the following:

1. Today's undertaking reflects the demands of our people for justice, morality, survival, and prosperity. Therefore, we will act solely in the spirit of liberty, never in the spirit of enmity.

2. To the last person and to the last moment, we will forthrightly express the will of the Korean people.

3. We will respect order in all our actions and ensure that our demeanor and claims are always honorable and upright.

The first day of the third month of the 4252nd year of the founding of Korea,

The Representatives of the Korean people:
(the names of 33 signatories)

Appendix B

In the following article, the noted historian, Lee Young-hwa, places the lifelong work of Yuktang Ch'oe Nam-sŏn in its historical context–a period of unprecedented change and tumult in Korea during the first half of the twentieth century.

Who Is Yuktang Ch'oe Nam-sŏn?

by Lee Young-hwa, Ph.D.

translated by Yer-ae K. Choi

Yuktang Ch'oe Nam-sŏn was born in 1890 in Korea, just as traditional East Asian civilization was reeling under the onslaught of Western civilization. In 1910, he saw his country fall into the hands of Japan, a newly Westernizing neighboring power already emulating the imperialist ways of the West. By his late twenties, Yuktang had become widely known in Korea as its foremost intellectual and historian, his fame reaching its height in 1919 with his drafting of the Korean Declaration of Independence. However, certain choices he made during the latter part of the 36-year-long colonial rule gained him another sort of fame because they were perceived as "collaboration" with the Japanese authorities. Ever since, Yuktang's legacy has been relegated to a problematic place in Korean history and historiography, a situation later reinforced by simplistic and polarized nationalist narratives upheld by both South Korea and North Korea.

With Korea's sovereignty lost, Yuktang faced myriad challenges as he struggled to protect East Asian civilization from the encroachment of Western civilization, to extricate Korea from its deeply rooted sinocentrism, and to gain Korea's political independence from Japanese rule.

When World War II came to an end in 1945, Korea regained its sovereignty, but Yuktang's trials did not end there. Korea had turned into a battleground for two Western ideologies, capitalism and communism, sowing the seeds of national division and fratricidal carnage.

Yuktang yearned to see a unified nation on the Korean peninsula, with its citizens bound together by a common culture. His notion of a Korean nation was inclusive of the Korean people who had settled in various parts of Northeast Asia, beyond the borders of the peninsula. Throughout his life, Yuktang strove to lay a scholarly and theoretical foundation in support of this idea. A systematic study and objective evaluation of Yuktang's lifelong work is essential for historians of Northeast Asia–and of Korea in particular–in order to understand and explain the region's passage from its sinocentric past into modernity.

In this book, Hak Joo Choi traces the steps Yuktang took at the beginning of the twentieth century in order to establish Korean identity as a cultural entity. The identity of Korea, as formulated by Yuktang, was rooted in its indigenous culture and civilization. Today, amidst the accelerating pace of globalization, it is more important than ever to firmly establish a Korean national identity. Moreover, with the issue of Northeast Asia brought to the fore once again, it is time to put past contentions to rest. A century ago, Yuktang set out to resolve the dilemma of "modernity" and "Korea" by exploring a Korean identity based on the common culture of Northeast Asia. Today, such an endeavor may still hold the key to solving the dual dilemma of national identity on the Korean Peninsula and stability in Northeast Asia.

Yuktang's modernization efforts in Korea began with the compilation of a Korean dictionary, the vernacularization of the written language, and the raising of a modern consciousness in the Korean people through various publishing projects. Consistently running through these efforts was the establishment of Korean identity based on the idea of *minjok*, a people with a common culture, as he defined it. To this end, Yuktang engaged in the preservation of ancient Korean classics, the paean of the Korean land, and the writing and publication of Korean history, all while under the intense scrutiny of Japanese censorship. He then proceeded to discover the nexus point between the cultural history of the world and that of Northeast Asia. With this broad stance, he took on the ambitious task of compiling an encyclopedia of Korean cultural history, completing only the first of his ten planned volumes before his death in 1957, at age 67.

As timely material for the study of the development of modern Korea, as well as all of Northeast Asia, the importance of *Yuktang Ch'oe Nam-sŏn and Korean Modernity* cannot be overstated. As the very first memoir/biography to come out of Ch'oe Nam-sŏn's immediate family, the book contains detailed information that adds fresh insight into the life and work of Yuktang. The author offers new interpretations of Yuktang's work, which diverge significantly from existing evaluations, pointing to many new areas for scholarly inquiry.

Yuktang Ch'oe Nam-sŏn and Korean Modernity is divided into three parts. In Part One, the author reveals the multi-generational involvement of the Ch'oe family in modern Korean history, from the "enlightenment movement" to the "modernization movement." In particular, the members of Yuktang's grandfather's generation opposed Taewŏn'gun's seclusionist policies at their peril and actively supported the movement to bring new knowledge to the Korean people. At their behest, Yuktang's father, Ch'oe Hŏn-gyu, supported his young son's cultural projects, depleting his hard-earned fortune to finance his son's publications and other modernization efforts. In effect, Ch'oe Hŏn-gyu served as a bridge between the end of the nineteenth century and the early twentieth century during Korea's modernization process.

In addition, the author's detailed accounts of Yuktang's family members create a microcosm of the world inhabited by Korean intellectuals during the modern era. Yuktang formed an in-law relationship with Yi Ik-sang, the leader of the Korean Artists Proletarian Federation. His youngest son, Ch'oe Han-gŏm, engaged in various leftist activities and voluntarily went to North Korea when the Korean War broke out. His brother-in-law, Pak Sŏk-yun, a supporter of autonomy, held the highest-ranking position for a Korean in the Japanese imperial hierarchy. His younger brother, Ch'oe Tu-sŏn, was a major player in the education efforts led by nationalist-industrialist Kim Sŏng-su. Yuktang's family history, riveting in itself, encapsulates the political and intellectual life of Korea during the colonial era.

In Part Two, the author offers a summary of Yuktang's lifelong work, pointing out that the main objective of Yuktang's scholarly endeavors was to free Korea from its sinocentric past and to move its people instead to embrace globalism. The author asserts that Yuktang conducted his study of Korea, as well as his compilation of an encyclopedia of Korean history, with this objective foremost in mind. For Yuktang, Korean history was an integral part of world history, and he approached it through the lens of continuous interchanges between Eastern and Western cultures.

After revealing the hitherto unknown family history of Yuktang in Part One and presenting Yuktang's work as a series of "globalization" efforts in Part Two, the author explores the present-day significance of Yuktang's work in Part Three. As the author points out, the crux of Yuktang study lies in the full understanding of his concept of nationalism, or *minjok chuŭi*. It is important to note that, in the context of his time, Yuktang's *minjok chuŭi* was an instrument he used to fight imperialism and sinocentrism. Far from being exclusionist, his *minjok chuŭi* was an "open" nationalism, which stood, in his own words, "side by side" with the world.

In recent years, the "global" aspect of Yuktang's work has been highlighted within the postmodern discourse on modern Korean history. The postmodernists' appreciation of Yuktang's work stems from his focus on the interactions between Korean history and world history. Yuktang implicitly rejected a narrow-minded, exclusionist view of Korean history, circumscribed by the country's immediate physical borders. Instead, he viewed Korean history as a unique current in the vast flow of world history. Thrust into the most intricate confluence of historical currents, Yuktang articulated a distinctive yet open Korean identity and, at the same time, envisioned, one hundred years ago, a Korean historiography that scholars all over the world would recognize for its originality and universality.

Today, as evidenced by the ongoing controversy in both academic and political circles in Korea, Yuktang is still very much alive. His work remains highly relevant in the larger East Asian context as well. It is my belief that a comprehensive, objective study of Yuktang will give impetus to the effort already underway to confer upon him his rightful place in Korean historiography. Once his voice is clearly heard and evaluated, it will make an important contribution to the academic community, both in Korea and abroad, as its members continue to inquire into one of the most complex and least understood periods in modern history.

Bibliography

Books in Korean (chrolonogical order)

The Maritime History of Korea. The Committee for the Compilation of Korean Naval History, 1954.

Kim, Chong-kwŏn. *A Survey of Wars in Korean History.* Pŏpchosa, 1957.

Hong, Il-sik. *The Study of Yuktang.* Ilsinsa, 1959.

Cho, Yong-man. *Yuktang Ch'oe Nam-sŏn.* Samchungdang, 1964.

Chang, Jun-ha. *Stone Pillow: The Record of My Anti-Japanese Struggles as a Youth.* Hwada Publishing Company, 1971.

The Research Society on Asian Issues, Korea University. *The Complete Works of Yuktang Ch'oe Nam-sŏn,* vol. 1-15. Hyŏnamsa, 1973-1975.

Yang, Sang-kyŏng, et al. *In Memory of Sunsŏng Chin Hak-mun,* 1975.

Kim, Sun-yŏng. *Following the Light.* The Asssociation of University Women, 1976.

Yi, Kwang-rin. *The Study of the Englightenment Party.* Ilchokak, 1979.

The Geneology of the Dongju Ch'oe Family, Hoesangsa, 1981.

The Complete Works of Chŏng In-bo. Yonsei University Press, 1983.

Ch'oe, Han-ung. *Yonghŏn Miscellany.* Tongmyŏngsa, 1986.

The Society of Korean Philosophy. *The History of Korean Philosophy.* 3 vols. Tongmyŏngsa, 1987.

Hong, Il-sik. *The National Cultures as Defined by Cultural Borders.* Yukmunsa, 1987.

The Committee for the Commemoration of Yuktang. *A Hundred Years After the Birth of Yuktang*. Tongmyŏngsa, 1990.

Yun, Kyŏng-ro. *The Study of the "105 Incident" and Sinminhoe*. Ilchisa, 1990.

Kim, Il Sung. *With the Century*. vols. 1-5. Chosŏn Labor Party Press, 1992.

Yi, Kyun-hyŏng. *The Study of Singan'hoe*. Yŏksabipyŏngsa, 1993.

Chŏng, Pyŏng-chun. *A Biography of Mong'yang Hong Myŏng-hi*. Hanul, 1993.

Kang, Yŏng-ju. *A Study of Byŏkch'o Hong Myŏng-hi*. Ch'angjak gwa Bipyŏngsa, 1999.

Kim, Sŏng-ho. *The Study of the Minsaengdan Incident in Yanji*. Paeksan Records, 1999.

Song, Byŏng-gi, et al. *The Diary of Yun Ch'i-ho in Korean Translation, vol. 1-4*. Yonsei University Press, 2001.

The Complete Works of Yuktang Ch'oe Nam-sŏn, vol. 1-14. Yŏknaksa, 2003.

Pak, Kyŏng-su. *Chang Jun-ha: The Road Taken by a Nationalist*. Tolbege, 2003.

Lee, Young-hwa. *The Historiography of Ch'oe Nam-sŏn*. Kyŏng'in Munhwasa, 2003.

Yi, Ŏryŏng. *The Spirit of Korea in Its Myths*. Munhwasasangsa, 2003.

Yun, Ch'ung-nam. *Studies on the Korean Materials in the Harvard-Yenching Library*, Kyŏng'in Munhwasa, 2004.

Song, Kŏn-ho, et al. *Understanding Korean History Before and After Liberation*, rev. Hangilsa, 2004.

Kim, In-sik. *An Chae-hong: A Moderate Nationalist*. Yŏksakong'gan, 2006.

Pak, Chi-hyang, et al. *A Re-evaluation of the History of Korean Liberation*. Ch'aeksesang, 2006.

Choi, Hak Joo, et al. "An Explanation of Yuktang's Activities." The Committee for the Inquiry into Pro-Japanese Anti-National Activities, 2007.

Yi, Yŏng-hun. *The Story of the Republic of Korea.* Kiparang, 2007.

Ko, Chŏng-il. *A Comparative Study of Sinmun'gwan's Ch'oe Nam-sŏn and Kodan's Noma Seiji.* Tongsŏmunhwasa, 2007.

Chŏn, Sŏng-gon. *The Identity of Modern Korea and Ch'oe Nam-sŏn.* J&C Publishing Corporation, 2008.

The Textbook Forum. *Alternative Textbooks for the History of Modern and Contemporary Korea.* Kiparang, 2008.

The Yuktang Research Society. *Rereading Ch'oe Nam-sŏn: The Birth of Chosŏn Studies Through the Eyes of Ch'oe Nam-sŏn.* Hyŏnsilmunhwa, 2009.

Ryu, Si-hyŏn. *The Study of Yuktang Ch'oe Namsŏn.* Yŏksa Bipyŏngsa, 2009.

Choi, Kook-ju, et al. "A Letter of Disagreement on the Decision Regarding Ch'oe Nam-sŏn's Activities." The Committee for the Inquiry into Pro-Japanese Anti-National Activities," 2009.

Books in Japanese

The Japanese Government-General of Korea. *A Summary of the Compilation Project for the History of Chosŏn,* 1938.

Ch'oe, Nam-sŏn. *The History of Chosŏn.* Trans. Syouzi Yamada. Tokyo: Sanichi Shobo, 1988.

Chŏn, Sŏng-gon. *Ch'oe Nam-sŏn: Establishing the Nationalism of Korea Under Japanese Rule.* J&C Publishing Corporation, 2005.

Books in English

The Academy of Korean Studies, ed. *Nationalism and History Textbooks in Asia and Europe.* Seoul, 2005.

Cox, Michael, ed. *E.H. Carr: A Critical Appraisal.* Palgrave, 2000.

Cumings, Bruce. *Korea's Place in the Sun: A Modern History.* New York: W.W. Norton, 1997.

________. *The Origins of the Korean War.* Vol. 1: *Liberation and the Emergence of Separate Regimes 1945–1947.* Princeton, NJ: Princeton University Press, 1981.

________. *The Origins of the Korean War.* Vol. 2: *Roaring of the Cataract 1947–1953.* Princeton, NJ: Princeton University Press, 2000.

Duus, Peter. *The Rise of Modern Japan,* Boston, MA: Houghton Mifflin Company, 1976.

Eckert, Carter, Ki-baik Lee, Young Ick Lew, Michael Robinson, and Edward Wagner. *Korea Old and New: A History.* Cambridge, MA: Korea Institute, Harvard University Press, 1990.

Foreign Language Press, ed. *Selected Readings from the Works of Mao Tsetung.* Peking, 1971.

Shin, Gi-Wook, and Michael Robinson, eds. *Colonial Modernity in Korea.* Cambridge, MA: East Asia Council Publications, 1999.

Huntington, Samuel P. *The Clash of Civilizations and the Remaking of World Order,* Simon & Schuster, New York, 1997.

Kang, Ellen S. *Tiger, True to Form.* PublishAmerica, Baltimore, 2006.

Kissinger, Henry A. *Diplomacy,* Simon & Schuster, New York, 1994.

Korean National Commission for UNESCO, ed. *Anthology of Korean Studies.* Vol. v: *Korean History: Discovery of Its Characteristics and Developments.* Elizabeth, NJ: Hollym International Corp, 2001.

Lee, Ann S. *Yi Kwang-su and Modern Korean Literature:* Mujŏng. Ithaca, NY: Cornell University East Asia Program, 2005.

McCann, David R. *Korea Briefing: Toward Reunification.* Armonk, NY: M.E. Sharpe, 1997.

Myers, Ramon H. and Mark R. Peattie, eds. *The Japanese Colonial Empire, 1895-1945,* Princeton, NJ: Princeton University Press, 1984.

Oberdorfer, Don. *The Two Koreas: A Contemporary History, rev.* Basic Books, 2001.

Palmer, R.R. and Joel Colton. *A History of the Modern World.* New York, NY: McGraw-Hill, 1995.

Robinson, Michael E. *Korea's Twentieth-Century Odyssey: A Short History.* Honolulu, HI: University of Hawaii Press, 2007.

Shirer, William L. *The Rise and Fall of the Third Reich.* New York: Fawcett Crest Publications, 1959.

Volkogonov, Dmitri. *Stalin: Triumph and Tragedy.* Rocklin, CA: Prima Publishing, 1992.

Wilson, Edward O. *Consilience: The Unity of Knowledge.* New York: Random House, 1998.

Yi, Tae-jin. *The Dynamics of Confucianism and Modernization in Korean History.* Ithaca, NY: Cornell University East Asia Program, 2007.

Index